WALKING TOWARD THE SUNSET

WALKING TOWARD THE SUNSET

The Melungeons of Appalachia

Wayne Winkler

Mercer University Press

Macon, Georgia

ISBN 0-86554-919-2   0-86554-869-2
MUP/H647   MUP/P250

©2005 (Paperback edition)
© 2004 Mercer University Press
1400 Coleman Avenue
Macon, Georgia 31207

First paperback edition.

∞The paper used in this publication meets the minimum
requirements of American National Standard for Information
Sciences—Permanence of Paper for Printed Library Materials, ANSI
Z39.48-1992.

Library of Congress Cataloging-in-Publication Data

Winkler, Wayne, 1956-
Walking toward the sunset : the Melungeons of Appalachia /
Wayne Winkler.
p. cm.
Includes bibliographical references and index.
ISBN 0-86554-919-2 (hardcover)
0-86554-869-2 (paperback) : alk. paper)
1. Melungeons—History. 2. Melungeons—Race identity. 3.
Appalachian Region—History. 4. Appalachian Region—Race
relations. 5.Melungeons—Historiography. I. Title.
E184.M44W56 2004
305.8'05074--dc22
2003026712
4 5 6 7 8 9

CONTENTS

FOREWORD

When my book, *The Melungeons: The Resurrection of a Proud People* was published in 1994, my deepest hope was that it would inspire, or ignite, additional public and academic interest in the Melungeons and other mixed-ethnic, mixed-race groups. My feeling was that too little attention and too few resources had been devoted to preserving and understanding the history, traditions, and culture of the various so-called "little races" of the South. My own gut instinct, strengthened by my own research, was that the numbers of, and kinship between, these groups were higher and more complex than any of us had originally thought, or been taught. I still believe that to be the case and continuing research efforts and publications are proving this to be the case. This nation was culturally and ethnically diverse from day one and that fact undoubtedly underlies our rise to greatness.

Wayne Winkler's book, *Walking Toward the Sunset: The Melungeons of Appalachia*, is a prime example of precisely what I had hoped would happen. Winkler, himself of Melungeon heritage, has taken firm hold of the Melungeon topic and exercised great care and considerable writing talent to give us as complete a history of these people as we have seen to date. From the earliest encounters to the most popular theories to an exploration of the scanty documents that tie a handful of Appalachian families to the core of this fascinating population, Winkler covers just about every imaginable aspect of what some now call "Melungia." This is not to say that Mr. Winkler and I agree on every aspect of Melungeon history, or even on who or what a Melungeon or a Melungeon-related individual might, or might not, be: we disagree on a number of topics, as one will see when reading this book. But, and crucially, we agree whole-heartedly on the importance of these early, virtually ignored pioneers in the shaping of this country and we agree that their story as a people—and their stories as individuals—both need and deserve to be told.

From beginning to end, Wayne Winkler's book presents a fair and balanced account of what we know, and do not know, of these fascinating people and his own insights flesh out in a logical manner what much of the extant evidence tells us. I am proud to introduce *Walking Toward the Sunset: The Melungeons of Appalachia*, as the latest acquisition to the Mercer University Press's groundbreaking series, *Melungeons: History, Ethnicity, Culture and Literature*. Thank you, Wayne, for a job well done.

N. Brent Kennedy, Ph.D.
Series Editor

INTRODUCTION

This is not a book about me or my family. However, since my family is the reason I became interested in this story, I will explain that connection at the outset.

My parents, like hundreds of thousands of others, left Appalachia in the 1950s for better opportunities in the industrial Midwest. For many of these transplants, "home" still meant "back home"—the hills of Appalachia. School holidays usually found our family on the road for the Hancock County, Tennessee farm where my father was born and where his mother and brother still lived.

Hancock County in the 1960s was one of the poorest counties in America. It's still economically depressed, and is also the least populated county in the state of Tennessee. Located just below the southwestern tip of Virginia, Hancock County is a rugged, mountainous area drained by the Clinch River. For a city boy like me, Hancock County seemed backward and dull.

In the summer of 1968, when I was twelve years old and visiting the family farm in War Valley, I read a copy of the Hancock County *Post* with great interest. The second page had an article entitled "Melungeons" which began, "One of the most fascinating mysteries in Tennessee lore concerns the unknown origin of the Melungeons, a dark-skinned people whom some romanticists compare in appearance to Othello immortalized by Shakespeare in *Othello, the Moor of Venice*."

The article mentioned many possible origins for the Melungeons, but strongly suggested a Portuguese ancestry. Quoting writer Will Allen Dromgoole, who visited Hancock County in the 1890s, the article suggested that some of the Melungeons had African-American ancestry. Now my curiosity was piqued: where could I see some of these mysterious Melungeons?

As it turns out, I didn't have to look far. Dad had told me long before that his family was part Indian, which seemed pretty obvious. When I asked about Melungeons, nobody had much to say until my mother told me that my dad's mother—my grandmother—was one of these mysterious people. (I recently discovered that my grandfather—who died when my father was two— had Melungeon as well as Native American ancestry.) In other words, Dad was a Melungeon, and so was I. So were many of the people with whom I came into contact when my family visited Tennessee. As I learned more about the Melungeons, I learned some of the reasons I had never heard the word up to that point.

There were many legends and theories about the origin of the Melungeons, ranging from "survivors of the Lost Colony of Roanoke Island" to "one of the Lost Tribes of Israel." However, most whites considered the Melungeons a mix of "white trash, renegade Indians, and runaway slaves," as one Hancock County resident expressed it. Whatever the origin of the people and name—even the term is mysterious—"Melungeon" was an insult.

That is, until 1968. Incredibly, a group of Melungeons took the epithet and embraced it proudly. According to the *Post*, plans were being made in Sneedville for an outdoor drama focusing on the Melungeons. Organizers hoped that the play, slated to open the following summer, would attract a portion of "the hundreds of thousands of tourists who pass through our state each year."

Although I had just learned of the existence of a people called Melungeon (not to mention my own membership in that group), I was fascinated by the subject and proud to be a part of this unique ethnic group. As my uncle said, "Used to be, nobody said the word 'Melungeon;' now everyone wants to be one." Not everyone shared this positive view of Melungeons, but I wouldn't learn the depth of their animosity until much later.

I was born at the beginning of the modern, post-World War II civil rights movement. Although I can remember segregation in the South, I grew up in the North where segregation and discrimination were not so obvious. Learning that I might have African-American ancestry was not at all upsetting to me, not in the summer of James Brown's hit record "Say It Loud, I'm Black And I'm Proud." In later years, as I learned of the years of discrimination and legal sanctions against our people, I realized how fortunate I had been. Even in my father's time, the heritage I proudly embrace was shameful, something to be hidden.

In high school I wrote a paper on the Melungeons for an English class. My teacher, of course, had never heard of the Melungeons, and I received an "A." I wrote essentially that same paper for other classes whenever the opportunity arose. By the time I was in college, I could—and sometimes did—write that paper from memory, changing the focus only slightly for each assignment. Even in the South, the Melungeons were not widely known; north of the Ohio River, the very novelty of the subject guaranteed an "A" paper.

After college, I embarked on a career in radio, eventually becoming manager of WETS-FM, a public radio station licensed to East Tennessee State University in Johnson City, Tennessee. Less than 100 miles from Sneedville, the Melungeons were considered by many to be a folktale or a legend, the Appalachian equivalent of the bogeyman or the headless horseman. When I met the woman who became my wife, she asked about my ethnic background. When I replied "Melungeon," she reacted as if I had said "Leprechaun." She was not the first person I'd met, and wouldn't be the last, who didn't believe in Melungeons.

In 1997, I read an article in the *Wall Street Journal* about an Internet website and an e-mail group devoted to the discussion of Melungeons, particularly a book written by Dr. N. Brent Kennedy three years earlier. *The Melungeons: The Resurrection of a Proud People; An Untold Story of Ethnic Cleansing in America* presented new theories about the origin of the Melungeons, theories that cast new light on pre-Colonial America.

I interviewed Brent Kennedy (and some of his critics) and produced a radio piece that aired on National Public Radio's *All Things Considered* in September 1997. The Melungeon story seemed far too complex for an eight-minute piece, however, so during the next year, I conducted more interviews and began producing an hour-long documentary. Simultaneously, I worked with a wonderful group of dedicated people who incorporated as the Melungeon Heritage Association.

While producing my documentary, I was keenly aware of all the information that had to be left out for one reason or another—and of how many more questions I had about my own heritage. I had barely scratched the surface of the Melungeon story.

I do not have a theory of origin I wish to promote. Personally, I like the idea that I come from a "mysterious" background. This book will attempt to present the theories that have been advanced about the

Melungeons, to record as accurately as possible the history of our people, and to report on the research that has been conducted in an effort to solve the mystery of these "sons and daughters of the legend."

One of the purposes of this book is to help shatter the notion of "race." Anthropologists have long discounted the concept of "race." That concept, however, is at the heart of this story; it is why the Melungeons and other mixed-race people were subjected to sometimes-harsh legal sanctions and isolation. America has had an unhealthy obsession with race and the notion of "purity." The Melungeon story is a celebration of the diversity of America.

Most importantly, I want to document, as best I can, the lives of those who struggled against racism and a rigidly enforced class system to survive. Those of us who descend from the Melungeons owe much to our ancestors who worked hard to provide their children with a quality of life that they themselves would never enjoy. A great deal of what has been written about our people is legend, intended only to sell newspapers and magazines, and the Melungeons who came before us deserve better than that.

The title of this book refers, of course, to the outdoor drama *Walk Toward the Sunset*, which was performed in Sneedville from 1969 to 1976. This drama marked a turning point in the history of the Melungeons in terms of the way they were perceived by themselves and by outsiders. In an incredibly brief span of time, the word "Melungeon" was transformed from an epithet rarely spoken to a name worn proudly.

The title of this book also refers to the fact that the Melungeons, sadly, are rapidly disappearing as a cohesive, identifiable group. Writers have spoken of the eventual disappearance of the Melungeons, through out-marriage and assimilation, for over half a century. The process may be taking longer than some of these writers believed it would, but it is still taking place. The Melungeons are no longer the social outcasts they were a half-century ago, and this is a positive development—but one which marks the elimination of one of the primary factors that made the Melungeons distinguishable from their neighbors.

An image stays in my mind: at the Wise County, Virginia courthouse on the last Saturday in July of 1997, city officials, Melungeon researchers, and visiting dignitaries are gathered on the steps to open First Union, a gathering that eventually led to the formation of the Melungeon Heritage Association. Many in this group of educated professional people are celebrating their Melungeon heritage, a heritage they only recently discovered.

On the fringes of the crowd that has gathered to watch and listen are an elderly, swarthy Melungeon couple, dressed in rough farm clothes. These people remind me of the Melungeons I knew as a child; they've come to town because it is Saturday and they always come to town on Saturday. Intuition and imagination tell me that they are not educated people, but they have known of their Melungeon heritage all their lives—and for them, it has never been a source of pride. That heritage has set them apart, made them the objects of scorn and derision, and has never been a heritage that they acknowledge, at least not out loud and in public. They listen to the words of the college-educated Melungeons, most of whom have been considered upstanding white citizens their entire lives, but the elderly couple stays on the edge of the crowd. They don't feel comfortable among the professional people in expensive clothes, but they listen with interest because of the topic and because these obviously well-educated people claim to be Melungeons just like themselves. They are interested, but puzzled that people are now embracing the heritage that has kept them on the fringes of society their entire lives.

"Melungeon" is no longer the epithet it once was, and the Melungeons themselves are no longer the people they once were. We can hope that coming generations will celebrate their Melungeon heritage while being thankful that they will never know first-hand what that heritage has meant. In order for coming generations to appreciate what it once meant to be Melungeon, however, the story of their ancestors must be told.

To tell this story, it is necessary to quote and paraphrase the words and thoughts of people of different generations and sensibilities. Terms such as "colored," "Negro," "black," and "African-American" have all, at one time or another, been considered the proper or polite term for Americans of African descent, but these terms have not always been synonymous. For that reason, I tend to use the terms that were in popular use during the time period in question. Uglier epithets are sometimes quoted; they are regrettably necessary to convey the thoughts and attitudes of society during various periods in our history.

Although this is an objective study of the Melungeons, I cannot pretend to be neutral or impartial about this subject; the people involved are my family and friends. At the time of this writing, I am president of the Melungeon Heritage Association. Readers are entitled to judge my writing with the knowledge of my associations.

On that note, I wish to thank those who have helped make this book possible, including Brent Kennedy, Claude Collins, DruAnna Overbay, Jim Callahan, Connie Clark, S. J. Arthur, Audie and Alisa Kennedy, Jim and Phyllis Morefield, Mattie Ruth Johnson, James Nickens, Jonah and Elene May, Scott Collins, Bob Greene, Mike Nassau, Bill Fields, Darlene Wilson, Dennis Maggard, Eloy Gallegos, Manuel Mira, Hazel (Winkler) Turner and the late Elmer Turner, Calvin Beale, Paul Brodwin, Kevin Jones, R. C. Mullins, Jack Mullins, Charles Sizemore, Troy Williams, Katie Doman, David Collins, Katherine VandeBrake, Kathy Lyday-Lee, John Lee Welton, Jack Goins, Cleland Thorpe, Seven Gibson, Johnnie Mullins Rhea, Arlee Gowen, Carroll and Betty Goyne, Helen Campbell, Joe Scolnick, Turan Yasgan of the Turkic World Research Foundation, Aslihan Arul, Vural Cengiz, Robin Benke, Ernie Martin, Joe Scolnick, Virginia DeMarce, David Henige, Donna Shields of the Monacan Indian Nation, Turker Ozdagon, the University of Virginia's College at Wise, National Public Radio, the Melungeon Heritage Association, and the Vardy Community Historical Society. I would especially like to thank my colleagues at East Tennessee State University, who have been invaluable in the research and writing of this book, including Judy Harwood, Fred Sauceman, Dr. Paul Stanton, Rick LaRue and the staff at the Charles G. Sherrod Library, and Norma Myers and the staff of the Archives of Appalachia.

Most of all, I wish to thank my mother, Wanda Barker, who was the first to tell me about this subject and has encouraged me ever since; my father, the late Willis Winkler, who taught me more than he ever could have known; and my wife, Andrea, whose proofreading, advice, and support have been invaluable. Finally, I dedicate this book to my daughter Claire, who was not yet born when I began this book but has provided a strong motivation for its completion.

PHOTOGRAPHS

Legendary Melungeon matriarch Mahala Mullins lived in this cabin on Newman's Ridge. In 1999, the Vardy Community Historical Society bought the cabin, moved it off the Ridge to a location across the road from the Vardy Church and restored it.

MAHALA (1824-1898) WITH BURTON AND MILLIE

MAHALA WAS THE DAUGHTER OF SOLOMEN COLLINS AND HIS WIFE, GINCIE GOINGS. MAHALA MARRIED JOHN MULLINS. THEIR CHILDREN WERE: JANE (1841), SALLY (1843), LARKIN (1844), BURTON, ADOPTED (1846), MILLIE (1846), ELBE (1848), RICHARD (1852), MARY ANN (1853), JERRY (1854), JOHN JR. (1855), RUBEN (1856), OLLIE (1859), LEWIS (1859), CALVIN (1860). SIX CHILDREN DIED IN INFANCY.

MAHALA AND JOHN LIVED ON TOP OF NEWMAN'S RIDGE IN A TWO STORY, DOUBLE LOG CABIN.
THE FAMILY MADE A GOOD LIVING FARMING, HUNTING, TRAPPING, SELLING TIMBER AND MAKING WHISKEY.
THE CABIN WAS BURNED IN THE CIVIL WAR AND REBUILT ON THE SAME LOCATION.
IN 2000, IT WAS MOVED TO ITS PRESENT LOCATION AND RESTORED BY THE VARDY COMMUNITY HISTORICAL SOCIETY.

BOOKS AND OTHER INFORMATION AVAILABLE FROM
THE VARDY COMMUNITY HISTORICAL SOCIETY.

Newman Ridge, Hancock County, Tennessee.

The Vardy School, left, was erected in 1929. The Presbyterian mission school served Melungeon school until it closed in 1973. The Vardy Church is in the foreground. (Courtesy of Vardy Historical Society.)

The Vardy School building today. The building was too far gone for restoration by the VCHS.

Plaque erected by the Vardy Community Historical Society.

The Vardy Church,
restored as a museum
by the Vardy
Community Historical
Society.

Researcher Calvin Beale (left) with Wayne Winkler, June 2002.

W. C. "Claude" Collins, recipient of a Lifetime Achievement Award from the Melungeon Heritage Association, June 2002.

Brent Kennedy on Melungeon Mountain, Cesme, Turkey, July 1998.

1

A RACELESS PEOPLE

melungeon, also malungeon: (me' lenjen-s) usu. cap [origin unknown]: one of a group of mixed Indian, white, and Negro ancestry in the southern Appalachians esp. of eastern Tennessee.
Webster's Third International Dictionary (1981)

These are raceless people, neither fish nor fowl, neither white, nor black, nor red, nor brown. They bear a heavy cross…These folks…are indeed America's outcasts. They, more than any other class, might properly be called "forgotten men." They spend their lonely lives in a social limbo—not quite white, not quite Negro, not quite Indian. They are ignored, derided, rejected, tolerated.

Brewton Berry, 1963[1]

A Malungeon isn't a nigger, and he isn't an Indian, and he isn't a white man. God only knows what he is.
Unnamed Tennessee legislator, circa 1890[2]

The core of reality within the legend is not easily discovered. There is no group of people who call themselves Melungeons or who would recognize themselves as thus separated from the rest of the country population. Non-Melungeons, however, are in general agreement as to who are Melungeons.

Edward Price, 1951[3]

---

[1] Brewton Berry, *Almost White* (New York: Macmillan, 1963) vii, 9.
[2] Will Allen Dromgoole, "The Malungeons," *The Arena* 3 (March 1891): 472.

Hancock County is located in the rugged terrain of northeastern Tennessee, adjacent to the Virginia state line. It has the smallest population of any county in the state, less than 7,000, and is one of the poorest counties in Tennessee and in the nation. The county was formed in 1844 from parts of two neighboring counties, Claiborne and Hawkins, and was named after John Hancock, the first signer of the Declaration of Independence. Clinch Mountain, a long, low ridge, makes up the southern border of Hancock County, with Powell Mountain on the northern border with Virginia. The Clinch River flows through the county, and the farms in its small valleys grow primarily tobacco and cattle.

The county is similar to dozens of Appalachian counties except for one thing: Hancock County is known as the home of the Melungeons, a mixed-race people who have fascinated anthropologists, social scientists, and (especially) feature writers for newspapers and magazines for nearly two centuries. The most common adjective used to describe the Melungeons is "mysterious;" no one knows where the Melungeons originated or how they wound up in Hancock County. Writers and researchers have developed theories to explain their origins, but the Melungeons themselves usually told outsiders they were Portuguese and/or Indian.

Despite the romantic legends surrounding the Melungeons, many of their neighbors considered them untrustworthy, unfriendly, and inferior to whites. Their precise racial status in society, however, was somewhat murky; Melungeons did not fit into any of the racial and ethnic categories which define an individual or group within American society. This uncertain status caused problems, both for the Melungeons themselves and for officials who were forced to categorize them. At various times, Melungeons were restricted in their educational opportunities and their choice of marriage partners. They caused confusion for military officials who were required to segregate black soldiers from white soldiers. Their right to vote was sometimes challenged and they faced hostility from their white neighbors. Perhaps most importantly, in a society whose members were defined in large part by their ethnic category, the Melungeons simply did not fit.

---

[3] Edward Price, "The Melungeons: A Mixed-Blood Strain of the Southern Appalachians," *Geographical Review* 41/2 (1951): 258.

Some of the questions surrounding the Melungeons may never be answered. Other questions can be answered, at least to a reasonable degree, through information available in historical records, census and tax records, and even in press accounts of the Melungeons.

Separating fact from fiction in the Melungeon story is no easy task. The Melungeons have been called by many writers "sons and daughters of the legend." Twentieth century writers have primarily seen the Melungeons as an interesting feature story, one that lends itself more to legend than to fact. As the newspaper editor in the film, *The Man Who Shot Liberty Valance,* said, "When the legend conflicts with the facts, print the legend." This philosophy has, intentionally or not, influenced most of the published work on the Melungeons, and has sold many newspapers, magazines, and books.

While this work will attempt to distinguish between fact and legend, both fact and legend are important facets of the Melungeon story. Some of the legends can be traced to specific sources and were introduced for specific reasons. Others have origins as ethereal as the Melungeons themselves. When examined in its historical context, the Melungeon story sheds new light on the history of America and the complex relations between its people of various colors.

Melungeon Identity

The definition of the word "Melungeon" has always been a bit vague. Scholars, journalists, and even Melungeons themselves disagree on who is and who is not a Melungeon. Some anthropologists have limited the term to a few families located near Newman's Ridge in Hancock County, traditionally considered the home of the Melungeons. More recent researchers have expanded "Melungeon" to include settlements of people related to the Hancock County group who migrated elsewhere in Tennessee and in Kentucky and Virginia.

Edward Price, a geographer who wrote about the Melungeons in the early 1950s, pointed out that Melungeons themselves did not usually associate themselves with that term, which they considered a vile epithet. However, whites who lived near Melungeons knew exactly who was and who was not a Melungeon. "Melungeon-ness" was based on family affiliations: Melungeon family names included Collins, Gibson, Mullins, Bunch, Bowlin, and a few others. Not everyone with a "Melungeon" name was considered a Melungeon by neighbors, however. The definition was very subjective, with lots of gerrymandering for particular individuals. Thus, the earliest practical definition of "Melungeon" was anyone whose neighbors referred to them as such.

Even using that very limited definition, Melungeons were not restricted to Hancock County. They were also found in neighboring Lee County, Virginia, as well as in the Virginia counties of Scott and Wise, where they were sometimes known as "Ramps." Groups of Melungeons also lived in Graysville, Tennessee, Magoffin and Letcher Counties in Kentucky, and even in Highland County, Ohio. Post-World War Two migrations have resulted in enclaves of "urban" Melungeons in Maryland, Indiana, and Michigan.

Today there is debate over whether the term can, or should, be applied to only the limited core families of Hancock County, Tennessee and surrounding areas. Genealogist Virginia DeMarce, in an article on Melungeons, complained, "Some writers today use the term generically, embracing the entire constellation of tri-racial groups. Technically, however, it belongs to the interrelated families along Newman's Ridge in Hawkins County, where they lived for forty years or so prior to 1844, when the area was cut away into the new county of Hancock."[4]

Limiting the definition of "Melungeon" only to those who were traditionally known by that name ignores the fact that these people had ancestors and descendants who shared their genetic background but not their geographic location or their name. Although some accounts place the Melungeons on Newman's Ridge prior to the arrival of the first white pioneers, everyone agrees that the Melungeons came there from somewhere else. And many Melungeons moved to the Newman's Ridge area only to move elsewhere soon afterward.

Similar groups of "mysterious" people, or at least remnants of these groups, are found all along the Atlantic seaboard. While these other groups have no known connection to the Melungeons, they have suffered similar problems due to the difficulty of placing them within an established racial category. These mixed-race groups will be examined in the following chapter. It is very likely that the Melungeons and these other groups originated with the large number of mixed-race families that developed in Colonial America.

---

[4] Virginia Easley DeMarce, "Looking at Legends—Lumbee and Melungeon: Applied Genealogy and the Origins of Tri-racial Isolate Settlements," *National Genealogical Quarterly* (March 1993): 24–45.

Over the years, many theories have been proposed to explain the origin of the Melungeons. These theories have suggested descent from Spanish or Portuguese explorers, from the "Lost Colonists" of Roanoke Island, from shipwrecked sailors or pirates of various nationalities, from one of the Lost Tribes of Israel, or from ancient Phoenicians or Carthaginians. More recent theories have proposed that the Melungeons descended from Mediterranean or Middle Eastern ancestors.

None of these theories originated with the Melungeons themselves. Early accounts reflect the Melungeons' self-description as "Indians." Some Melungeons reportedly described themselves a "Portuguese," or, as many pronounced it, "Portyghee." Most of their white neighbors considered the Melungeons a mixture of black and Indian, or white, black, and Indian.

The widely-held belief that the Melungeons had African ancestry was the source of most of their difficulties. The status of non-whites in America has always been problematic, and at times the Melungeons have had to defend their right to vote, to attend school, and to enjoy other privileges denied to African-Americans. To do this, they have consistently, until recently, denied having African ancestry. However, the myriad theories meant to explain their swarthy skins and generally non-European appearance have come from whites, most of whom were sympathetic to the Melungeons and wanted to help them avoid the social stigma associated with African ancestry.

The debate continues today. While most academics consider the Melungeons a mixture of European-American, African-American, and Native American ancestry, some Melungeons still vehemently reject any suggestion of African ancestry. Modern theories of Melungeon origin have generated controversy but have also inspired further research. Recent genetic studies have shed some light on the ancestry of the Melungeons, but have not answered all the questions.

By the early 1960s, newspaper articles predicted the disappearance of the Melungeons; out-migration and intermarriage with whites had nearly rendered the Melungeons indistinguishable from their white neighbors. However, by the end of that decade, Melungeons in Hancock County were acknowledging and celebrating their heritage with an outdoor drama. By the mid-1990s, the phenomenon C. S. Everett called "the exotic origins craze" was fueled by a "virtual community" on the

Internet.[5] Amateur genealogists and researchers sought to redefine "Melungeon" into a term broad enough to include their own families, and in doing so have blurred and distorted the term as it was originally used.

A Mysterious Word

One question which has been examined by nearly every writer on this subject is the origin of the name "Melungeon."[6] The most commonly accepted theory is that the word derived from the French *mèlange*, meaning mixture. In 1793 and 1794, Baron François de Tubeuf acquired thousands of acres in southwestern Virginia, near an area where many Melungeon families lived. Several French families attempted to create a city on the Clinch River, and before their colony failed, reportedly met with a band of "friendly Indians." This French colony may have dubbed these Indians with the plural form of *mèlange,* which is *mèlangeon* or *mèlangeons,* which could conceivably have been corrupted to "Melungeon." As we will see, the first written record of the term "Melungin [sic]" occurred just a few miles from this French settlement. Other possible sources for this term include French and Swiss settlers in northeastern North Carolina, or Huguenots in Virginia and North Carolina.[7]

Another proposed theory for the origin of "Melungeon" is the Afro-Portuguese term *melungo,* supposedly meaning "shipmate." Yet another is the Greek term *melan,* meaning "black." Author Brent Kennedy, in arguing a Turkish origin for the Melungeons, maintains that "Melungeon" derives from the Arabic *melun jinn* and the Turkish *melun can*, both pronounced similarly to "Melungeon" and both translating to "cursed soul" or "one who has been abandoned by God." Kennedy maintains that the Melungeons identified themselves by that name.[8]

Researcher C. S. Everett suggests another possible origin for the term: *melongena,* originally an Italian term related to the more modern *melanzane* (pronounced meh *lun'* zhen eh) which means "eggplant." The eggplant has a dark skin, and the term was used to describe sub-Saharan

---

[5] C. S. Everett, "Melungeon History and Myth," *Appalachian Journal* 26/4 (Summer 1999): 384.

[6] The word "Melungeon" was often spelled "Malungeon" in the nineteenth and early twentieth centuries.

[7] Everett, "Melungeon History and Myth," 360–61, 367–68.

[8] Brent Kennedy, Wayne Winkler, in-person interview, July 1997, Wise VA.

Africans. Everett argues that the term was used in the Carribean as a racial epithet, and is still in use in Italian-American communities to describe someone of real or presumed African heritage. The Melungeons, suggests Everett, may have acquired the name from late eighteenth-century Italian settlements in Albemarle County, Virginia.[9]

Karlton Douglas and Joanne Pezzullo believe the word "Melungeon" originated as the old English term "malengin" (singular) or "malengine" (plural). An old copy of Webster's Dictionary defines "malengine" as "evil machination; guile; deceit."[10] John Gower, who lived from 1330 to 1408, referred to "malengin" in his *Confession Amantis or Tales of the Seven Deadly Sins*. Edmund Spenser used both forms of the word in *Fairie Queen*, published in 1589:[11]

> Thereto both his owne wylie wit, (she sayd)And eke the fastnesse of his dwelling place, Both vnassaylable, gaue him great ayde: For he so crafty was to forge and face, So light of hand, and nymble of his pace,So smooth of tongue, and subtile in his tale, That could deceive one looking in his face; Therefore by name Malengin they him call, Well knowen by his feates, and famous ouer all.[12]

Spenser's *Fairie Queen* was well known by literate English-speakers at the time of the first European colonies in America. And, as Douglas and Pezzullo wrote, "It is well known the people of Appalachia, and Melungeons in particular, used words that were becoming archaic, and not much in use beyond Appalachia." Furthermore, "malengin" is very close in spelling to the first recorded reference to Melungeons in the Stony Creek Church Minutes of 1813, spelled "melungins."[13]

The term "Melungeon" did not always refer entirely to ethnic identity. The common usage of the term had an element of socio-economic status attached to it; families who were financially successful

---

[9] Everett, "Melungeon History and Myth," 373.

[10] Webster's Revised Unabridged Dictionary, 1913.

[11] Karlton Douglas and Joanne Pezzullo, "Melungeon or Malengine?" *The Appalachian Quarterly* 7/1 (March 2002): 99; "Edmund Spenser," http://www.notredame.ac.jp/~at93e184/Amoretti-html/html/spenser.html.

[12] Edmund Spenser, *The Fairie Queen* (New Haven and London: Yale University Press, 1978) 825.

[13] Douglas and Pezzullo, "Melungeon or Malengine?" 99–100.

often avoided the label, no matter who their ancestors were. In Reconstruction-era Tennessee politics, "Melungeon" was synonymous with "sneaky," and was often applied to East Tennessee Republicans by Middle and West Tennessee Democrats. While working for a Tennessee legislator, Nashville writer Will Allen Dromgoole overheard her employer mention that a fellow lawmaker was "tricky as a Melungeon."[14]

With the notable exception of Kennedy, nearly everyone who has written about the Melungeons agrees that they fiercely resented the name. Even in the mid-twentieth century, to call a Hancock Countian a Melungeon was to insult him. The stigma attached to the name "Melungeon" leads most researchers to the conclusion that the name was imposed upon these people and that it was not a name they used for themselves. Accounts of anyone calling himself or herself a Melungeon before the 1960s are extremely rare—although on several occasions individuals identified someone else as such. Usage of the word itself was rare; as William Worden wrote in a 1947 *Saturday Evening Post* article, "A lovely woman…may talk for some time and tell much that is written in no books, some fact, some hearsay, some the most fanciful legend. But one word she will never say. She will never say 'Malungeon.'"[15]

Melungeon Physical Characteristics

For years, curious individuals have made their way to Hancock County, Tennessee, with the intention of seeing a Melungeon. Inspired by newspaper and magazine articles, they have driven over the switchback roads of Newman's Ridge, explored Blackwater Creek and Snake Holler, and have even knocked on doors to ask where they might find some Melungeons. Many of these Melungeon-seekers have gone away convinced that looking for Melungeons was the Hancock County version of a snipe hunt. Others were puzzled at the unfriendliness of those whom they queried, completely unaware of the serious breach of local etiquette they had committed. Hardly anyone could say for certain they had seen a Melungeon.

---

[14] Jean Patterson Bible, *Melungeons Yesterday and Today* (Rogersville TN: East Tennessee Printing Company, 1975) 13; Dromgoole, "The Malungeons," 472.

[15] W. L. Worden, "Sons of the Legend," *Saturday Evening Post* (18 October 1947).

John Shelton Reed, author and former sociology professor at the University of North Carolina, wrote of hearing about Melungeons while growing up in Kingsport, Tennessee, "thirty-five miles from Sneedville as the crow flies, but an hour and a half on mountain roads." As a teenager during the 1950s, Reed and a friend decided to drive to Sneedville, the Hancock County seat, to find some Melungeons. Having heard that Melungeons had "olive" skin, Reed and his companion looked for green people. Of course, they found none, and "left Sneedville no wiser than we'd come." Reed's sister, novelist Lisa Alther, also made a trip to Hancock County in search of Melungeons. Those whom Alther questioned either denied knowing what she was talking about or insisted that the Melungeons no longer existed.[16]

Chances are good that both Reed and Alther saw some Melungeons without recognizing them as such. Most Melungeons in Hancock County look very much like their "white" neighbors, many of whom are quite swarthy from a lifetime of outdoor work. In 1963, Brewton Berry wrote, "[N]either in their culture nor their economy are they distinguishable from other mountain folk. Among those bearing the telltale surnames are individuals of dark complexion and straight black hair...But the physical features of most of them suggest no other ancestry than white."[17]

The current Melungeon gene pool, as chapter six will show, is quite diverse. In the absence of DNA testing on the remains of a known Melungeon from the early nineteenth century. We cannot know the genetic background of the earliest Melungeons, the original families who moved to Newman's Ridge between 1780 and 1820. Observers have attempted to describe the Melungeons since the mid-nineteenth century. These descriptions of Melungeon physical characteristics, however, present a confusing picture:

> They are tall, straight, well- formed people, of a dark copper color, with Circassian features, but wooly heads and other similar appendages of our negro.[18]

---

[16] John Shelton Reed, "Mixing in the Mountains," *Southern Cultures* (Winter 1997): 25–36; Lisa Alther, "The Melungeon Melting Pot," presentation at Third Union, Wise VA, 20 May 2000.

[17] Berry, *Almost White*, 18.

[18] "The Melungeons," *Littel's Living Age* 254/31 (March 1849).

Their complexion is reddish-brown, totally unlike the mulatto. The men are very tall and straight, with small, sharp eyes, high cheek bones, and straight black hair, worn rather long... their features are totally unlike those of the negro, except in cases where the two races have cohabitated, as is sometimes the fact.[19]

They are of swarthy complexion, with prominent cheek bones, jet black hair, generally straight but at times having a slight tendency to curl, and the men have heavy black beards...Their frames are well built and some of the men are fine specimens of physical manhood. They are seldom fat.[20]

They have swarthy complexion, straight black hair, black or gray eyes—and are not tall but heavy-set.[21]

Most Melungeons have oily skin and kinky hair, hardly typical characteristics of either the red or white race.[22]

While some of them are swarthy and have high Indian cheekbones, the mountain whites, too, often display these same characteristics. Also, many of the Melungeons have light hair, blue eyes, and fair skin.[23]

The color of the skin of a full-blooded, pure Melungeon is a much richer brown than an Indian's skin. It is not the color of a part Indian and part white, for their skin is lighter. The full-

---

[19] Dromgoole, "The Malungeons," 473.

[20] Paul D. Converse, "The Melungeons," *The Southern Collegian* (December 1912): 59–69.

[21] Will T. Hale and D. L. Merritt, *A History of Tennessee and Tennesseans* (Chicago: Lewis Publishing Company) 1913.

[22] Anonymous, "Crawford Story Brings Comment," *The Coalfield Progress* (Norton VA): 4 July 1940.

[23] Leo Zuber, "The Melungeons," WPA Federal Writers' Guide MSS, McClung Historical Collection, Lawson-McGhee Library, University of Tennessee, Knoxville, Tennessee.

blooded, pure Melungeon had more the color of skin of a person from India and Egypt.[24]

No wonder so many Melungeon-seekers have been disappointed in their pilgrimages to Hancock County. Based on this variety of descriptions, creating a mental portrait of a "typical" Melungeon is virtually impossible. Obviously, there is no Melungeon archetype; all of the above descriptions are accurate to some degree. While most Melungeons have been described as resembling a mixture of Indian and European, some Melungeons display a distinct African heritage.

While outsiders may have had difficulty in identifying Melungeons, neighboring whites have not. Traditionally, those living near Melungeons have known exactly who "belonged" with white people and who did not. The history of nearly all tri-racial groups has been marked by their efforts to overcome their inferior social status.

The Concept of Race

Although the traditional concept of race has been discredited by much (but not all) of the scientific community, race has been an obsession in American life. The presumed "superiority" felt by Europeans over Africans and Native Americans has played a dominant role in American history and culture. An understanding of the prevailing notions of race is helpful in putting the Melungeon story in context.

In the past, anthropologists have categorized humans into one of three general racial categories: Caucasian, Negroid, and Mongoloid. The Caucasian, or white, race was associated with Europe, while the Negroid, or black, race originated in Africa. The Mongoloid race included both Asians and American Indians. These categories included several sub-categories, but for the Europeans who colonized America, there were three races with distinct social positions. The white race was considered by whites to be superior and the Negroid race inferior. The Mongoloid race occupied a social position somewhere in between.

American society had strict taboos against the mixing of the races, taboos that still exist in some degree today. Richard McCulloch is the

---

[24] William P. Grohse, papers, (Microfilm Roll # 7) East Tennessee State University.

author of "The Racial Compact," a website which advocates racial pride and the maintenance of "racial purity."

> [R]acial separation is necessary for the long-term preservation of the Northern European race, the founding and still the majority American racial type, which I refer to as the Nordish race. It is a simple matter of either-or—either racial separation or racial death... For the Nordish race, with its many recessive genetic traits, the consequences of extensive intermixture are racial destruction, and as intermixture is unavoidable in a multiracial environment, the inevitable consequence of multiracial conditions is the destruction or extinction of the Nordish race... Since the Nordish race requires racial separation for its continued existence or preservation, to oppose racial separation is to effectively oppose the preservation or continued existence of the Nordish race, to effectively propose and support Nordish racial destruction or extinction, and this is the position of the presently dominant or "mainstream" elements.[25]

McCulloch espouses views that seem dated to many Americans today, but were widely held in the not-so-distant past. The Commonwealth of Virginia passed a Racial Integrity Act in 1924 banning marriage between whites and non-whites, a law that was not repealed until 1971. The notion of "racial purity" reached its zenith with the policies of Adolf Hitler and Nazi Germany. Since then, the idea of "racial purity" has been largely—but not completely—discredited.

Today, a majority of scientists reject the entire notion of race, feeling that the concept is more a reflection of societal attitudes than it is of science. From the Emory University Anthropology web page:

> The concept of race was constructed long before scientists understood the role of the genes or the fact of evolutionary change. In the beginning, race was a divinely ordained concept that wedded social, psychological and biological characteristics to describe people and explain behavior. Race was used to justify

---

[25] Richard McCulloch, "Separation: The Preservationist Imperative," http://www.racialcompact.com/preservationimperative.html.

the exploitation of populations that were assumed lack the biological and cultural ability to survive.

Anthropology was part of the "scientific" approach to race that to "biologize" the concept by eliminating the social and psychological descriptors. This attempt to make the concept more valid scientific construct had little impact on how racial groups were viewed. Prior to Darwin, racial inferiority was God's will; after Darwin, the result of natural selection. Furthermore, classifications based on biological traits are still strongly influenced by the social system and race is of little use in understanding biological diversity. Racial classifications tell us more about society than biology. Accordingly, many anthropologists have discarded the concept. However, the sociopolitical use of race and racism continues and its use has dramatic biological consequences. Anthropological study of race and racism from a historical, political, economic, and biocultural perspective remains a vital area of interest.[26]

In 1998, the Executive Board of the American Anthropological Association officially rejected the concept of race.

In the United States both scholars and the general public have been conditioned to viewing human races as natural and separate divisions within the human species based on visible physical differences. With the vast expansion of scientific knowledge in this century, however, it has become clear that human populations are not unambiguous, clearly demarcated, biologically distinct groups...Historical research has shown that the idea of 'race' has always carried more meanings than mere physical differences; indeed, physical variations in the human species have no meaning except the social ones that humans put on them. Today scholars in many fields argue that "race" as it is understood in the United States of America was a social mechanism invented during the 18th century to refer to those populations brought together in colonial America: the English

---

[26] Emory University, "Race and Racism," http://www.emory.edu/COLLEGE/ANTHROPOLOGY/research/race.html.

and other European settlers, the conquered Indian peoples, and those peoples of Africa brought in to provide slave labor.

From its inception, this modern concept of "race" was modeled after an ancient theorem of the Great Chain of Being, which posited natural categories on a hierarchy established by God or nature. Thus "race" was a mode of classification linked specifically to peoples in the colonial situation... How people have been accepted and treated within the context of a given society or culture has a direct impact on how they perform in that society. The "racial" worldview was invented to assign some groups to perpetual low status, while others were permitted access to privilege, power, and wealth. The tragedy in the United States has been that the policies and practices stemming from this worldview succeeded all too well in constructing unequal populations among Europeans, Native Americans, and peoples of African descent. Given what we know about the capacity of normal humans to achieve and function within any culture, we conclude that present-day inequalities between so-called "racial" groups are not consequences of their biological inheritance but products of historical and contemporary social, economic, educational, and political circumstances.[27]

While this statement did not reflect the beliefs of all members of the AAA, the Executive Board believes that it represents generally the contemporary thinking and scholarly position of a majority of anthropologists today.

Race, therefore, is not a valid means by which to categorize groups of human beings. "Ethnicity" is a much more precise term, as it considers cultural as well as genetic factors. The genetic differences between an Irishman and an Arab may be very slight, but the cultural differences are far more pronounced. Even more significantly, the notion of race as an influence on behavior, intelligence, and personality traits has been discredited by most (but certainly not all) scientists.

For most of American history, however, race has been the primary factor in determining social status. In practical usage, the concept of race in our nation's history has been much simpler: a person is white, black,

---

[27] American Antropological Association, "Statement on Race," http://www.aaanet/stmts/racepp.htm.

or Indian (or Mexican, depending on location). Within those groups, there was a feeling of community, of shared problems and hopes, even for those at the bottom of the social ladder. Most people who are a mix of two of these "races" have identified with one or the other. Sometimes the identification is externally mandated; mixtures of black and white in America have traditionally (and legally) been associated with the African-American community, whether the individuals desired that identification or not.

Tri-racial people are, or are at least considered to be, a mixture of the Negroid, Caucasoid, and Mongoloid races. For the purposes of this study, however, "tri-racial" does not refer to simply a mixture of the three races. Many Americans, particularly African-Americans, have a tri-racial background, but they usually identify themselves as "black" and are accepted as such in the community. Traditionally, "tri-racials" have not been identified as members of any of those three racial categories. They have shunned identification as blacks, primarily to avoid the legal and social restrictions such an identification entailed. They have not, for the most part, maintained a tribal identity with recognized Indian groups. And because the predominant white society in America has, until recently (and this is arguable), denied social acceptance to all but "pure" Caucasians, tri-racial people have usually not been considered "white."

If the idea of race in general is dubious, the notion of a "pure" race is downright ludicrous. For millennia, human beings have been blending genes with other human beings. A cursory study of world history reveals countless examples of genetic mixing between diverse people who made contact through exploration, trade, and warfare. There is no such thing as a "pure" race—yet notions of racial purity still exist.

In a society which believed that whites were supreme, and that racial mixtures were to be avoided, the Melungeons and other tri-racial groups were a nightmare, a dirty little secret to be kept hidden. Most of the tri-racial groups would have been content to remain hidden, forgotten, and most of all, left alone. In a race-obsessed and Negrophobic America, that was not possible.

Marginal Peoples, Racial Islands, and Isolates

In America, dozens of distinct groups of people have inhabited a racial and ethnic no-man's land. Throughout the eastern United States, small communities of "mysterious" people struggled to survive in a society that insisted on categorizing its citizens but had no convenient category for them. These were people who had Native American ancestry, but no remnants of Native language, culture, or connection with a recognized tribe. They had (or were believed to have) African-American ancestry, but were often looked down upon by nearby black communities for trying to "pass" as white or white-and-Indian. And while they undoubtedly had European-American ancestors, they were commonly denied the rights and privileges available to white Americans.

There is no commonly-accepted word or phrase to describe these people. In the late 1950s, demographer Calvin Beale dubbed them "tri-racial isolates." Writer Brewton Berry calls them "mestizos," and researcher Mike Nassau refers to them as "mestees." Others have used the terms "racial islands," "little races," and "marginal peoples."[28] These are terms meant to describe people whose ancestry is a mix of European-American, African-American, and Native American. Although the concept of race is no longer accepted by most anthropologists, American history has largely been the story of conflicts between the "races" popularly identified as white, black, and Indian. The term "mixed race" seems inexact because it usually indicates far more common mixture of two of the "races." The same could be said of the terms "mestizo" and "mestee." The term "tri-racial" has been resented by some for its implication of African ancestry, and Beale's term "tri-racial isolates" has been criticized by some modern-day Melungeon activists because the "isolate" part of the phrase is taken to imply inbreeding.

The term "tri-racial," while perhaps controversial, is useful to describe those who, in the eyes of their neighbors, were a mixture of white, black, and Indian. It is that three-way mixture, or at least the perception of that mixture, which makes these groups unique in the eyes of their communities and to scientists and feature writers alike.

"Tri-racial" is not a term that will please everyone to which it refers. Many of these groups have struggled for years to obtain state and/or

---

[28] Calvin L. Beale, "American Triracial Isolates: Their Status and Pertinence to Genetic Research," *Eugenics Quarterly* 4 /4 (December 1957): 187; Berry, *Almost White*, 40–41; Mike Nassau (McGlothlen), "Melungeons and Other Mestee Groups," http://www.multiracial.com/readers/nassau.html, 9; Lynwood Montell, "The Coe Ridge Colony: A Racial Island Disappears," *American Anthropologist* 74 (1972): 710; J. K. Dane and B. Eugene Griessman, "The Collective Identity of Marginal Peoples: The North Carolina Experience," *American Anthropologist* 74 (1972): 694.

federal recognition as Indian tribes. Often the suggestion of African ancestry has prevented such recognition. Also, many individuals resent any implication that they have African ancestry. Given America's once-restrictive racial laws and customs, not to mention racial attitudes still held today, this attitude is unfortunately understandable. Few people would choose to occupy the social position held by African-Americans through most of American history. A very important fact to remember, however, is that, as far as American society was concerned, *it did not matter* if these "tri-racials" did or did not actually have African antecedents. The majority (white) opinion was that these people had at least a degree of African or African-American ancestry. Even if false, the argument that these mixed-ethnic peoples had "Negro blood" carried much weight.

The Melungeons, like all the groups in this study, were thought by most to have at least some African-American ancestry. American popular thought in the nineteenth and most of the twentieth century subscribed to the "one drop" rule expressed often by Southern novelist Thomas Dixon: "One drop of 'Negro blood' makes one a Negro," "blood" referring not to the bodily fluid but to all aspects of one's genetic background. In many cases, the law considered tri-racials black; they attended segregated schools and were drafted into the military as blacks. Given these circumstances, the specific genealogy of an individual identified as a Melungeon or other "tri-racial" mattered not at all. Not all groups suffered the same legal and social discrimination as African-Americans, but all were consigned to a lower social status than whites. They were truly "marginal people," consigned to the fringes of life in the Piedmont towns and mountain communities where they lived, accepted as equals by none but their own kind.

Tri-racial groups are remnants of America's early colonial history that, to varying degrees, still exist as identifiable communities in the twenty-first century. A 1953 study showed such communities spread throughout the eastern United States from New England to Louisiana.[29] Mike Nassau estimated that 200 such groups existed in 1994.[30] Many members of these groups have migrated away from their traditional

---

[29] Edward T. Price, "A Geographic Analysis of White-Negro-Indian Racial Mixtures in the Eastern United States," Association of American Geographers, *Annals* 43 (June 1953): 139.

[30] Nassau, "Melungeons," 4.

communities to urban areas and have lost identification with their unique ethnic heritages. Some of these traditional communities have disappeared. Others, however, have survived and many are currently in the process of reclaiming their respective heritages.

Several tri-racial groups were directly descended from particular Native American tribes. Despite the mixture of European and African genes, some groups have maintained a semblance of tribal culture and have recently abandoned the pejorative names by which their neighbors once knew them, adopting traditional tribal names and striving for recognition as Indians.

Mike Nassau writes of tri-racial people:

> What are Mestees? Brewton Berry, in *Almost White*, wants to make most of them white. Of course, he was a white liberal being big hearted and offering them the most advantageous classification. William Gilbert, in his treatment of Indian and part-Indian groups in the eastern US, wants them all considered Indian. Terry Wilson, in his chapter on Native American mixed bloods, gives some details of the contribution of these peoples to the history of native peoples of the United States. He mentions the Mestee groups, citing Berry's *Almost White*; he prefers to consider them as mixed blood Indian communities rather than as marginal whites. He describes the uneasy relationship between mixed and putatively full blooded Indians, suggesting that it is time for the Indians to reject the racial classification imposed by the whites and accept all those of Indian or part Indian culture as Indians. G. Reginald Daniel, in the same book, *Racially Mixed People in America*, treats Mestees a part of the light skinned blacks who have passed or attempted to pass for white or Indian in order to escape the lower status accorded blacks. He is sympathetic to their lot, noting that blacks have resented Mestees denying their black ancestry, but sees it as a result of their attempt to avoid white racism rather than symptomatic of their own bigotry. Jack Forbes considered them as a black-Indian mix, a bridge between the two groups, but not to the whites.[31]

---

[31]Ibid, 5.

In 1946, William Gilbert presented the first comprehensive survey of tri-racial groups in the US. He estimated that there were at least 50,000 persons who were "complex mixtures in varying degrees of white, Indian, and Negro blood."[32]

Gilbert lists ten major tri-racial groups with several related groups. These include:

1. Brass Ankles and allied groups in South Carolina, including Red Bones, Red Legs, Turks, Marlboro Blues, and others.
2. Cajans and Creoles of Alabama and Mississippi.
3. Croatans of North Carolina, South Carolina, and Virginia.
4. Guineas of West Virginia and Maryland. (Other names included "West Hill Indians," "Cecil Indians," and "Guinea niggers.")
5. Issues of Amherst and Rockingham Counties, Virginia.
6. Jackson Whites of New York and New Jersey.
7. Melungeons of the Southern Appalachians.
8. Moors and Nanticokes of Delaware and New Jersey.
9. Red Bones of Louisiana.
10. Wesorts of southern Maryland.[33]

In addition to their uncertain ethnic background, Gilbert notes that "These small local groups seem to develop especially where environmental circumstances such as forbidding swamps or inaccessible and barren mountain country favor their growth."[34]

Gilbert saw little evidence that these groups were being absorbed by either the white or black communities, and noted, "Their native breeding grounds furnish a seemingly inexhaustible reservoir of population which periodically swarms into cities and industrial areas." Gilbert did not fear that further investigation of these tri-racials could "prejudice their social prospects since the vast majority cannot possibly hope to pass as 'white' under the present social system."[35]

---

[32] William Harlan Gilbert, Jr., "Memorandum Concerning the Characteristics of the Larger Mixed-Blood Racial Islands of the Eastern United States," *Social Forces* 24/4 (1946): 438.

[33] Ibid., 438–47.

[34] Ibid., 438.

[35] Ibid.

Several researchers believe there are ethnic and genetic links between the various tri-racial groups. However, the primary groups identified by Gilbert in 1946 have their own unique histories, common family names, and characteristics. While Melungeons have been the subject of much interest in the past decade, their history is intertwined with that of the other tri-racial communities. Therefore, a general familiarity with all the tri-racial groups is necessary.

Brass Ankles: Gilbert uses this term to identify several groups of people, numbering from 5,000 to 10,000, who were known by various names in South Carolina. The term "Brass Ankle" was used in some counties; terms used in other counties included Red Bones, Turks, Marlboro Blues, Croatans or Cros, Greeks, Portuguese, Yellow Hammers, Clay Eaters, Summerville Indians, or simply "those yellow people." Common family names include Boone, Braveboy, Bunch, Chavis, Creek, Driggers, Goins,[36] Harmon, Russell, Scott, Shavis, Swett, and Williams.[37]

The name "Brass Ankle," like the names of so many tri-racial groups, is shrouded in mystery. One possible origin is the Spanish *abrasado*, meaning "toasted brown." Other possible origins include a reference to brown skin showing between the cuff of the pants and the shoe, or from brass shackles used to keep slaves from escaping.[38]

Gilbert observes that, although some Brass Ankles had African-American features and others seemed to be Native American, they were recognized as "near white:" they were drafted into the segregated 1940s military as whites, and they voted. However, although their schools were classified as "white," Brass Ankles usually did not attend school with whites. While they claimed to be descended from Native Americans, neighboring whites were skeptical, as Brewton Berry noted in 1963.

"Around here," said a county lawyer, "these Brass Ankles will tell you they are Indians, descended from Pocahontas. Pocahontas? Why, poky nigger would be more like it." And from a deputy sheriff came this opinion, "If a man ain't white, he's a nigger, as far as I'm concerned.

---

[36] The name "Goins" (including such variants as Goyne, Goynes, Gowen, Gowan, etc.) is the most common family name among the tri-racials, and appears in most of the major groups, including the Melungeons. If there is a common genetic denominator among the various tri-racial groups, the Goins family may be the key.

[37] Gilbert, "Memorandum," 439.

[38] Ibid; Berry, *Almost White*, 38.

These Brass Ankles ain't white, so they're niggers. They're nothin' but niggers to me." Finally, there was the banker who said, "Brass Ankles are part white, part nigger, and part S.O.B."[39]

Today, the Brass Ankles of the White Oak community in South Carolina are known as the Santee Indian Association, while the Creeltown and Four Holes communities have incorporated as the Edisto Indian Association.[40] Another group included by Gilbert as associated with the Brass Ankles have formed the Summerville Indian Association.

Cajans and Creoles: These groups are not related to either the Cajuns (Acadians) of Louisiana nor the mixed-race French Creoles of Louisiana and the Caribbean. According to Gilbert, "The term 'Cajan' is derived from a fanciful resemblance to the Louisiana Cajuns. The "Creole" name derived from 'Creole colored' or 'Creole mixed.'"

The Cajans, with such family names as Byrd, Carter, Chestang, Johnson, Jones, Reed, Rivers, Smith, Sullivan, Terry, and Weaver, were located in southwestern Alabama, in the hilly areas of Washington, Mobile, and Clarke counties, as well as adjoining counties in Mississippi. Common family names among the Creoles include Allen, Andry, Balasco, Battiste, Chastang, Collins, Gomes, Hiner, Gomez, Laurent, Nicholas, Perez, Pope, Reid, Taylor, and Trenier. Creoles were found in Mobile and Baldwin counties in Alabama.[41]

Gilbert believed the Cajans descended from a free mulatto from Jamaica named Reed who settled in the Mobile Bay area and operated a cattle business and an inn. Two other families, named Byrd and Weaver, significantly contributed to the Cajan population: of the 2,000 or so Cajans enumerated in a 1953 study, over half bore the names Reed, Byrd, or Weaver. Their white neighbors borrowed (with modified spelling) the term "Cajan" from Louisiana to describe them.[42]

While the Cajuns are predominantly Protestant, the Catholic Creoles reflected a Latin aspect of their heritage that is not apparent among the Cajans. The Creoles operated their own fire companies and schools.

---

[39] Gilbert, "Memorandum," 439; Berry, *Almost White*, 58.

[40] John S. Kessler and Donald B. Ball, *North From The Mountains: A Folk History of the Carmel Melungeon Settlement, Highland County, Ohio* (Macon GA: Mercer University Press, 2001) 47.

[41] Gilbert, "Memorandum," 439.

[42] Price, "Racial Mixtures," 144–45.

However, both groups were socially isolated from both black and white neighbors.[43]

Croatans of North Carolina, South Carolina, and Virginia: Most of those described as "Croatans" in Gilbert's study are now recognized by the Federal government as Lumbee Indians. They have in the past been recognized by the state government as "Cherokee Indians of Robeson County" and "Sioux Indians of Lumber River." Their struggle for recognition as Indians has been complex.

The center of this population is in Robeson County, North Carolina, and in neighboring counties. Family names within this group include Allen, Bennett, Berry, Bridger, Brooks, Brown, Butler, Chapman, Chavis or Chavez, Coleman, Cooper, Dare, Gramme, Harris, Harvie, Howe, Johnson, Jones, Lasie, Little, Locklear, Lowry, Lucas, Martyn, Oxendine, Paine, Patterson, Powell, Sampson, Scott, Smith, Stevens, Taylor, Viccars, White, Willes, Wilkinson, Wood, and Wright. They numbered 3,640 in 1890 and over 13,000 only 40 years later.[44]

According to Gilbert, the name "Croatan" originated from the word "Croatoan," which was found carved on a tree or fencepost on Roanoke Island after the mysterious disappearance of Sir Walter Raleigh's "Lost Colony." Actually, "Croatan" was the name of a tribe that lived in the Pamlico Sound region, and was also the name of an island in the Outer Banks. While several tri-racial groups, including the Melungeons, are linked in legend with the English survivors of the Lost Colony (who supposedly intermarried with Indians), the Croatans or Lumbees probably have the strongest claim to that tradition.

The Croatans were disfranchised in North Carolina in 1835 but were allowed to vote after the Civil War. In 1946, they had separate schools, were forbidden by law from intermarrying with whites, and occupied a social status somewhat higher than blacks, but decidedly lower than whites.[45] Researcher Mike Nassau considers the Lumbee to be "the most Indian of the Mestee groups and the only one to be accepted as Indian by recognized Indian groups. Some of them are recognized as Indian by the Bureau of Indian Affairs; however, the BIA does not consider the

---

[43] Gilbert, "Memorandum," 439–40.

[44] Ibid., 440.

[45] Ibid.

Lumbee to be descended from any historical Indian tribe and denies them any federal benefits."[46]

Guineas of West Virginia and Maryland: Gilbert numbered this group at between 8,000 and 9,000 in 1946. They were centered in Barbour, Taylor, and surrounding counties in West Virginia, with a small group in Garrett County, Maryland. Family names included Adams, Collins, Croston, Dalton, Dorton, Kennedy, Male (or Mayle, Mahle, and Mail), Minard (or Miner), Newman, Norris, and Pritchard.

Although the Guineas had voted since West Virginia was organized and had been drafted as "whites," courts in West Virginia had pronounced them "colored." The Guineas at one time had their own schools, but by the 1940s were attending white schools. This caused considerable tension in their home territory, and two schools were burned, presumably by irate whites, as a result.[47]

Issues of Virginia: Now known as the Monacan Indian Tribe, the people once known as "Issues" still live in Amherst and Rockbridge counties in Virginia. In the mid-1920s, they numbered about 500, with the primary family names being Adcox, Branham, Johns, Redcross, and Willis.

The name "Issues" is derived from "free issues," a derogatory term referring to free blacks prior to the Civil War. The epithet accurately reflected the attitude of neighboring whites about the ancestry of this group. The Issues were the subject of a 1926 book entitled *Mongrel Virginians*. The book referred to the group as the "WIN Tribe," an acronym of "White-Indian-Negro."[48] Gilbert notes that the group had a tradition of Indian descent; in 1989 the group received state (but not federal) recognition as Monacan Indians.[49]

Jackson Whites of New Jersey and New York: One of the many legends about this group is that they descended from prostitutes brought to serve British troops in Manhattan during the American Revolution. "Jackson" was said to be the name of the procurer. These women—some white, some black—were said to have moved into the Ramapo

---

[46] Nassau, "Melungeons," 16.

[47] Gilbert, "Memorandum," 442.

[48] Arthur H. Estabrook, and Ivan E. McDougal, *Mongrel Virginians* (Baltimore: Williams & Wilkins, 1926).

[49] Gilbert, "Memorandum," 442; Karenne Wood, and Diane Shields, *The Monacan Indians: Our Story* (Madison Heights VA: Monacan Indian Nation, 2000) 33.

Mountains of New Jersey, where they intermarried with Tuscarora and Delaware Indians and runaway slaves.

Another explanation for the name is "Jacks and whites," i.e., blacks and whites, indicating a mixture. The Jackson Whites seemed to suffer no legal discrimination in New Jersey and sent their children to school with whites, according to Gilbert, but had a lower social status.[50]

However, Jackson Whites were barred from attending school with white children in New York State. Several families sued the state Department of Education for admission to white schools. Their case was supported by the NAACP and presented by Thurgood Marshall two years before the landmark Brown vs. Topeka Board of Education case, making it a forerunner in the fight for school integration.[51]

Some Jackson Whites have organized as the Ramapough Mountain Indians and have applied for recognition as Native Americans. However, writer David Cohen has largely discounted their claims to Native American identity, having traced most of the families back to free blacks and mulattoes.[52]

Melungeons of the Southern Appalachians: The original center for this population was Hancock County, Tennessee, but the Melungeons were also found in neighboring counties in northeast Tennessee, southwest Virginia, and southeast Kentucky. In some Virginia counties they were known as "Ramps." Core-group family names included Collins, Gibson (or Gipson), Goins, and Mullins. Other family groups included Bolen (or Bowlin), Denham, Freeman, Graham, and others, and Gilbert estimated their numbers at from 5,000 to 10,000.

Melungeons were disfranchised in 1834, but regained the right to vote just prior to the Civil War. Although Melungeons had attended separate schools in the past, by 1946 most were attending white schools—when they attended at all, according to Gilbert. For some Melungeons, however, the right to attend white schools came only after lawsuits. Melungeons were, for the most part, drafted as whites, although Gilbert notes that illiteracy kept many out of the military.[53]

---

[50] Gilbert, "Memorandum," 443.

[51] Nassau, "Melungeons," 16.

[52] David S. Cohen, *The Ramapo Mountain People* (New Brunswick NJ: Rutgers University Press, 1974) 25–58.

[53] Gilbert, "Memorandum," 444.

Moors and Nanticokes of Delaware and New Jersey: Although there is no direct link between these two groups, their small numbers and geographic proximity seem to argue for pairing the two. The Moors, numbering about 550 in 1946, were centered in Kent County, Delaware, and Bridgeton in southern New Jersey. Family names included Carney, Carter, Carver, Coker, Dean, Durham, Hansley, Hughes, Morgan, Mosely, Reed, Ridgway, and Sammon. The Nanticokes were found in Sussex County, Delaware, and numbered about 700. Nanticoke family names included Bumberry, Buton, Cormeans, Coursey, Drain, Hansor, Harmon, Kimmey, Layton, Miller, Morris, Norwood, Reed, Ridgway, Rogers, Sockum, Street, Walker, and Wright.

The name "Moor" is derived from the belief that this group is descended from shipwrecked Moorish sailors. The Nanticokes claim descent from the Nanticoke Indians of the region, and have attempted to gain recognition as Native Americans. The remnants of the original Nanticoke tribe, who now live in Canada, resent the use of the name "Nanticoke" by the Delaware group, which Nassau describes as "the blackest of all the Mestee groups; some members appear to be pure African." While the children of the Moors attended "colored" schools, Nanticokes had their own school.[54]

Red Bones of Louisiana: The Red Bones are found in the parishes of Natchitoches, Vernon, Calcasieu, Terrebonne, La Fourche, and St. Tammany in Louisiana. They were also known as "Houmas" along the coast and "Sabines" farther west. Another term used was "Cane River Mulattoes." Gilbert estimated their numbers at over 3,000, bearing a limited number of French family names. Their ancestry almost certainly includes French, and they are primarily Roman Catholic. Gilbert observes that they were once treated as equals by the French, but their status slipped to that of mulattoes. They attended "colored" schools or had their own separate schools.[55]

Wesorts of Southern Maryland: In 1946, the Wesorts numbered from 3,000 to 5,000, primarily in Charles and Prince Georges counties in southern Maryland. Their social status was ambiguous; while they apparently always had the right to vote, the draft board considered some to be black and others to be white. They attended black schools and were considered to be of lower status than whites. Family names include

---

[54] Ibid., 445; Nassau, "Melungeons," 18.

[55] Gilbert, "Memorandum," 446.

Butler, Harley, Linkins, Mason, Newman, Proctor, Queen, Savoy, Swan, and Thompson.[56]

The name "Wesort," according to popular legend, came from a matriarch of the community who referred to "we sort of people."[57] Forced by social pressures to marry within their own group, the Wesorts are known for several genetically-transmitted conditions, including albinism, hereditary deafness, short teeth, and nervous disorders.

Gilbert also cites several other "mixed Indian peoples" worthy of notice, including the Mashpee, Pequot, and Wampanoag of Massachusetts, the Narragansetts of Rhode Island, Connecticut's Mohegan and Pequot, and the Shinecock and Poosepatuck of New York. Many of Virginia's pre-colonial Indian groups were included in Gilbert's tally, among them the Chickahominy, Mattaponi, Nansemond, Pamunkey, Potomac, Rappahanock, and others.[58]

Common Characteristics Among Tri-Racials

These groups comprise America's tri-racial communities. Whether each group, or each individual within the group, actually has a mix of white, black, and Indian ancestry is, in a sense, not important. As far as their neighbors were concerned, they were a mixture of all three. The law, in most areas, considered them subject to the same restrictions as African-Americans. They were not considered white, and that is the primary characteristic each of these groups shares with the others. There are more.

Among these tri-racial groups, we see some overlap of family names: the names Collins appears among the Melungeons, the Cajans, and the Guineas; "Scott" and "Chavis" (or "Shavis" or "Chavez") are names found among the Brass Ankles and the Croatans; and the name "Goins" or one of its variants appears in most tri-racial groups. No connection, however, has been made tying these various groups together.

In 1953, geographer Edward T. Price of Los Angeles College estimated the members of tri-racial groups to number between 50,000 and 100,000. Price recognized many common factors in each of these groups, but also observed that each group was seen as a local

---

[56] Ibid.

[57] Berry, *Almost White*, 35.

[58] Gilbert, "Memorandum," 447.

phenomenon, "a unique demographic body, defined only in its own terms and only by its own neighbors. A name applied to one group in one area would have no meaning relative to similar people elsewhere."[59]

Like Gilbert, Price noted that one characteristic shared by each of these groups is the prevalence of frequently repeated family names. Another is that they were presumed by neighbors to be part white, with varying degrees of Negro and Indian ancestry, and were accepted by neither the Negro nor white communities. Yet another typical trait is that most of these groups were recognized by an unusual name; i.e., "Melungeon," "Brass Ankle," "Wesort," etc.[60]

Some researchers have noted another common characteristic of tri-racials: a tendency to ascribe their origin to migrations in the distant past. Brewton Berry writes:

> Sometimes these outcasts are thought to be descendants of certain well known nationalities and are named accordingly. For instance, we have the Arabs in New York State, the Moors in Delaware, the Cubans in North Carolina, the Turks and Greeks in South Carolina, and the Portuguese in Tennessee. Invariably the story is told—but rarely believed—that their distant ancestors reached these shores by some accident; and the monotonous theme of shipwrecked sailors recurs again and again.[61]

Researcher David Henige is another who discounts the oral traditions of the tri-racial groups. He notes that most (but not all) historians who deal with oral historical traditions have become convinced that these traditions have served a practical purpose: to deny African ancestry and therefore escape the harsh social and legal sanctions faced by African-Americans. "Congenial 'traditions,' of origin," Henige writes, "combined with and supporting local political and social exigencies, served to deflect this danger."[62]

Demographer Calvin Beale observed in 1957 that the areas where tri-racials were found were "typically rural and geographically isolated.

---

[59] Price, "Racial Mixtures," 138.

[60] Ibid.

[61] Berry, *Almost White,* 35–36.

[62] David Henige, "Origin Traditions of American Racial Isolates: A Case of Something Borrowed," *Appalachian Journal* (Spring 1984): 210.

It is difficult to find such a settlement that is not associated with a swamp, a hollow, an inaccessible ridge, or the back country of a sandy flatwoods." The majority of the groups had originated in the Atlantic Coastal Plain. While some groups had segregated schools of their own, other groups had "achieved a measure of acceptance as white."[63]

Beale lists several stereotypes associated with tri-racials, including "illegitimate origin; the use of stigmatic group names by the general society; proscription from social intercourse with others on terms of equality;... a reputation for violence, drunkenness, and crimes of passion within the group, and for petty thievery against outsiders;... [and] a reputation for laziness."[64]

Beale concluded in a 1972 article that the tri-racials were "a highly inbred class of people" due to their social and physical isolation and limited choice of marriage partners. He projected, however, that because of the high fertility rates cited among the members of these groups, their population would increase two-and-a-half times in each generation and would disperse more widely in the population.[65]

This dispersal had been occurring for over two decades when Beale published his study. Tri-racials, especially in the South and in Appalachia, were moving *en masse* from their rural communities to urban and industrialized areas. In leaving their traditional home, the tri-racials also left behind a heritage many of them regarded as unsavory. A Melungeon who moves from Hancock County to Detroit is, in a very real sense, no longer a Melungeon. His unique racial status does not move with him; his new neighbors have never heard of a Melungeon and consider him just another swarthy Appalachian. Losing the stigma of being tri-racial was often as much an incentive to move away from home as the prospect of better jobs, and few parents were willing to tell their children about their family's low social status back at home. As a result, the latest generations of tri-racials have, for the most part, grown up with little or no knowledge of their unique ethnic heritage.

Yet many of the children of these urbanized, transplanted tri-racials are reclaiming their heritage, embracing the group names which stigmatized their parents and grandparents. Many of these newly-aware

---

[63] Beale, "American Triracial Isolates," 188.

[64] Calvin Beale, "An Overview of the Phenomenon of Mixed Race Isolates in the United States," *American Anthropologist* 74 (1972): 705.

[65] Beale, "American Triracial Isolates," 192.

tri-racials are happy to reject the "white" status their ancestors sought in vain. Certainly, proclaiming a non-white ancestry is much easier in 2004 than it was in 1904 or even 1954, and carries far fewer penalties. Some of those seeking to document a tri-racial heritage are obviously "wannabes;" many have been unsuccessful in past attempts to establish an Indian background. Racial attitudes have obviously changed, however, when people who are secure in their status as "white people" will go to considerable effort to prove a non-white ancestry.

The similarity of their respective situations has not led tri-racial groups toward unity. Many tri-racials have opted for recognition as Native Americans, while others, such as the Melungeons and the Guineas, have no tradition of tribal affiliation to fall back upon. Instead, they, or at least many of them, are embracing a unique heritage, one which is not tied specifically to any of the "established" ethnic groups. During the census of 2000, several members of a Melungeon e-mail group reported writing in "Melungeon" as their ethnic classification.

Despite predictions that the Melungeons and other tri-racial groups would eventually disappear through outmigration and intermarriage, there is a growing number of people who choose to identify themselves as a mixture of ethnicities. Some of these people, until quite recently, considered themselves white; some considered themselves black, and others Indian. Some grew up with the knowledge of their mixed heritage, and many have only just discovered it. Some are not comfortable with the "tri-racial" designation, and there are widely divergent views on the specific origins of their respective groups. Despite their differences, and despite the number of "wannabes" among their ranks, these people are helping to demolish the existing notions of race in America.

2

RACE AND CONQUEST
ON THE EASTERN SEABOARD

The history of the Melungeons is closely intertwined with the history of the European conquest of the North American continent. Many of the theories of the Melungeons' origin relate to the earliest European contact with Native Americans. While this chapter will not attempt to duplicate the excellent work done by the authors cited within, an understanding of the history of the Melungeons requires at least a basic understanding of the earliest European settlers and their interaction with the Indians they found here and with the Africans they imported.[1]

Prior to 1600, several attempts were made by Europeans to establish colonies on the North American continent. As researcher and author Pat Elder writes, "[F]rom the moment Europeans stepped on North American soil, the seeds of white supremacy were sown."[2] While England, France and Spain battled for domination of the continent, the Natives saw their status shift from dominant to subservient, and finally irrelevant.

From the very beginning, English, Spanish, and French colonists depended on the Natives for labor, either as voluntary workers or as slaves. With governmental sanction, the Spaniards began enslaving Indians upon the arrival of Columbus in 1492. The first English settlers in what is now Virginia and North Carolina found Indian slave labor

---

[1] The idea that Europeans "settled" or brought civilization to the North American continent is an ethnocentric concept, which ignores the complex Native civilizations which had existed for generations before the arrival of Europeans. The Europeans who came to America considered themselves "settlers" and "pioneers" in a land that was already "settled" and known by its current occupants.

[2] Pat Spurlock Elder, *Melungeons: Examining an Appalachian Legend* (Blountville TN: Continuity Press, 1999) 50.

essential to their colonies. France never authorized the enslavement of Indians.

English colonists dealt with native populations differently than did the French or Spanish. Since most of the earliest European arrivals were men, the contacts between cultures frequently occurred between European men and Indian women. Indians, at least in the early days of European contact, encouraged alliances between the two cultures through marriage. Spanish men married Indian women and assimilated them into Spanish culture. French men married Native women and joined Indian societies. The British encouraged marriage to Indian women only briefly in an attempt to promote alliances with Indians. Soon the British banned interracial marriages. Anglo/Indian couples generally found greater acceptance in Indian society; their descendants were stigmatized as "half-breeds" and denied acceptance in white society. Later, the offspring of Anglo/African couples would suffer even greater stigmatization in (white) American society.

The following is a brief overview of some of the natives and Europeans who came into contact in the earliest days of the European colonization of what is now the southeastern United States.

The Spanish

The Spanish were the first Europeans to establish colonies in the Western Hemisphere. Hernando DeSoto first visited what is now Tennessee in 1540. One theory of Melungeon origin speculates that members of his expedition were either lost, captured, or deserted, then intermarried with Indians and left descendants in the mountains of east Tennessee.[3] However, no evidence exists to link these particular Spaniards with the Melungeons. The Spanish attempted to establish missions in the Chesapeake Bay area, and in 1561, founded a colony on Port Royal Sound in what is now South Carolina. They named their colony Santa Elena.

In the spring of 1566, Captain Juan Pardo left Spain with seventeen ships, 1,500 men, fourteen women, and supplies for the main Spanish colony at San Agustin (present-day St. Augustine, Florida). Most of the men and women were recruited from Galicia, Northern Portugal, and the

---

[3] Bible, *The Melungeons*, 93–95.

Asturias. Pardo himself was most likely of Portuguese origin.[4] Upon arrival in San Agustin, Pardo learned that the colony at Santa Elena needed men and supplies. Pardo took 250 men to bolster the fledgling colony. Soon after his arrival, Pardo was given the task of completing the road to New Spain. In 1559, the road was opened from what is now Pensacola, Florida to Chiaha in what is now northwestern Georgia. Pardo was to open the road from Chiaha to Santa Elena, creating an overland route from the Atlantic coast to the Gulf of Mexico. Pardo intended to establish forts along the route and station men there to hold the road.

Pardo took 125 men into the interior at the end of 1566. His travels took him into what is now the Appalachian region of South Carolina, Georgia, Tennessee, Alabama, and North Carolina. He and his men built four or five forts and two settlement towns. Scholars dispute the location of these forts, but they were probably located in northern Georgia, eastern Tennessee, and southwestern North Carolina, near the route of the road.[5]

These Spanish colonists in the interior never returned to Santa Elena. Records indicate that they and their families still occupied these interior forts twenty years later, marrying men and women of the Cherokee, Creek, and Catawba tribes. Eloy Gallegos speculates that as the half-Indian children of these Spanish and Portuguese began to multiply, they formed a separate culture, one more European than Indian. A 1584 account tells of an Indian attack on one of the Spanish communities. In 1598, a Spanish expedition reached the vicinity of Stone Mountain, Georgia, where an Indian told them of men who wore their hair short, used axes, and lived in houses four days' travel to the north. The Spanish in these interior forts remained even as the colony of Santa Elena was being abandoned by the Spanish. Pressure from the English forced the colony at Santa Elena to abandon that location in 1587 and move to the more easily defended settlement at St. Augustine in present-day Florida. Those in the forts were apparently left behind to survive as

---

    [4] Eloy J. Gallegos, *The Melungeons: The Pioneers of the Interior Southeastern United States, 1526–1997* (Knoxville: Villagra Press, 1997) 27; N. Brent Kennedy with Robyn Vaughan Kennedy, *The Melungeons: The Resurrection of a Proud People; An Untold Story of Ethnic Cleansing in America* (Macon GA: Mercer University Press, 1994, revised 1997) 114.
    [5] Gallegos, *The Melungeons*, 27–67; Kennedy, *The Melungeons*, 114–15.

best they could.[6] There is evidence that all the forts had been overrun by Indians by 1568, but determining whether all the Spanish were killed is impossible.[7]

The Yuchi

The people encountered by the Pardo expeditions were primarily the Yuchi, a tribe little studied by historians. The Yuchi had villages scattered from present-day states of Illinois to Florida, and from the Carolina coast to the Mississippi River. The tribe was known by many names. The Spanish knew them as the Chisca, while other tribes and other Europeans knew them variously as the Tongora, Oustack, Westo, Tomahittans, Tahogalewi, and Hogoheegee.

The Yuchi were distinct from the neighboring tribes, both in their language, which is unique and has never been classified with any certainty, and in their belief that they were descended from the sun. They lived among several other tribes, but maintained a distinct and separate culture.

Hernando De Soto visited the Yuchi in 1540, and fought battles with them. Juan Pardo's expedition in 1567 also fought the Yuchi. The Europeans were badly outnumbered by this large tribe, but had a weapon far more powerful than their firearms. Like most natives, the Yuchi were especially vulnerable to European diseases; never having been exposed to them, they had no natural immunity. Like many native people, the Yuchi would be virtually destroyed by an enemy they could not see.[8]

"The Lost Colony"

In 1584, English captains Philip Amadas and Arthur Barlowe began to explore the North American coast for Sir Walter Raleigh. The English coveted the riches being taken out of the New World by the Spanish, and English privateers—pirates with official sanction—plied the waters of

---

[6] Gallegos, *The Melungeons*, 60; Elder, *Melungeons*, 38–39; Kennedy, *The Melungeons*, 114–18.

[7] Charles Hudson and Paul E. Hoffman, *The Juan Pardo Expeditions, Explorations of the Carolinas and Tennessee, 1566–1568* (Washington: Smithsonian Institution, 1990) 175.

[8] "Who Were The Mysterious Yuchi of Tennessee and the Southeast?" http://www.geocities.com/Capitol Hill/Lobby/3486/tenn-asi.html.

the Atlantic, preying on treasure-laden Spanish ships. England wanted a foothold in the Western Hemisphere; more immediately, they wanted a secure base on the American coast from which to conduct raids against Spanish ships. Amadas and Barlowe landed on the Atlantic coast, about seven leagues above Roanoke Island, and took possession of the country for Queen Elizabeth and for the use of Sir Walter Raleigh, according to the Queen's charter.[9]

Amadas and Barlowe took glowing reports about the area back to Raleigh. The Indians they met had been friendly, and two of them, Wanchese and Manteo, were brought back to England. England's "virgin" Queen Elizabeth named the new possession "Virginia."

The next spring, Raleigh sent 108 persons to establish a colony on Roanoke Island. The expedition was commanded by Raleigh's cousin, Sir Richard Grenville. The two Indians, Wanchese and Manteo, returned to America on this voyage. The Grenville party came to the new colony by way of the Spanish West Indies. England and Spain were virtually at war at that time, and that war was to become an actuality within three years.

Upon the colonists arrival at Roanoke Island, Ralph Lane became governor, and Grenville returned to England for supplies. At first, relations with the Indians were friendly. However, the English attitude toward the natives became clear when, during an expedition to the island of Ocracoke prior to Grenville's return to England, Grenville burned the Indian village of Aquascogok in retaliation for the presumed theft of a silver cup by one of the Indians. During the spring, before crops were harvested, English supplies ran low and the Indians were unable to provide food. The colonists responded by robbing the Indians' fish traps. By mid-1586, the colonists and Indians were in open conflict.[10]

Grenville's delayed return from England left the Roanoke colony in a desperate situation. In June of 1586, the colonists learned that Sir Francis Drake was off the coast with a fleet of 23 ships, rich with booty from his attack on the Spanish West Indies and Florida. Drake offered to either leave supplies with the colony or take the colonists back to England. Lane at first opted for the supplies, but a storm arose and blew the supply ship out to sea. The delay of Grenville's supply fleet, along

---

[9] "First English Settlement," http://statelibrary.dcr.state.nc.us/nc/ncsites/english1.htm.

[10] Ibid.

with the inevitability of war between England and Spain, caused Lane to request passage back to England. Drake sailed on 18 June, carrying the colonists home with him.

Prior to his arrival at Roanoke Island, Drake had attacked several Spanish fortresses and captured a number of individuals who had been slaves of the Spaniards. At Cape Verde Island, Drake freed 150 Negro slaves. He then freed 200 Moorish and Negro galley slaves at Santa Domingo. At Cartagena, Drake liberated more Negro slaves, as well as 300 Indians, most of whom were women. These liberated slaves were on board Drake's ships when they arrived at Roanoke Island. While some may have died on the way, it seems likely there were as many as 400 liberated persons with Drake, and Drake collected supplies for Roanoke, indicating his intent to use these people to reinforce the colony.[11]

Author and Melungeon researcher Brent Kennedy, citing the research of David Beers Quinn, suggests that this group included a number of Ottoman Turks who had been captured by the Spanish and liberated by Drake, and that Drake left these captives on Roanoke Island. In his 1994 book *The Melungeons: The Resurrection of a Proud People*, Kennedy argues that the Melungeons have a Turkish origin, and a possible source for this ancestry is this group of liberated slaves.[12]

Quinn notes that Drake did not have enough time to put many of this group ashore between the meeting of Drake and Lane on 11 June and the beginning of the four-day storm on 13 June. Written records shed little light on this aspect of Lane's colony, but it is unlikely all were lost during the storm. Drake was able to reorganize his ships and arranged to bring Lane's colonists home to England. Records indicate about 100 Moorish galley slaves were later returned to the Mediterranean. Quinn concluded that a large number of Indians and blacks must have been left behind. Drake probably took advantage of the possibility of collecting ransom for the Moors; there was no one to pay ransom for the Indians and Negroes.[13]

There is no direct evidence that Drake actually left these people on Roanoke, and certainly no record of what became of them. In addition to

---

[11] David Beers Quinn, "The Lost Colony In Myth and Reality," *England and the Discovery of America, 1481–1620* (New York: Alfred A. Knopf, 1974) 433.

[12] Kennedy, *The Melungeons*, 120–21, citing David Beers Quinn, ed., *The Roanoke Voyages*, 1/104 (The Hakluyt Society, 1952) 251, 255.

[13] Quinn, "The Lost Colony," 434.

the Indians and Negroes who may have been left on Roanoke Island, three of Lane's colonists were left behind; these men had probably been taking a message to a nearby Indian village.[14] Soon after Lane and the colonists left Roanoke Island, a supply ship sent by Sir Walter Raleigh searched for the colonists but found no one. Later, Grenville arrived with three ships but found no colonists—or South American Indians, Negroes, Moors, or Turks. Grenville left 15 men and provisions for two years on Roanoke Island to hold the country for the Queen.

In 1587, Raleigh sent another colony to Virginia, this one containing women and children The pilot leading the expedition was Simon Fernandez, a Spanish-trained Portuguese navigator who led the first two Roanoke expeditions. This colony intended to settle, not on Roanoke Island, but northward on Chesapeake Bay. They meant only to stop on Roanoke to retrieve Grenville's 15 soldiers. Roanoke Island itself was not a promising agricultural site, and hostilities between Lane's colony and the Indians made Roanoke a poor choice for settlement.

Author Lee Miller argues that the third Roanoke colony—the "Lost Colony"—was doomed from the start. She speculates that the colonists were separatists from the Church of England and were willing to move to a strange and potentially hostile land because they feared imprisonment or even death for their religious beliefs. The hostility of the Church of England, compounded by the jealousy felt by many in the royal court toward Sir Walter Raleigh, a favorite of Queen Elizabeth, ensured that the colony would not be successful. Simon Fernandez may well have been assigned to guarantee the colony's failure.

The expedition started badly and got worse. One of the ships in the fleet, a small flyboat, became separated from the main group off the Portuguese coast. Fernandez did not wait or search for the flyboat, but sailed for Santa Cruz in the Virgin Islands. Some of the group were poisoned by a strange fruit, and the colonists discovered the only available water was poisonous as well. A mysterious person named Darby Glande jumped ship in Puerto Rico and was taken into Spanish custody, where he evidently informed authorities of the latest English attempt at colonization in what the Spanish regarded as *their* territory.

Fernandez refused to send boats ashore where fresh food and cattle were available, even though these commodities were essential to the

---

[14] Ibid., 434–35.

colonists' survival. Fernandez also delayed the fleet until late in the summer, too late for the colonists to plant crops. And, although their stop at Roanoke Island was intended only to retrieve Grenville's soldiers, Fernandez refused to take the colonists to Chesapeake Bay and left them on Roanoke Island to survive as best they could.[15]

The 15 soldiers left by Grenville were nowhere to be found. The colonists found only one skeleton and no trace of the other 14 soldiers. The Indians of the area were more hostile than before. Through the intercession of the English-speaking Manteo, who had accompanied the group, the colonists established friendly relations with the Secotans, but other tribes remained hostile or suspicious. The Secotans accused the remaining Roanoke Island Indians of killing an Englishman, George Howe, as well as the 15 men left on the island by Grenville. Governor John White led a force which attacked and burned the town of Dasamonquepeuc. However, the Roanoke Indians had already fled. Instead, the town was occupied by the friendly Secotans who had come to take whatever corn and fruit might have been left behind. The Secotans never forgave the colonists for what was apparently a case of mistaken identity.

On 18 August 1587, Governor White's daughter, Eleanor, wife of Ananias Dare, gave birth to a daughter who was named Virginia. She was the first English child to be born on American soil. Another child was born to the Harvie family shortly afterwards. On 27 August Governor White, at the urging of the colonists, sailed to England to obtain supplies for the colony.

At this point, events in the colony on Roanoke Island become a mystery. The colonists had discussed moving inland about 50 miles, and Governor White arranged for signals to indicate their whereabouts if they had to leave the island before his return. However, the Governor's return was delayed by the outbreak of war with Spain. The Spanish Armada threatened England in 1588. Sir Richard Grenville, preparing a fleet to sail for the Roanoke Island colony, was ordered to make his ships available for use against the Armada. On 28 April, Governor White was permitted to use two small ships to resupply the colony, but these ships never arrived at Roanoke.

---

[15] Lee Miller, *Roanoke: Solving The Mystery of the Lost Colony* (New York: Arcade, 2000).

The Armada was defeated in the summer of 1588, but Spain continued to use its navy against the English. The Spanish also planned to attack the English colony at Roanoke Island. The attack never materialized, but Spanish reconnaissance on the island indicated that the colony was still active in June 1588.

Governor White continued his attempts to raise a supply fleet for Roanoke Island, but was unable to return to the colony until mid-August of 1590, three years after he left. Upon his arrival at Roanoke Island, White and his party searched in vain for any colonists. They found the word "CRO" carved on a tree. Traveling further, they found that all of the houses had been taken down and the area enclosed with a palisade of tree trunks. One of the trees, or posts, had the bark peeled off, and carved on it was the word "CROATOAN." However, the message lacked the Maltese cross that White had asked the settlers to use in such messages in the event they were in danger. The messages reassured White that his daughter, granddaughter Virginia Dare, and the colonists would be found at Croatan Island.[16]

White and his party did not reach Croatan Island; a storm forced the boats to stay well clear of the treacherous Outer Banks. The group planned to go to the West Indies to take on fresh water, then return to Croatan Island, but the wind blew their ships to the Azores instead. From there, they made their way to England.

Governor White could not raise the funds for another expedition to America. Raleigh was expending his wealth colonizing his properties in Ireland, and he was later disgraced and imprisoned for marrying Elizabeth Throckmorton without the Queen's knowledge or consent. Raleigh was alternately in and out of favor with the Crown for years afterward but continued to send expeditions in search of the Lost Colony. These expeditions engaged in trading with the Indians along the coast, and probably did not expend much energy searching for the lost colonists. After the Jamestown settlement was established in Virginia in 1607, those colonists expressed deep interest in the Lost Colony and

---

[16] Crotatan Island is today the lower part of Hatteras Island. The Outer Banks are constantly shifting; some of the inlets that existed in Raleigh's time are now closed, with other inlets having appeared.

continually attempted to learn from the Indians the whereabouts of the Roanoke colonists.[17]

The theory that the Melungeons may be descended from the Lost Colonists of Roanoke Island was popularized by writers in the twentieth century. The colonists, some researchers have suggested, moved to the interior and intermarried with Indians. However, the Lost Colony tradition is more commonly associated with the Lumbees. The Lumbees have an oral tradition of descent from the Lost Colonists, and many family names of the Lost Colonists are still present among Lumbees today, including Allen, Berry, Chaven, Graham, Martin, Samson, White, and Wilkinson.[18] In 1889, Dr. Swan Burnett suggested a possible connection between the Lumbees, then known as the Croatans, and the Melungeons. Researcher Edward Price discounts that possibility, however, saying that "no present mixed-blood group appears to be the specific source of the Melungeons."[19]

The earliest accounts of Melungeons noted that they spoke English and had English-sounding names. This certainly points to an English element in the ancestry of the Melungeons. However, there was no shortage of Englishmen on the North American continent, many European colonies along the eastern coast were lost without a trace, and the possibility of a connection between the missing Roanoke Island settlers and the Melungeons seems remote at best.

Word would eventually filter back to England that Raleigh's Lost Colonists had found refuge with the Chesapeake Indians, only to be slaughtered along with the Chesapeakes by the Powhatan Indians, led by the powerful chief Wahunsenacawh. This explanation seems to have been a convenient means of stirring English sentiments against the Powhatans. There is evidence that some of the Lost Colonists survived along the Indian trading route, possibly held as slaves by Eno Indians. Jamestown colonist John Smith told the Virginia Council in London in 1609 that the Lost Colonists were alive. Explorers from the Jamestown colony came tantalizingly close to finding these survivors, but eventually the English came to accept the story that the Lost Colonists had been

---

[17] "First English Settlement," http://statelibrary.dcr.state.nc.us/nc/ncsites/english1.htm.

[18] Elder, *Melungeons*, 307.

[19] Swan M. Burnett, "A Note on the Melungeons," *American Anthropologist* 2 (October 1889): 347; Price, "The Melungeons," 270.

killed by the Powhatans. What became of the Lost Colonists and their descendants is anyone's guess. These colonists, along with the South American Indians, Negroes, and Turks that may have been left by Drake, represent the possibility of a group of non-native inhabitants that could conceivably have survived through alliance or amalgamation with local Indians. This possibility continues to fascinate researchers to this day.

Jamestown

In May 1607, 101 English men and boys established a colony at Jamestown in what is now Virginia. They constructed a large triangular fort on the banks of a river the Indians knew as "Powhatan's River," or "Powhatan's Flu." The settlers named the river, and their colony, after King James.

The colonists were soon plagued by bad water, blistering heat with swarms of insects spawned in the nearby wetlands, fierce winters, typhus, starvation, and Indian attacks. The colonists themselves were particularly unsuited to pioneer life. Some of the men were the younger sons of noblemen who had no future in England. They were lured to Virginia by promises of land and wealth, and knew nothing of farming or hunting.

In August 1609, 400 more colonists arrived after being caught in a hurricane. One of the ships reportedly carried the plague, and most of the new colonists were injured or sick, unable to care for themselves. Most of the proposed leaders of the new colony were stranded in Bermuda. Captain John Smith, the only colonist able to keep the peace, both within the colony and with the neighboring Indians, was injured in a gunpowder explosion and returned to England. The colony fell into chaos.

The winter of 1609–1610 was particularly brutal; it was known by colonists as the "Starving Time." The residents of Jamestown survived on mice and rats, and some even turned to cannibalism. By the time the remaining colonists, who had been stranded in the relative paradise of Bermuda, arrived at Jamestown, only 60 survivors were left. Nearly 90 percent of the colony had died. The newly-arrived Englishmen helped the survivors onto their ships and sailed down the James River, the colony abandoned. Before they reached the mouth of the river, however, they learned that three ships were on the way to Jamestown, loaded with supplies and 150 new colonists.[20]

The colonists' situation vastly improved by 1619, as Jamestown had found a profitable enterprise: tobacco. The colony had shipped 10 tons of the leaf to England, and that year they imported the first African slaves.[21]

The Powhatans

Upon their arrival, the Jamestown colonists came into immediate contact with several groups of Algonquian-speaking Natives, known collectively as the Powhatans. The Powhatan Indians were a collection of 32 tribes under the *mamanatowick,* or "Great King," Wahunsenacawh, also known as Powhatan.[22] At the time of the Jamestown settlement, there were an estimated 13,000 to 14,000 people under Wahunsenacawh's leadership. The Powhatan villages were located on rivers or on the Chesapeake Bay on Virginia's coastal plain. The Powhatan empire stretched from the Potomac River west to the fall line and south to what is now the Virginia/North Carolina border.[23]

Wahunsenacawh had inherited control of six tribes: the Powhatan, Arrohateck, Appamattuck, Pamunkey, Mattaponi, and Chiskiak. Other tribes were brought under his control either through conquest or intimidation. Two exceptions were the Chesapeakes, who were exterminated by Powhatan in the summer of 1608, and the Chickahominies, who maintained their independence with a large force of warriors and periodic payments to Wahunsenacawh.[24]

Wahunsenacawh had more than 100 wives and many children. The best-known of his children was a daughter named Matoaka, better known by the nickname "Pocahontas," meaning "little wanton." She was born about 1595. In December 1607, Wahunsenacawh's brother, Opechancanough, captured John Smith. As Smith told the story many years later, he was brought to Wahunsenacawh and sentenced to death. According to

---

[20] "Jamestown," http://www.tobacco.org/History/Jamestown.html#aa2.

[21] Ibid.

[22] Wahunsenacawh is commonly called "Powhatan" in most histories. However, to avoid confusion between the man and the larger body of people, he will be referred to herein as Wahunsenacawh.

[23] "Pocahontas," http://www.apva.org/history/pocahont.html.

[24] Helen C. Rountree, *Pocahontas's People: The Powhatan Indians of Virginia Through Four Centuries* (Norman: University of Oklahoma Press, 1990) 10–11.

Smith, Pocahontas saved his life by throwing herself down and cradling his head before he was clubbed to death.[25]

While some historians have accepted Smith's account, others are skeptical. Smith did not write about this incident—or even mention Pocahontas—until 1624. Although it is probable that Pocahontas met Smith at this time, it is highly unlikely that Smith's life was in danger. Smith also claimed in his 1624 account that in 1617 he had written to Queen Anne on Pocahontas' behalf. By 1617, Pocahontas had no need of Smith's endorsement because she was already a court favorite in England. Pocahontas later married John Rolfe, a tobacco planter. The marriage led to a period of peace between the colonists and the Powhatans. Pocahontas visited England, was presented to the royal family, and died (possibly of pneumonia or tuberculosis) in 1617.[26]

Although the English and the Powhatans frequently clashed, both Native and English leaders realized that peaceful relations could benefit both peoples. The marriage of Pocahontas to John Rolfe ensured a few years of peace. However, with the death of Pocahontas in 1617 and the death of Wahunsenacawh a year later, conflicts erupted again. The new Powhatan leader, Opechancanough, led an attack on English settlements throughout Virginia in 1622. The English colonists retaliated; for over a decade, the English systematically razed villages, seizing or destroying crops and killing as many Indians as possible. In 1644, Opechancanough made a final attempt at driving the English away. Hundreds of colonists were killed before the English captured and shot Opechancanough. Treaties with Opechancanough's successor severely restricted the Powhatan people's territory to small reservations. By 1669, the population of Powhatan Indians in the area had dropped to about 1,800 and by 1722, many of the tribes comprising the Powhatan Nation had become extinct. The remaining Powhatans, now known as Pamunkeys, were living on reservations.[27]

Africans in America

---

[25] "Pocahontas," http://www.apva.org/history/pocahont.html.

[26] Rountree, *Pocahontas's People,* 38–39; "Pocahontas," http://www.apva.org/history/pocahont.html.

[27] Rountree, *Pocahontas's People,* 15–88; Elder, *Melungeons,* 165; "Chief Powhatan," http://www.baydreaming.com/powhatan.htm.

The first Africans arrived in the colony of Virginia in 1619. Records do not specify whether they were indentured servants or slaves. Indentured servants were expected to provide labor for a specified period of time, after which they were free, while slaves served for life. The English did not originally enslave Africans exclusively; they enslaved non-Christians or captives taken in war. These slaves could gain their freedom by converting to Christianity.

In the early days of the Virginia colony, imported slaves were not in great demand. Labor was vital to Virginia's growing tobacco industry, but English workers were in plentiful supply and were willing to become indentured servants for a period of time to pay their passage to Virginia. By the middle of the seventeenth century, however, the Black Plague in England had reduced the available labor pool considerably, and the effort to rebuild London after the Great Fire absorbed much of what remained. Following the example set by the Spanish and Portuguese a century before, England began looking toward Africa for labor.

African laborers were often indentured and could become free after their term of servitude was completed. Soon Virginia contained a relatively large population of free African-Americans, many of whom owned property.

The system of indentured servitude had many flaws in the eyes of plantation owners. Servants became free workers and had to be paid or they would move on. These free workers posed a threat to Virginia's property-owning elite. The colony restricted the availability of land in order to maintain the power of these property owners, but that caused resentment among former indentured servants; in 1676, free workers burned Jamestown.

The permanent enslavement of Africans seemed like the logical solution. They would not become free to compete with English laborers for paid work. Africans could not easily escape bondage because their skin color marked them as slaves. And even if they converted to Christianity (as many did), the English did not believe them to have the same human rights as white men—in fact, did not consider them human in the same way a white man was human—and could thus keep them enslaved without being bothered by conscience.

In 1662, the colony of Virginia decreed that all children born of slave mothers were to be enslaved as well. By 1672, England was a full participant in the African slave trade, eventually bringing as many as 45,000 slaves into America each year.[28]

Although most African-Americans were slaves, several African-American families were free throughout the colonial period and afterward. Paul Heinegg contends that most of these families descended from white servant women who had children by slaves or free African Americans. Others descended from slaves who were freed prior to Virginia's 1723 law which required legislative approval for freeing a slave. Many families that later turned up in various tri-racial groups, including the Gowens, Cumbos, Nickens, and Driggers families, are included in this group.[29]

The English Meet the Cherokee

English colonial officials discussed exploration of the Appalachian mountain region as early as May 1626, when Virginia's colonial council hoped to discover not only the "riches of the mountains," but a river route to the Gulf of Mexico. English, Spanish, and French traders had established contact with the Cherokees (originally known by the English as the Rickahockans), some as early as 1612, and established trading posts on the fall line of Virginia's rivers. Reports of great rivers to the west inspired entrepreneurs and investors to mount expeditions to the mountains.[30]

Abraham Wood operated a trading post at the falls of the Appomattox River, at Fort Henry, now Petersburg. He sent expeditions to the New River area in 1671, and in 1673 Wood chose James Needham to lead an expedition into the unknown mountains. Needham came to Carolina from Barbados in 1670. Soon thereafter, he participated in an expedition to capture a traitor who was attempting to escape from Carolina through the wilderness to Spanish territory.[31]

---

[28] "From Indentured Servitude to Racial Slavery," *Africans in America*, http://www.pbs.org/wgbh.aia.part1/1narr3.html.

[29] Paul Heinegg, "Free African Americans of Virginia, North Carolina, South Carolina, Maryland and Delaware," http://www.freeafricanamericans.com/introduction. htm.

[30] Samuel Cole Williams, *Early Travels in the Tennessee Country, 1540–1800* (Johnson City TN: The Watauga Press, 1928) 17–18.

[31] Ibid., 20–21.

Needham set off from Wood's trading post in April 1673, accompanied by Gabriel Arthur, who was presumably Wood's indentured servant, and eight Indians. This journey resulted in the first recorded English visit to the Tennessee Valley and the Overhill Cherokees.[32]

The Cherokee were an Iroquoian people who came into the region now known as Tennessee, North Carolina, and Georgia in about 1450. They overpowered or absorbed many smaller tribes and dominated a large territory. Hernando deSoto's expedition visited the Cherokee in 1540. Records of that expedition refer to the "Chalaque," a word from the common Indian trade language which probably meant "cave people." The Cherokee pronounced the word either "tsa-la-gi" or "tsa-ra-gi." The Cherokee called themselves "Ani-Yun-wiya," meaning "the principal people." The Spanish began gold smelting operations in Cherokee territory, some of which continued as late as 1690.[33]

As Needham prepared to return to Fort Henry, he left Gabriel Arthur with some Cherokees in order that Arthur might learn the Cherokee language. Another band of Cherokees accompanied Needham on his journey to Fort Henry. On their second day out, Needham was killed after an argument with "Indian John" on the Yadkin River. "Indian John" sent a message that Arthur was to be killed as well, and Arthur was tied to a stake which was then surrounded by dry brush in preparation for his execution by fire. He was rescued at the last minute by the chief and later managed to gain favor with the Indians. He accompanied them on expeditions to Florida and the Carolina coast, and into present-day Kentucky and West Virginia. Wounded in a skirmish with the Shawnee near the Ohio River, Arthur managed to befriend his Shawnee captors. After his wounds healed, Arthur traveled the ancient war trail through Cumberland Gap to the Cherokee towns on the Little Tennessee River. A chief accompanied Arthur to Fort Henry, where he arrived in May 1674 and reported his experiences to his employer, Abraham Wood.[34]

In 1674, Wood wrote a letter to John Richards, the treasurer of the Lords Proprietors of Carolina in London. Several writers cite a passage from that letter as an early reference to Melungeons: "Eight days jorny

---

[32] Ibid, 21.

[33] Ken Martin, "First European Contact," *History of the Cherokee*, http://cherokeehistory.com/firstcon.htm.

[34] Williams, *Early Travels,* 22–23.

down this river lives a white people which have long beardes and whiskers and weares clothing, and on some of ye other rivers lives a hairey people."[35]

The "white people" were almost certainly Spaniards, who had been in contact with the Cherokee for several years. Samuel Cole Williams, in his *Early Travels in the Tennessee Country*, refers to a Cherokee tradition regarding the presence of a "white race" in Tennessee. Many writers would later cite Wood's account of the journey of Needham and Arthur as evidence of an early Melungeon presence in the Appalachian region. Undoubtedly there were European groups and individuals in close contact with the Indians of the interior mountains. Their fate is unrecorded, however, and any connection with the Melungeons is speculative at best.

Wood's account refers to the Tomahitans, a "broken tribe" that incorporated with the Cherokee about 1632. As Europeans settlements continued to encroach upon Indian territory, smaller and weaker tribes found it necessary to merge with larger, more powerful tribes. Those that failed to do so soon became virtually extinct.[36]

The English Meet the Monacans

The Monacan Nation, a group of Siouan tribes including the Catawba and the Saponi, lived in the Piedmont and mountain regions of Virginia. The Monacan and Mannahoac tribes, numbering over 10,000 individuals, were loosely organized into a confederation ranging from the Roanoke River Valley to the Potomac River, and from the Fall Line at present-day Richmond and Fredericksburg west through the Blue Ridge Mountains.

While the Powhatans maintained an appearance of friendly relations with the English, the Monacans tried to avoid contact with the colonists. No English explorers remained in their villages long enough to learn their language or culture, and the historical record of the Monacans is sparse.[37]

A series of encounters between the colonists and the Monacans between 1607 and 1720 convinced the Monacans to move westward,

---

[35] Abraham Wood to John Richards, 22 August 1674, cited in Williams, *Early Travels,* 28–29.

[36] Williams, *Early Travels,* 24.

[37] "History Corner," http://www.monacannation.com.History/hispage1.htm.

away from the advancing settlers. The Saponi, one of the Monacan tribes that had been willing to live among Europeans, were forced out of the Roanoke area and found themselves caught in the middle of a war between the British and the Tuscarora. The Saponis maintained their neutrality and remained in Bertie County, North Carolina. In 1714, the British opened Fort Christiana, Brunswick County, Virginia, three miles below present-day Lawrenceville. The fort was located on a main trading route, and in addition to its usefulness in trade and military security, Fort Christiana operated as a mission and school for Indians. As agreed by treaty, remnants of the Catawba, Eno, Meherrin, Meipontsky, Nottoway, Occaneechi, Saponi, Stenkenock, and Tutelo tribes, among others, settled at the fort. Regardless of their tribal affiliation, the Indians at Fort Christiana were all known as Saponi. Within two years, nearly 400 people were living in the village outside the fort.[38]

Fort Christiana officially closed in 1717, but the Saponi remained at the fort until 1729, when conflict arose between them and the remaining Tuscarora and Meherrin. By 1740, the village was completely deserted. Many of the Indians had taken European names. Among the Saponi and other Monacan people who dispersed from the fort were individuals with the surnames Collins, Bolten, Bell, Goins, and Minor—all later recognized as Melungeon names.[39]

Some of the Saponi moved to the region controlled by the Catawba Indians in present-day South Carolina, but by 1733 they had moved back into Virginia. Some eventually moved into Pennsylvania and finally to Canada, where they were adopted by a division of the Iroquois Confederacy. Others moved to North Carolina. Some settled in what later became Louisa County, Virginia, and others occupied the region around Bear Mountain in present-day Amherst County. There, in 1790, William Johns, designated a "free person of color," married Molly Evans, and Ned Branham married Molly's sister Nancy. William Johns was sometimes referred to as "Portugue." These individuals, along with Raleigh Penn, represented the primary family groups that would dominate this community for generations.[40]

---

[38] Elder, *Melungeons*, 165.

[39] Ibid., 295.

[40] Ibid., 167–68; Karenne Wood, and Diane Shields, *The Monacan Indians: Our Story* (Madison Heights VA: Monacan Indian Nation, 2000) 20.

Most of the Monacan people—the Saponi, the Occaneechi, the Tutelo, and others—found themselves frequently on the move during the eighteenth century, moving to various locations in Virginia and North Carolina.

By 1780, nearly all the tribes in the southeastern United States were either extinct, dispersed, or had merged with the Creek or Cherokee. Many of the tribes in Virginia and elsewhere along the Eastern Seaboard had intermarried with free blacks, and many people believed that some of the tribes had more African ancestry than Indian. This belief would have a tremendous impact on the descendants of these tribes in the twentieth century.

At about the beginning of the eighteenth century, English colonists realized that African slaves and indentured white servants proved a more stable source of labor than did Indians, and the practice of enslaving Natives began to decline. By this time, a sizable population of mixed-race people had already formed. Virginia and Maryland prohibited marriages between blacks and whites in 1662 and prohibited any union between free whites and Indians in 1691. North Carolina prohibited any type of mixed marriage in 1715. That prohibition was intended to prevent whites from marrying any Indian, Negro, mulatto, or person of mixed race.[41]

The Spanish, French, and English were the main players in the European colonization of America. But there were others.

Virginia imported Armenian and Turkish workers to help develop the silk trade. In 1656 the Virginia Assembly set aside 4,000 pounds of tobacco to encourage "George the Armenian" to stay in the colony to produce silk. A Virginia document from 1652 refers to a Turk who wrote in the Turkish language, and a 1686 letter from Governor William Byrd described a Turkish merchant. Other documents from the colonial period refer to individuals as Turks and East Indians.[42]

Gypsies were also a part of the American "melting pot" from the earliest days. Although commonly believed to have arrived in America in

---

[41] Elder, *Melungeons*, 131–33, 305–306.

[42] Edward, D. Neill, *Virginia Carolorum: The Colony Under the Rule of Charles the First and Second, A.D. 1625–A.D. 1685* (Albany NY: Joel Munsell's Sons, 1886) 240; *Virginia Magazine of History and Biography* 5 (1898): 36; *Virginia Magazine of History and Biography* 25 (1917): 250.

the nineteenth century, Gypsy, or Romany, people were noted in the colonies as early as 1647.

> 1647. Aug 8: There hath suddenlie come among vs a companie of strange people, wch bee neither Indjan nor Christian. And wee know not what to liken them vnto. Some will have it yt they bee Egyptians or Jypsjes, wandering thieves, jugglers and beggars...Never hearing yt any such people were in ye Dutch settlements or Virginia, I surmised yt hee did mean yt they came from ye Spanish settlements, thousands of leagues awaie...They doe use palmistry and other devilish arts and witchcrafts...[43]

The Romany people originated in northern India and migrated to Turkey about 1000 A.D. They continued to migrate throughout Europe, reaching the Great Britain by about 1500. Historian Ian Hancock noted the common use of Gypsies as slaves.

> Spain had already begun shipping Gypsies to the Americas in the 15th century; three were transported by Columbus to the Caribbean on his third voyage in 1498. Spain's later *solucion americans* involved the shipping of Gypsy slaves to its colony in 18th century Louisiana. An Afro-Gypsy community today lives in St. Martin's Parish, and reportedly there is another one in central Cuba, both descended from intermarriage between the two enslaved peoples. In the 16th century, Portugal shipped Gypsies as an unwilling labor force to its colonies in Maranhão (now Brazil), Angola and even India, the Romas' country of origin which they had left five centuries earlier. They were made Slaves of the Crown in 18th century Russia during the reign of Catherine the Great, while in Scotland during the same period they were employed "in a state of slavery" in the coal mines. England and Scotland had shipped Roma to Virginia and the Caribbean as slaves during the 17th and 18th centuries...[44]

---

[43] Obadiah Oldpath, *Jewels of the Third Plantation* (Lynn MA: Thomas Herbert and James M. Munroe, 1862) 71–74.

[44] Ian Hancock, *Roma Slavery*, http://www.geocities.com/Paris/5121/slavery.htm

Genealogist David Hobson documented Gypsies, many with English surnames, who were expelled from the British Isles as early as 1682.[45]

As the English consolidated their hold on North America, the contributions of these individuals and families of non-English origin were often overlooked or forgotten. The racial attitudes of the dominant English society forced many of these swarthy or mixed-race people to keep a low profile, band together in extended family groups, and often to migrate to more sparsely-populated areas where racially-restrictive laws had not yet been enacted.

The Melungeons Arrive on Newman's Ridge

Legend has it that the Melungeons were in the Hancock County area prior to the arrival of the white settlers. The best evidence, however, places the first Melungeon families in the area at about the same time the first white settlers arrived. As in most other aspects of Melungeon history, legend competes with documented fact for popular attention.

Hancock County, Tennessee was formed from portions of Hawkins and Claiborne counties in 1846. White settlers first entered the area encompassed by the county in about 1795. Settlements sprang up along the Clinch River and at Mulberry Gap. Newman's Ridge runs north of the river and was reportedly named after a member of one of the first hunting parties to come through the area.[46]

In 1673, James Needham and Gabriel Arthur traveled into the Tennessee Valley and the domain of the overhill Cherokee. Samuel Cole Williams quoted an account of this trip in his *Early Travels in the Tennessee Country* which was cited earlier in this chapter: "Eight days journey down the river lives a white people which have long beards and whiskers and wear clothing."[47] Williams concluded that the white people in question were Spaniards. This information is sometimes cited as proof that the Melungeons were in present-day Hancock County at that date.

---

[45] Thomas A. Acton, "Gypsies in the United Kingdom," *Patrin Romani Web Journal*, http://www.geocities.com/~patrin/patrin.htm

[46] Lewis M. Jarvis, *Hancock County Times,* 17 April 1903, cited in Elder, 74.

[47] Williams, *Early Travels*, 28–29.

Most researchers believe, however, that Needham and Arthur never came close to the Newman's Ridge area.[48]

In 1891, journalist Will Allen Dromgoole wrote, "When John Sevier attempted to organize the State of Franklin[49], there was living in the mountains of Eastern Tennessee a colony of dark-skinned, reddish-brown complexioned people, supposed to be of Moorish descent, who affiliated with neither whites nor blacks, and who called themselves Malungeons, and claimed to be of Portuguese descent. They lived to themselves exclusively, and were looked upon as neither negroes nor Indians."[50]

This alleged account is often used to "prove" that the Melungeons were in eastern Tennessee at that early date. However, no one has found an original copy of this account. Dromgoole got the story from a letter written by one Dan W. Baird, who offered no source for the information.[51] Neither Baird nor Dromgoole state that Sevier actually saw these dark-skinned people, and the term "Portuguese" is absent from copies supposedly made of Sevier's journals.[52]

The 1790 census of the Southwest territory (the eastern tip of present-day Tennessee) cited 361 "other free persons." Some writers have concluded that these free, non-white individuals must have been Melungeons, assuming that there could not have been that many free blacks, mulattoes, or Indians at that time. Genealogist Virginia DeMarce disagrees, maintaining that such a proportion of free blacks, mulattoes, or Indians was consistent with the population of Virginia and North Carolina, from where most of the territory's settlers came. Of the Melungeons enumerated in the 1850 census, none were born in Tennessee prior to 1800.[53]

---

[48] Elder, *Melungeons*, 114.

[49] The State of Franklin was an unsuccessful attempt in 1784 by settlers in what is now Tennessee to break away from North Carolina and form a new state. Sevier later became the first governor of Tennessee.

[50] Will Allen Dromgoole, "The Malungeons," *The Arena* 3 (March 1891): 470.

[51] *Nashville Daily American*, Monday, 15 September 1890, 2.

[52] Elder, *Melungeons*, 114–15.

[53] Virginia Easley DeMarce, "Looking at Legends—Lumbee and Melungeon: Applied Genealogy and the Origins of Tri-racial Isolate Settlements," *National Genealogical Quarterly* (March 1993): 33–34; Price, Edward, "The Melungeons: A Mixed-Blood Strain of the Southern Appalachians," *Geographical Review* 41 (2) (1951): 266.

It is not possible to trace with total accuracy the migrations of the various families that ended up on and near Newman's Ridge. However, names of some of early Melungeon settlers, and those of their probable ancestors, can be found in the tax and census records of North Carolina and Virginia The Orange County tax list of 1755 includes several names associated with Melungeon families, including Collins (with various spellings), Bunch, and Gibson— most listed as "mulatto." Melungeon names are also found in the 1782 tax lists for Montgomery and Grayson Counties in Virginia, and Wilkes County, North Carolina. Vardemon Collins, one of the original Melungeon settlers on Newman's Ridge, can be found on the Wilkes County list for 1787.[54]

Lewis Jarvis was an attorney in Sneedville, the Hancock County seat. He was born in Scott County, Virginia, in 1829 and spent most of his life near Melungeons. In 1903 Jarvis gave an interview which placed the arrival of the Melungeons simultaneously with the white settlers.

> These people, not any of them, were here at the time the first white hunting party came from Virginia and North Carolina in the year 1761…Vardy Collins, Shepherd Gibson, Benjamin Collins, Solomon Collins, Paul Bunch and the Goodmans, chiefs and the rest of them settled here about the year 1804, possibly about the year 1795, but all these men above named, who are called Melungeons, obtained land grants and muniments of title to the land they settled on and they were the very first and came here simultaneous with the white people not earlier than 1795. They had lost their language and spoke the English very well. They originally were the friendly Indians who came with the whites as they moved west.[55]

Jarvis makes no mention of any claims of Portuguese ancestry; he states that they were Indians. He traced the migration of these families, white and Indian, from Cumberland County and the New River area of Virginia. Some of the family members stopped at various points along the Blue Ridge Mountains, while others came to Stony Creek in Scott County, Virginia. "The white emigrants and friendly Indians erected a fort on the bank of the river and called it "Fort Blackmore'…From here

---

[54] DeMarce, "Looking at Legends," 34–35; Bible, 20–21.

[55] Jarvis, cited in Elder, *Melungeons,* 75.

they came on to Newman's Ridge...They all came here simultaneously with the whites from the State of Virginia between the years 1795 and 1812..."[56]

Researcher Pat Elder suggests that these "friendly Indians" were mostly descended from the Monacan Nation, with a few remnants of Algonquian peoples. She traces the Collins and perhaps the Gibson families to the Saponi and contends that the first Melungeons settlers came in two groups, or "waves." The first wave, made up of the Collins and Gibson families, set out from the New River area and met French Huguenots, who Elder suggests may have dubbed these mixed Indian people *melange*, or mixture—a label that could easily have been corrupted into "Melungeon." A second wave, involving the Bell, Going, and Minor families, originated farther east in the vicinity of Charles City and New Kent counties, and came to Newman's Ridge separately.[57]

The first white settlement in what became Tennessee was at Sycamore Shoals on the Watauga River in 1769. Another settlement at Carters' Valley in Hawkins County was established in 1772, and was the westernmost American settlement at the time.

North Carolina had passed a series of "Land Acts" in 1777 to finance the war with England and to "settle" the frontier. Another Land Act in 1783 eased restrictions on land purchases. Since the border between Virginia and North Carolina was not certain, Virginia also issued land grants for Tennessee land. When Tennessee became a state in 1796, it also issued land grants. While this situation caused some confusion, land in Tennessee remained fairly easy to get. Since land on and near Newman's Ridge was not considered particularly desirable, Melungeons were able to buy large tracts for relatively little money.[58]

Millington Collins is the first presumed Melungeon recorded in the area, having filed a deed with the Hawkins County Registrar's office in 1802. Tax records indicate that Collins was in Montgomery County, Virginia from 1787 to 1789. His name reappears on the tax lists for Wythe County. Virginia in 1793 and in Grayson County in 1795. Millington Collins appears to have moved in stages down the Appalachian range before settling in Hawkins (now Hancock) County.[59]

---

[56] Ibid.

[57] Elder, *Melungeons*, 298–99.

[58] Bible, *The Melungeons*, 25–26.

[59] DeMarce, "Looking at Legends," 34; Bible, 25.

Newman's Ridge is the location most often associated with Melungeons. Today, one can turn north at the courthouse in Sneedville, go past the new elementary school, and immediately begin climbing the Ridge. The Ridge runs parallel to the Clinch River and extends into Lee County, Virginia. There are two Blackwater Creeks associated with Newman's Ridge, one in Virginia and the other in Tennessee. Sycamore and Snake Hollow are at the northwest foot of the Ridge, and Vardy Valley (named after Vardemon Collins) is between Snake Hollow and the Blackwater Community. All of these areas were settled by both Melungeons and whites. A list of landowners prior to 1812 in Vardy Valley includes Vardemon Collins, Shepherd Gibson, Solomon Collins, Benjamin Bunch, Joseph Gibson, Thomas Miser, James Mullins, Mourning Gibson, Joseph Goins, and Benjamin Collins. While some of the residents of Newman's Ridge and the surrounding areas had land grants dating back to 1780 or earlier, this is not proof that those individuals lived on the property at that time. Often, those who possessed grants would wait years before moving to the property, or might pass the grant on to their offspring at a later date.[60]

Contrary to later legends, the Melungeons did not arrive penniless after being driven from better land in Virginia and North Carolina. They purchased their land, sometimes using cash gleaned from the sale of property in their former states of residence, sometimes using credit. Vardemon Collins' original land grant was for 110 acres. By 1850, he owned property worth $1,500, which was a considerable sum at the time. He owned a hotel/boarding house on Blackwater Creek near Vardy Springs and was considered a reasonably prosperous man. Many other Melungeons had relatively substantial holdings prior to moving to Tennessee and acquired more property after moving. As Pat Elder writes, "This should cause researchers to question twentieth century stories of poverty, ignorance, and supposed land confiscation."[61] Individual family traditions of being forced from land may have their roots with the confiscation of Indian lands several generations prior to the migration to Newman's Ridge.

---

[60] William P. Grohse, "Brief History (Revised) of Vardy Community, Hancock County, Tennessee," 6 October 1967, William Grohse papers (Microfilm Roll # 7) East Tennessee State University.

[61] Elder, *Melungeons*, 208–209.

Not all the Melungeons moved to the vicinity of Newman's Ridge, and not all of those who did move to that area moved at the same time. Newman's Ridge does, however, seem to be the focal point of the migration and the point of dispersal for other family groups. Researcher Edward Price suggests, based on census information, that the migration of Melungeons from their North Carolina and Virginia homes continued over a generation or more. Some families stayed in a given area along the route while the others moved on. The paths of migration taken by Melungeon families can be traced in part by the existence of Melungeon communities along the routes.[62]

One important early Melungeon settlement is the Stony Creek area, near Fort Blackmore in present-day Scott County, Virginia. The Stony Creek Baptist Church records include several people with Melungeon surnames who joined the church between 1801 and 1804. The church minutes provide a unique picture of community life, and give a reasonable estimate of the dates when individuals joined, and later left, the community and the church.

In November of 1801, Stephen and Jemina Osborn joined the Stony Creek Baptist Church. The following month, Comfort Osborn was received, but was not baptized. Nancy Gibson was "received by letter," and Valentine Collins (who was probably Vardemon Collins' brother) was "received by experience" and baptized. The following February, David Gipson, "a backslider" was "received on a relation of the work of God upon his soul." In the next few months, Riley Collins joined the church, along with several Gipsons, including Elizabeth, Rachel, Thomas, Beter, George, Charles, Mary, Henry, Vina, and Fanny.[63]

Even as more Melungeon families moved into the Stony Creek area, others were moving on to the Blackwater, Newman's Ridge, and Mulberry areas of present-day Hancock County, Tennessee. In February of 1803, the Stony Creek Church minutes indicate that Vina Gibson[64] was dismissed from the Stony Creek Church after the church received a letter from her new church in Blackwater. Mary Gibson was also dismissed in February, presumably to join another church. Charles

---

[62] Price, "The Melungeons," 266.

[63] "Stony Creek Baptist Church Minute Books, 1801–1814," http://searches.rootsweb.com/usgenweb/archives/va/scott/church/stonycrk.txt (32 pages). 2–4.

[64] The minutes seem to use the spellings "Gipson" and "Gibson" interchangeably.

Gibson, Valentine Collins, and their wives applied for letters of dismission in April 1803.[65]

Some individuals with Melungeon surnames were excommunicated for various offenses, some unstated in the minutes. Henry Gibson was excommunicated on November 25, 1802, and Tiny Collins and Thomas Gibson placed on censure. The next month, Tiny Collins was restored, but Thomas Gibson remained under censure; he was excommunicated in February 1803. Spicey Moore was excommunicated for "going off with a married man" in April 1804. The following month, George Gibson was excommunicated for "a disorderly walk." In September, Rheuben Gibson was excluded from membership at Stony Creek Church "for persevering in wickedness such as cursing and swearing and getting drunk." Gibson lived at Blackwater and had joined another church while retaining membership at Stony Creek.[66]

The case of Charles Gibson is curious. The minutes give no indication whether there was more than one Charles Gibson (or Gipson), but if this is in fact one individual, he certainly had a checkered career at Stony Creek Baptist Church. A Charles "Gipson" was received into the church in June of 1802, but the following April Charles "Gibson" asked to be dismissed, along with his wife. In September 1803, Charles "Gipson" and his wife were received into the church, based on their old letters of membership. In January 1804, Charles "Gibson" was under censure for "getting drunk and fighting," but was restored the next month. The minutes for May of 1804 indicate Charles "Gibson" was under censure until the next church meeting, but the minutes for the following month indicate the case of Charles "Gipson" was laid over until the next meeting. This last case is obviously one person whose name was spelled both ways in the minutes, but that does not necessarily mean that the earlier entries refer to a single individual. Charles "Gipson" was restored to membership in July 1804, and the minutes have no further record of him until June 1806, when "Brother Gibson came and acknowledged being drunk and he was sorry for which the church forgave him." The next entry in the minutes is dated January 1806, which is either a mistake or the entry was misplaced within the minutes. In any event, Charles "Gipson," was excommunicated after testimony from "several witnesses from the Mulberry Church" who related that Gipson

[65] "Stony Creek Minutes," 3.

[66] Ibid., 3–5.

had been excommunicated from their church for "getting drunk, fighting and gaming."[67]

These individuals with Melungeon surnames were by no means the only people being excommunicated from the church, as the minutes bear out. After about 1808, Melungeon surnames appeared rarely in the church minutes. By then, many of the Melungeon families had relocated to nearby Tennessee locations such as Newman's Ridge, Blackwater, and Mulberry. Other Melungeons communities were being formed, including settlements in Lee County, Virginia, just north of Hancock County, Tennessee. Another group settled near Dungannon, Virginia, in the vicinity of Fort Blackmore, in Scott County, Virginia. Yet another group established itself on High Knob and Stone Mountain in present-day Wise County, Virginia. These Virginia Melungeons were sometimes known as "ramps," presumably after the rampion, an onion-like plant common in the southern Appalachians. Another Melungeon community formed in Hamilton County` in southeastern Tennessee.[68]

The minutes for September 26, 1813, long after many of the Melungeon-surname families had moved away, provide one last reference to these families—and the first written record of the word "Melungeon,"or at least a variant spelling.

> Then came forward Sister Kitchen and complained to the church against Susanna Stallard for saying she harbored them Melungins. Sister Sook said she was hurt with her for believing her child and not believing her, and she won't talk to her to get satisfaction, and both is "pigedish" ["prejudiced"?], one against the other. Sister Sook lays it down and the church forgives her.[69]

C. S. Everett cites an oral tradition that a band of "peaceable" Indians came to Stony Creek in 1817 for some undetermined ceremony. It is probable that "them Melungins" were former members of the congregation who had moved away. Everett suggests that returning "Melungins" in 1813 and "peacable Indians" in the same neighborhood in 1817 might be the same people.[70]

---

[67] Ibid., 3–7.

[68] Ibid., Price, "The Melungeons," 264.

[69] "Stony Creek Minutes," 20.

[70] Everett, "Melungeon History and Myth," 361–62.

The term "Melungin" was not used again in the minutes of Stony Creek Church. In referring to the Stony Creek church records, Everett notes that "while 'Negro' and 'black' are utilized in several instances throughout the minutes as descriptive terms for a few church members ('white' never being used), 'Melungins' was used but once and not when the people being referred to as such were sitting in Stony Creek church. Clearly, something about the word precluded it from being used in the presence of actual 'Melungins.'"[71]

A tantalizing suggestion of Melungeon migration west of the Mississippi River exists in a history of Baxter County, Arkansas. By 1811, large numbers of Cherokees had moved west in anticipation of their eventual removal; enough Cherokees were in the area to warrant the establishment of an Indian Agency. At about the same time, a man named Jacob Mooney, along with four slaves and four other men, poled a flatboat up the White River and established a store. In 1973, Mary Ann Messick, the great-great-granddaughter of Jacob Mooney, wrote, "The four men who had come with Mooney were men of mystery—referred to by oldtimers who knew of them as "Lungeons." They were neither Negro or Indian and in later years Jacob Mooney was ostracized for living with these "foreigners."[72]

While this snippet of information provides no solid link between these "Lungeons" and the Melungeons of the Clinch River region, the similarity between the two words is remarkable. Mooney was originally from McMinnville, Tennessee, and could conceivably have come into contact with one of the Melungeon communities near his home. Messick writes that by the 1830s, "his former slaves and the "Lungeon" men had died and most of their families had moved west with the Indians."[73]

If these "Lungeons" had any connection with the Melungeon settlements in the Clinch River region, they were an exception to the usual migration patterns. Melungeon surnames are found in the census records of southwestern Virginia counties as early as 1820. Many of these families seem to have moved there from the Hawkins/Hancock County, Tennessee area. The 1870 census enumerators in Lee County, Virginia, listed the county of birth; of the 46 families with Melungeon

---

[71] Ibid., 361–62, 392.
[72] Mary Ann Messick, *History of Baxter County, Centennial Edition, 1873–1973,* Baxter County Historical and Genealogical Society (1973, reprinted 1998): 6.
[73] Ibid., 7.

surnames, thirty had one or more members who were born in Hawkins or Hancock County. Eight had members born in Scott County, Virginia, and at least one of those families had members born in Hancock or Hawkins County. Other family members had been born in Ashe or Surry Counties, North Carolina. As Price said, "This is the best direct evidence available to confirm the relationship between several different groups of Melungeons and the importance of Newman's Ridge as a center of their dispersal, but it is also evident that the secondary Melungeon localities were also fed from North Carolina and Virginia."[74]

Whatever their actual ancestry, by the time the first Melungeon families settled on and near Newman's Ridge, they considered themselves white people with Indian ancestry. That opinion was not universally shared by their white neighbors, and their legal status would be questioned repeatedly.

"A Singular Species of the Human Animal"

Anyhow, in the early eighteen hundreds the Melungeons was here. So the white settlers commenced a-coming in and noticing what good creek-bottom farms the Melungeons had. Them great-grandpappies of ours just wanted them farms till they hurt. They was a breed that got what they wanted. If the Melungeons had been plain Injuns, it wouldn't been no trouble to kick them out. But here they was, a-speaking English, and on top of that they was Christians. Some of them fought in the war against the English, .

Well, the white settlers didn't want to do nothing that wasn't right with the Lord and the Law. So they scrabbled around and studied it from all sides and directions. They knowed the Melungeons, like the Cherokees, had let runaway slaves hide out amongst them. This with their dark skins was enough to make our grandpappies see pretty plain that the Melungeons was a niggerfied people. The more they looked at them good Melungeon bottom lands, the plainer they saw the nigger blood.

So they passed a law. They fixed it so that nobody with nigger blood could vote, hold office, or bear witness in court.

---

[74] Price, "The Melungeons," 267.

Then they got busy and sued for the bottom lands. Pretty soon
the Melungeons lost all their holdings in law suits.
    Folklore compiled by James Aswell[75]

When Tennessee became a state, its constitution provided that any
free man could vote, regardless of ethnic background. This fact
accounted for the migration of a good many free blacks and other "free
persons of color" from other states, particularly North Carolina and
Virginia. The right to vote may have played a large part in the decision
of the early Melungeon families to move to Tennessee. However, when
the state constitution was rewritten in 1834, voting rights were restricted
to free white men only; free blacks and other "free persons of color"
were denied the vote.

If Tennessee's formerly liberal voting laws had been part of the
motivation for the Melungeons' move from Virginia and North Carolina,
the revised constitution must have been a great disappointment. On the
other hand, since the Melungeons seem to have considered themselves
white, the ramifications of the new law may have gone unnoticed—at
least until someone questioned the degree of "whiteness" the
Melungeons possessed. Making that determination, though, would not
prove an easy task.

In the 1820 census, 310 "free persons of color" were listed in
Hawkins County. The 1820 census listed individuals in four categories:
whites, slaves, free persons of color, and all other persons not taxed.
Indians who were not taxed were not enumerated so the fourth class
seems to be intended for Indians who were, as Edward Price put it,
"living as ordinary citizens." No one in Hawkins county was listed in the
fourth class. Most of those listed as "free persons of color" had surnames
associated with the Melungeons.

In the 1830 census, Hawkins County had 331 "free persons of
color," more than any other county in the state except Davidson County,
which included Nashville. Again, most of those so designated had
Melungeon names. In addition, neighboring Grainger County had 130
"free persons of color" bearing Melungeon surnames. However, in the
1840 census, these same families are listed as "white. Since these people
probably did not undergo a change of complexion, there was evidently

[75] James Aswell, *God Bless The Devil*, Federal Writers' Project (Chapel Hill:
University of North Carolina Press, 1940) 207–208.

some question among census enumerators as to the ethnic status of these families. A family that seemed "white" to one enumerator may not have seemed "white" to another.

The same 1830 census which showed 331 "free persons of color" in Hawkins County, also noted the presence of four separate units of the Goins family in Hamilton County, in southeastern Tennessee. Some members of this family were enumerated as black, while others were considered white. One of these first Melungeons in southeastern Tennessee was David Goens, a veteran of the American Revolution who was born in Hanover County, Virginia. Following the war, Goens lived in Wythe and Grayson counties in Virginia, then in Grainger County, Tennessee, near Hawkins County and Newman's Ridge. From there, he moved to Hamilton County with his younger brother Laban. By 1840, the census listed 13 "free colored" families in Hamilton County. Eight of those families, a total of 53 people, were named "Gowin." The 1850 census recorded 16 families named Goins (or variations thereof) listed as "mulatto."Records indicate that two individuals from this group were born in Virginia and one in North Carolina; the rest were born in Tennessee.[76]

As Tennessee grew, word of this unusual colony of dark-skinned people began to spread around the state. The term "Malungeon" was used in an article printed in Jonesborough, Tennessee in 1840.

NEGRO SPEAKING!

We have just learned, upon undoubtable authority, that Gen. Combs, in his attempt to address the citizens of Sullivan County, on yesterday, was insulted, contradicted repeatedly, limited to one hour and a half, and most shamefully treated, and withall an effort was made, to get an impudent Malungeon from Washington City, a scoundrel who is half Negro and half Indian, and who has actually been speaking in Sullivan, in reply to Combs! Gen. Combs, however, declined the honor of contending with Negroes and Indians _ said he had fought against the latter, but never met them in debate! This is the party, reader, who are opposed to the gag-law, and to abolition!

---

[76] Ibid; E. Raymond Evans, "The Graysville Melungeons: A Tri-Racial People In Lower East Tennessee, *Tennessee Anthropologist* (Spring 1979): 5.

Bigotry and democracy in Sullivan County, well knowing that their days on earth are numbered, are rolling together their clouds of blackness and darkness, in the person of a free negroe, with the forlorn hope of obscuring the light that is beaming in glory, and a gladness, upon this country, through the able and eloquent speeches of Whig orators. David Shaver replied to Gen. Combs, we are informed. This is the same Davy, Mr. Netherland gave an account of, some time since, and who, Col. James gave us the history of, in an address, at our late convention. When Davy had finished, the big Democratic Negro came forward, and entertained the brethren. These two last speakers were an entertaining pair![77]

Tennessee politicians, particularly in the post-Civil War era, would use the term "Melungeon" to describe opposing politicians, particularly Republicans from the eastern third of the state. During the post-war Reconstruction era, bitter epithets flew freely between Democrats and Republicans. This particular epithet, however, seems never to have lost its suggestion of non-white ancestry. When Nashville writer Will Allen Dromgoole asked two Tennessee legislators of the 1890s to define "Malungeons," the answers were "a dirty Indian sneak" and "a Portuguese nigger."[78]

The 1840 article was printed in the Jonesborough *Whig*, a political newspaper edited by William Gannaway "Parson" Brownlow, later to become the controversial Reconstruction governor of Tennessee. Over the next two weeks, Brownlow's *Whig* made several references to the "Malungeon" which made clear that Brownlow considered a Melungeon to be "a scoundrel who is half Negro and half Indian." References to "the big Democratic Negro" were meant to associate the Democrats with the concept of racial equality, a notion repugnant of southern Whigs (and to southern Democrats as well).[79]

The origin of this "impudent Malungeon" is given as "Washington City." This raises some questions. Jonesborough, where the newspaper was published, is the seat of Washington County, Tennessee, and there is a Washington County nearby in Virginia. However, there is no city or

---

[77] *Brownlow's Whig* (Jonesborough, TN) 7 October 1840, 3.

[78] Dromgoole, "The Malungeons," 472.

[79] Everett, "Melungeon History and Myth," 375.

town named "Washington" anywhere near Jonesborough. In the 1840s, "Washington City" often referred to Washington, DC. If the "scoundrel who is half Negro and half Indian" came from the District of Columbia, the term "Melungeon" obviously had a far broader meaning and more widespread usage than anyone has suggested to date. If the term was being used in the nation's capital, one could reasonably assume the term would exist in numerous other records. It does not; as of this writing, the Jonesborough articles of 1840 are only the second known written record of the word, the first being the Stony Creek church minutes of 1813. The author may have been applying a local term to an outsider, someone who would not have been called a "Malungeon" anywhere else. The more likely explanation, however, is that the reference to "Washington City" is a mistake or a typographical error, and the origin of the "impudent Malungeon" was Washington County.

Wherever the "impudent" individual originated, the term "Melungeon" was clearly associated with African ancestry. The Tennessee Constitution of 1834 clearly prohibited voting by non-whites. The Melungeons may have considered themselves white, but that opinion was not shared by all of their neighbors, and in 1845, the voting rights of several Melungeon individuals were challenged in court.

Many years after the event, Swan Burnett wrote:

There was at least one record in which the matter was brought before the courts. Which was before the Civil War, during the period of slavery, that the right of a number of people in this group to vote was questioned. The matter was finally carried before a jury, where the question was decided by an examination of the feet. One was found sufficiently flat-footed to be regarded "a free person of color" hence not allowed to vote, while the others were determined to have enough white blood to permit them suffrage. The defense for the entire group was argued by Col. John Netherland, the Rogersville lawyer who was later instrumental in getting their citizenship rights restored.[80]

Jack H. Goins of Rogersville examined the court records and believes that Burnett's account of the trial came from "second or third

---

[80] Swan Burnett, "A Note on the Melungeons," *American Anthropologist* 2 (October 1889): 347.

hand information." The outcome of the trials, according to county records, is not quite as Burnett described. On January 25, 1846, eight Melungeons were charged with illegally voting in an election held the previous August. The defendants were Melungeon patriarch Vardemon "Vardy" Collins, Solomon Collins, Ezekial Collins, Levi Collins, Andrew Collins, Wiatt Collins, and brothers Zachariah and Lewis Minor. Each of the defendants posted $250 bond.[81]

Although Hancock County had been formed from parts of Hawkins and Claiborne Counties on January 6, 1844, it was not officially organized until 1846. The illegal voting, therefore, had taken place in Hawkins County, and the defendants were tried in the Hawkins County seat of Rogersville. The Attorney General for the district was the Honorable A.R. Nelson. The Melungeons were probably represented by the aforementioned Col. Netherland, although court records do not list the name of the attorney for the defense.

The trials were repeatedly postponed, and after two defendants were acquitted, the state declined to prosecute the others. No record has been found of the trial arguments, and if flat-footedness was an issue at all in the trial, the verdicts would suggest that the absence of flat-footedness proved in favor of the defendants. The use of this physical trait to prove—or disprove—African ancestry would surface in another Melungeon court case a quarter century later. The arguments used in the "Celebrated Melungeon Case" of 1872 may possibly have originated with the defense used in the 1844 Hawkins County case.[82]

In 1849, *Littel's Living Age* took note of the Melungeons. Although the unidentified correspondent evidently met Vardy Collins, no mention is made of the illegal voting charge; it is highly unlikely, though, that Vardy would have mentioned to a stranger that he had been accused of not being white enough to vote. *Living Age* was a popular magazine of the nineteenth century that reprinted articles from other publications for national distribution. No one has been able to provide a citation on the original article. It may have been published in Louisville, Kentucky, as early as 1847. It appeared as an unsigned article in the Knoxville *Register* of September 6, 1848.[83]

---

[81] Jack H. Goins, *Melungeons: And Other Pioneer Families* (Rogersville TN: Jack Harold Goins, 2000) 47.

[82] Goins, *Melungeons,* 38–47.

[83] Everett, "Melungeon History and Myth," 405.

THE MELUNGENS

(We are sorry to have lost the name of the southern paper from which this is taken.)

We give to-day another amusing and characteristic sketch from a letter of our intelligent and sprightly correspondent, sojourning at present in one of the seldom-visited nooks hid away in our mountains.

"You must know that within ten miles of this owl's nest, there is a watering-place, known hereabouts as 'Black-water Springs.' It is situated in a narrow gorge, scarcely half a mile wide, between Powell's Mountain and the Copper Ridge, and is, as you may suppose, almost inaccessible. A hundred men could defend the pass against even a Xerxian army. Now this gorge and the tops and sides of the adjoining mountains are inhabited by a singular species of the human animal called MELUNGENS.

The legend of their history, which they carefully preserve, is this. A great many years ago, these mountains were settled by a society of Portuguese Adventurers, men and women—who came from the long-shore parts of Virginia, that they might be freed from the restraints and drawbacks imposed on them by any form of government. These people made themselves friendly with the Indians and freed, as they were from every kind of social government, they uprooted all conventional forms of society and lived in a delightful Utopia of their own creation, trampling on the marriage relation, despising all forms of religion, and subsisting upon corn (the only possible product of the soil) and wild game of the woods. These intermixed with the Indians, and subsequently their descendants (after the advances of the whites into this part of the state) with the negros and the whites, thus forming the present race of Melungens. They are tall, straight, well-formed people, of a dark copper color, with Circassian features, but wooly heads and other similar appendages of our negro. They are privileged voters in the state in which they live and thus, you will perceive, are accredited citizens of the commonwealth. They are brave, but quarrelsome; and are hospitable and generous to strangers. They have no preachers among them and are almost without any knowledge of a

Supreme Being. They are married by the established forms, but husband and wife separate at pleasure, without meeting any reproach or disgrace from their friends. They are remarkably unchaste, and want of chastity on the part of females is no bar to their marrying. They have but little association with their neighbors, carefully preserving their race, or class, or whatever you may call it: and are in every respect, save they are under the state government, a separate and distinct people.

Now this is no traveler's story. They are really what I tell you, without abating or setting down in aught in malice. They are behind their neighbors in the arts. They use oxen instead of horses in their agricultural attempts, and their implements of husbandry are chiefly made by themselves of wood. They are, without exception, poor and ignorant, but apparently happy.

Having thus given you a correct geographical and scientific history of the people, I will proceed with my own adventures.

The doctor was, as usual my compagnon de voyage, and we stopped at 'Old Vardy's', the hostelrie of the vicinage. Old Vardy is the 'chief cook and bottle-washer' of the Melungens, and is really a very clever fellow: but his hotel savors strongly of that peculiar perfume that one may find in the sleeping-rooms of our negro servants, especially on a close, warm, summer evening. We arrived at Vardy's in time for supper, and thus despatched, we went to the spring, where were assembled several rude log huts, and a small sprinkling of the natives, together with a fiddle and other preparations for a dance. Shoes, stockings, and coats were unknown luxuries among them—at least we saw them not.

The dance was engaged in with right hearty good will, and would have put to the blush the tame steppings of our beaux. Among the participants was a very tall, raw-boned damsel, with her two garments fluttering readily in the amorous night breeze, who's black eyes were lit up with an unusual fire, either from the repeated visits to the nearest hut, behind the door of which was placed an open-mouthed stone jar of new-made corn whiskey, and in which was a gourd, with a 'deuce a bit' of sugar at all, and no water near than the spring. Nearest here on the right was a lank lantern-jawed, high cheekbone, long-legged fellow who seemed similarly elevated. Now these two, Jord Bilson (that was he,) and Syl Varmin, (that was she,) were destined to afford the amusement of the evening: for Jord, in cutting the pigeon-wing, chanced to light from one of his aerial flights right upon the ponderous pedal appendage of Syl, a compliment which this amiable lady seemed in no way to accept kindly.

'Jord Bilson,' said the tender Syl, 'I'll thank you to keep your darned hoofs off my feet.'

'Oh, Jord's feet are so tarnel big he can't manage 'em all by hisself.' suggested some pasificator near by.

'He'll have to keep 'em off me,' suggested Syl, 'or I'll shorten 'em for him.'

'Now look ye here, Syl Varmin, ' answered Jord, somewhat nettled at both remarks, 'I didn't go to tread on your feet but I don't want you to be cutting up any rusties about. You're nothing but a cross-grained critter, anyhow.'

'And you're a darned Melungen.'

'Well, if I am, I ain't nigger-Melungen, anyhow—I'm Indian-Melungen, and that's more 'an you is.'

'See here, Jord,' said Syl, now highly nettled, 'I'll give you a dollar ef you'll go out on the grass and right it out.'

Jord smiled faintly and demurred, adding—'Go home Syl, and look under your puncheons and see if you can't fill a bed outen the hair of them hogs you stole from Vardy.'

'And you go to Sow's cave, Jord Bilson, ef it comes to that, and see how many shucks you got offen that corn you took from Pete Joemen. Will you take the dollar?'

Jord now seemed about to consent, and Syl reduced the premium by one half, and finally came down to a quarter, and then Jord began to offer a quarter, a half, and finally a dollar: but Syl's prudence equalled his, and seeing that neither was likely to accept, we returned to our hotel, and were informed by old Vardy that the sight we had witnessed was no 'onusual one. The boys and gals was jist having a little fun.'

And so it proved, for about midnight we were wakened by a loud noise of contending parties in fierce combat, and, rising and looking out from the chinks of our hut, we saw the whole party engaged in a grand melee; rising above the din of all which, was the harsh voice of Syl Varmin, calling—

'Stand back here, Sal Frazar, and let me do the rest of the beaten of Jord Bilson; I haint forgot his hoofs yit.'

The melee closed, and we retired again, and by breakfast next morning all hands were reconciled, and the stone jar replenished out of the mutual pocket, and peace ruled where so lately all had been recriminations and blows.

After breakfast, just as the supper had been at old Jack's, save only that we had a table, we started for Clinch river for a day's fishing where other and yet more amusing incidents awaited us. But as I have dwelt upon this early part of the journey longer than I intended, you must wait till the next letter for the concluding incidents."[84]

The 'next letter" containing "the concluding incidents" was evidently not printed, for no record of a sequel to this article has turned up.

The *Living Age* piece is the earliest known reference to the Melungeons' supposed Portuguese ancestry. Since the article was written more than a decade after Tennessee constitutionally disfranchised all non-whites, those skeptical of the Melungeons' claim could assume that the claim of Portuguese ancestry was used to help them establish a European (white) ancestry. However, it is plain from the tone of the article that the writer did not consider Portuguese to be "white." The writer shared this attitude with many American Anglo-Saxons; had the Melungeons been trying to emphasize their white ancestry, they might have done better to stress an English-Indian mix.

The article described the Melungeons as having "a dark copper color, with Circassian [Caucasian?] features, but wooly heads and other similar appendages of our negro." Few of the later physical descriptions of the Melungeons would emphasize Negroid traits. Many of these articles portrayed the Melungeons as being "maligned" by the belief that they had Negro ancestry, and downplayed the obvious Negroid traits of some Melungeon individuals.

---

[84] "The Melungeons," *Littel's Living Age* 254/31 (March 1849): 618–19.

The *Living Age* article implied that the Melungeons differentiated between "Indian-Melungen" and "nigger-Melungen." James Aswell wrote in 1940, "The whites always claimed the Melungeons was a nigger breed and nobody can deny some of them really was. Some of them mixed and mingled with niggers and got the name of Blackwaters. The pure breed Melungeons wouldn't have nothing to do with the Blackwaters. They called themselves Ridgemanites or Hill Portughee, and today there's not any difference much betwixt the Ridgemanites and the rest of us."[85]

According to interviews conducted in the 1940s, a family named Pugsley moved from Virginia into Highland County, Ohio about 1858. The Pugsleys brought along several black servants to help them run an inn near the town of Carmel. Those servants, whose name was Nichols, later married into several families named Gibson and Perkins who moved up from eastern Kentucky.

This is the commonly-accepted genesis of a group of people known as the Carmel Indians. The Perkins family was reputed to have Indian ancestry, while the Gibson family can be traced to Melungeons in eastern Kentucky, who in turn can be traced to the families who settled Newman's Ridge. The most common names among the Carmel Melungeons were Nichols, Gibson, and Perkins.[86]

Melungeons and the Civil War

In the summer of 1852, Wilson Minor applied for a marriage license. Minor sent his brother, John Minor, to Rogersville to apply for the license. James Bloomer, the uncle of the proposed bride, forcibly took the license from John Minor, who filed an assault charge against Bloomer. Bloomer claimed that Wilson Minor had abducted his niece, Jane Bloomer, for the purpose of marriage, and that the Minors "free persons of color" and forbidden to marry whites.

The jury ruled against Bloomer, and the court fined him one cent and court costs. Bloomer appealed the case, but the Tennessee Supreme Court upheld the jury verdict. Wilson Minor received another marriage license in December of 1852, but there was no return of this license. Jane Bloomer would have been about 15 years old at the time; Wilson Minor

---

[85] Aswell, *God Bless The Devil*, 3.
[86] Kessler and Ball, *North From the Mountains*, 19–20, 31–57.

was 28. Wilson Minor's love for Jane may have been unrequited, or Jane may have been persuaded to drop the idea of marriage; in any event, the marriage never took place. No further record of Wilson Minor can be found, but Jane Bloomer married Shelby Bledsoe in 1860. Bledsoe was killed by "bushwhackers" during the Civil War, and Jane married Richard Wallen in 1870.[87]

"Bushwhackers" is a term used to describe participants in a particularly brutal form of guerilla warfare during the Civil War. Tennessee rejected secession in early 1861, and only reluctantly joined the Confederacy after Lincoln's call for troops following the attack of Fort Sumter. East Tennessee had relatively few slaves and had closer economic ties to the industrial North than with the planters of the South. The majority of east Tennesseans remained loyal to the Union, and the region was occupied by Confederate troops through the early years of the war.

> Well, first thing anybody knowed the Civil War busted out. Most of the men hereabouts joined up with the Union and started in fighting. But you can bet a pretty the Melungeons didn't burn up no shoe leather hotfooting it to the colors—the Stars and Bars nor the Stars and Stripes.
> Folklore compiled by James Aswell[88]

Many Hancock County Melungeons did serve their country in uniform. Like many East Tennesseans, however, they weren't completely of one mind as to which country was theirs. The loyalties of the Melungeons paralleled those of the neighboring whites; the majority fought for the Union, but a significant minority sided with the Confederacy. Hancock Countians who sided with the North made their way through nearby Cumberland Gap into Kentucky, which was officially still part of the Union despite its widespread Confederate sympathies.

The majority of Hancock County soldiers with Melungeon surnames served in the First Tennessee Cavalry of the Union Army, including Privates Bailey Collins, Simeon Collins, Calaway Collins (wounded at the Battle of Franklin in November 1864), Silas Collins

---

[87] Goins, *Melungeons*, 11–16.
[88] Aswell, *God Bless The Devil*, 3.

(who made it home to die in 1863 from wounds received in combat), Lewis Collins (who was wounded in the leg), Vardaman Collins, Ervin Collins (wounded in action), Thomas Anderson, Franklin Collins, Wilson Miser, James Delp, William Bell, and Alfred Goins. Conoway Collins was a captain in that unit. Privates McKinley Collins and Batey Collins (who was wounded and suffered a case of mumps) served in the 8th Tennessee Cavalry, and Britton Bowlin was in the 10th Tennessee Infantry. Vardyman [sic] Collins served in the 2nd Tennessee Infantry, while John Goins served in a Kentucky infantry unit and was a prisoner of war for 13 months. Corporal Harrison Collins of the 1st Tennessee Cavalry was awarded the Congressional Medal of Honor by President Lincoln at the White House in 1864. Morgan Goins, Howard Collins, Milum Collins, Christofer Mullins, and Alfred Goins also served in various Union companies.

On the other hand, Hancock Countians Armstrong Collins, Joseph Gibson, and Jerry Mullins served under the Stars and Bars. Collins was a private in the 10th Tennessee Confederate Infantry, while Gibson and Mullins went to nearby Virginia to enlist as privates in the 50th Virginia Infantry.[89]

The majority of Melungeon males, however, avoided serving in either army. In that, they were not at all different from their white neighbors in eastern Tennessee. Many east Tennesseans were divided in their loyalties between their country and their state. Many did not see that the war concerned them one way or the other. All realized that east Tennessee was considered a Union stronghold and was occupied by Confederate troops. Few were eager to leave their families during such a perilous time.

> After the war got a-going, a heap of them took up bushwhacking and made a proper good thing out of it. The old folks say for years after the war the Melungeons was still trying to get the blue and gray pants and coats they'd taken from supply trains wore out. They was plenty of killings enduring those bad old war times, but all of them can't be hung on the Melungeons. Too many gangs of white bushwhackers, draft dodgers, and

---

[89] Bible, *The Melungeons*, 44–45; Hallie Price Garner, 1890 Census of Union Veterans and their Widows, Hancock County, TN, htttp://www.rootsweb. com/~tnhawkin/1890vethan.html.

deserters rampaging about in the hills for that. But Lord knows they were up to enough mischief, though, as it is.
Folklore compiled by James Aswell[90]

If the Melungeons engaged in bushwhacking, they were not alone. East Tennessee saw relatively few major battles, but a great deal of informal activity, including bridge burnings and assassinations. East Tennesseans were by no means unanimous in their support of the Union, and the cliche "brother against brother" was often literally true in east Tennessee. Unionists were frequently persecuted by their former friends and neighbors who were now among the Confederate authorities. "Bushwhackers" were not part of a regular army, but carried out informal acts of retribution against their enemies. In the early years of the war, when east Tennessee was under Confederate authority, guerilla activity was primarily directed against that authority. Later, when Union troops occupied much of the area, Confederate guerillas emerged. However, the issue of Union versus Confederacy was not always a paramount consideration in the activities of bushwhackers; personal vendettas motivated many, if not most, bushwhackings.

This sort of brutal, personal warfare did not recognize non-combatants. Women and children from Unionist families were subjected to atrocities in many parts of the Confederacy, including Appalachia, and retribution for those atrocities was often in kind. The bitterness engendered by the Civil War lasted for generations, as did the Melungeons' reputation as bushwhackers.

Forty years later, journalist Will Allen Dromgoole wrote, "After the breaking out of the war, some few enlisted in the army, but the greater number remained with their stills, to pillage and plunder among the helpless women and children. Their mountains became a terror to travelers; and not until within the last half decade has it been regarded as safe to cross Malungeon territory."[91] A century after Dromgoole wrote those lines, Mike Nassau asked Rogersville, Tennessee attorney and historian Henry Price about these raids against neighboring whites. "I could not imagine a non-white group in the early nineteenth century conducting organized raids on whites and surviving. Mr. Price confirmed

---

[90] Aswell, *God Bless The Devil*, 3.
[91] Dromgoole, "The Malungeons," 472.

that, like the systematic dispossession of the Melungeons, these raids never occurred."[92]

However, in 1994, Brent Kennedy suggested that the Civil War provided Melungeons an opportunity to avenge the various wrongs committed against them. "Bands of Melungeon men formed what came to be known as the 'Melungeon Marauders,' spreading terror throughout east Tennessee…Now the white community's previously simple prejudice escalated to include an accompanying terror of these dark-complexioned people."[93]

Bushwhacking, raiding Union and Confederate supply trains, and using the war as a cover for personal vendettas were widespread during that time. Some Melungeons probably engaged in such activities; it would be surprising if they had not. There is no evidence of large-scale raids or any sort of paramilitary organization among the Melungeons of that era. Exaggerated reports of the "Melungeon Marauders" likely grew out of the imaginations of post-war storytellers.

William O. "Wild Bill" Sizemore was the most noted bushwhacker of the time in that region. His exploits may have been inflated in retelling; he is said to have become a bushwhacker when Rebel soldiers killed his brother Kit. A Rogersville newspaper reported, many years after the fact, that Sizemore had murdered seven Confederate prisoners near the end of the war.[94] After the war, Sizemore reportedly continued to terrorize the area with robberies and murder. Sizemore was finally killed by his cousin, Irdell Willis, in 1867. Researchers differ on whether or not Sizemore was a Melungeon. Pat Elder and Virginia DeMarce maintain that he was not; while Jack Goins asserts that he was. Either way, the activities of Sizemore and his fellow guerillas added to the sinister reputation the Melungeons had following the war.[95]

Most of the Union veterans from east Tennessee came home to vote Republican. Reconstruction in the state was less traumatic than in other states, but it was bitter enough. The Democrats of west and middle Tennessee began to use the term "Melungeon" as a generic slur against the eastern Republicans, implying that they were bushwhackers of

---

[92] Nassau, "Melungeons," 25.

[93] Kennedy, *The Melungeons*, 15–16.

[94] *Rogersville Herald*, 3 February 1892, cited by Goins, *Melungeons*, 21.

[95] Elder, *Melungeons*, 292–94; Goins, *Melungeons*, 21–36.

uncertain racial pedigree. The reputation of the Melungeon people grew even more sinister.

In North Carolina, the Confederate Army drafted Croatans (today known as the Lumbee), but only as laborers. Negroes were also drafted as laborers. Many Croatans deserted, and many others were suspected of aiding Union troops. In 1864, Confederate Home Guards captured and shot three members of the Croatan Lowry family. Henry Berry Lowry witnessed the incident, and soon led a band of "desperadoes." This group included not only Croatan Indians, but deserters from the Union army and several blacks as well. Lowry and his band terrorized the region for eight years before Lowry's associates were captured and killed. Lowry himself disappeared, to become a folk hero among his people. For years afterward, the Croatans had the same fearsome reputation as the Melungeons.[96]

> Whites left them alone because they were so wild and devil-fired and queer and witchy. If a man was fool enough to go into Melungeon country and if he come back without being shot, he was just sure to wizzen and perish away with some ailment nobody could name. Folks said terrible things went on back yonder, blood drinking and devil worship and carryings on that would freeze a good Christian's spine-bone
> Folklore compiled by James Aswell.[97]

Despite the folk tales and legends, the Melungeons lived lives almost identical to their white neighbors. Those who had tillable land lived the life of any small farmer. Those who lived on the mountains and ridges hunted and fished for food. For cash, the Melungeons, like mountain whites, gathered ginseng, which was sold for export to Asia. The manufacture of illegal liquor was a common occupation among Melungeons and whites alike. The Melungeons were primarily Protestant, and some of their churches engaged in snake handling, following a scriptural suggestion that those who "had the spirit" would not bitten. This practice was not limited to Melungeons, but was a feature in many mountain churches and still surfaces occasionally today.

---

[96] Berry, *Almost White*, 154–55.
[97] Aswell, *God Bless The Devil*, 212.

Likewise, superstition and a belief in witchcraft were common among both whites and Melungeons.

Unlike other tri-racial groups with significant Native ancestry, such as the Croatans and the remnants of the Virginia Powhatan and Monacan nations, the Melungeons had no tribal identity to fall back on. The mountains of northeastern Tennessee and southwestern Virginia had not had large plantations, and therefore few slaves. There was not a significant black community for the Melungeons to identify with even if they had desired to do so.[98] Attempting to join white society was possible only for Melungeons with relatively fair complexions who moved away from their home region to a location where their families were not known. In Melungeon country, even a blue-eyed blond-haired Collins was still a Collins, and therefore a Melungeon.

The Celebrated Melungeon Case

The "Celebrated Melungeon Case" of 1872 brought more attention to the Melungeons and their peculiar status. It also set a legal precedent which the Melungeons would use to their advantage in years to come.

The origin of the case dates to the early days of Chattanooga, Tennessee, when a wealthy Virginian bought a large tract of land in Moccasin Bend along the Tennessee River. Upon his death he left considerable property to his three sons. Two of the sons died without marrying, leaving their estates to the surviving brother. This young man, who remained anonymous in a later account of the case, went into business in Chattanooga while renting out his property and slaves. His mother, meanwhile, remarried and had three daughters with her second husband.

The young man fell victim to an unspecified mental illness that left him temporarily incapacitated. However, he was able to resume his business by 1848. On one of his farms lived a tenant, a Melungeon named Bolton. The young man fell in love with Bolton's daughter, who was "famed for her beauty." The couple planned to marry, but the young

---

[98] Some Melungeon families assimilated into the minuscule African-American communities of northeast Tennessee. Their descendants considered themselves African-American, but in recent years some have acknowledged and celebrated their Melungeon ancestry.

man's mother objected, knowing that she and her daughters stood to lose any chance of inheriting any of her first husband's property.

The mother threatened to sue the county clerk if he issued a marriage license to the couple, claiming not only that her son was mentally incompetent, but that the girl had Negro ancestry and the marriage would be illegal. Several days later, when the couple applied for a license, the clerk refused to issue one. The couple then went to neighboring Dade County, Georgia, where they received a license and were married on June 14, 1856.

The couple's first child, a son, died in infancy. A daughter was born in 1858, but the wife died of complications from childbirth. The husband never recovered from the loss and was placed under the care of a guardian. The mother of the stricken husband arranged for the child's "Aunt Betsy" to take the girl to Illinois, never to return. Aunt Betsy took with her the family Bible, including birth and marriage records. A friend of Aunt Betsy named Samuel Williams arranged to keep informed of the girl's welfare.

The insane man's guardian, a Mr. Foust, managed his ward's affairs well, and built up a handsome estate. However, in 1872, the man's surviving half-sisters and the children of his deceased half-sister charged Foust with mismanagement, and sued to have the ward and his estate turned over to them. At this point, Samuel Williams decided to produce the rightful heir. He tried to engage one of Chattanooga's more experienced lawyers, but found that nearly all of them were already involved in the case on one side or the other. Lewis Shepherd was available, however; he was a young attorney, new in his profession, and was eager to take a high-profile case such as this.[99]

Shepherd was born in Hamilton County, Tennessee in 1846. In June of 1861, at the age of 15, Shepherd was swept up in the wave of Southern war hysteria and left school to join the Confederate Army. Shepherd served in Company "A," Fifth Tennessee Cavalry, which surrendered at Washington, Georgia. Shepherd spent about a year at Camp Morton, near Indianapolis, Indiana. On November 15, 1864, Shepherd and several comrades escaped, but were soon recaptured. He

---

[99] S. L. Shepherd, "A Romantic Account of the Celebrated Melungeon Case," *Memoirs of Judge Lewis Shepherd* (Chattanooga: 1915): 82–86.

was exchanged in time to take part in the final actions in the war only to surrender again in the spring of 1865.[100]

Shepherd studied law, was admitted to the bar in 1866, and began practicing in Chattanooga in 1870. He saw this case as a means to make a name for himself, and filed suit on behalf of the child. Though the opposition claimed the girl was illegitimate and her father insane, Shepherd easily proved the validity of the marriage through the Dade County, Georgia, records. The judge ruled that, even if the girl's father was insane, only he or his wife could void the marriage contract—not an outside party.

If the bride had Negro ancestry, however, the marriage was illegal and the daughter illegitimate. The opposition produced several local Negroes who testified that the Boltons were also Negroes, that "the whole bunch of them had kinky hair, just like a mulatto Negro." They testified that Aunt Betsy and the girl's mother also had kinky hair. What the opposition did not know was that Shepherd had brought the girl, now almost 15 years old, from Illinois to Chattanooga.

The girl gave a deposition, and pinned a lock of her hair to the document. Her coal-black hair was perfectly straight and about four feet long, negating the earlier testimony about "kinky hair."[101] Shepherd then proceeded to "explain" the ancestry of the Melungeons:

> In truth, these people belonged to a peculiar race, which settled in East Tennessee at an early day and, in the vernacular of the country, they were known as "Melungeons," and were not even remotely allied to Negroes. It was proven by the tradition amongst these people that they were descendants of the ancient Carthagenians [sic]; they were Phoenicians, who, after Carthage was conquered by the Romans, and became a Roman province, emigrated across the straits of Gibraltar, and settled in Portugal. They lived for many years and became quite numerous on the southern coast of Portugal, and from thence came the distinguished Venetian general, Othello, whom Shakespeare made immortal in his celebrated play, "The Moor of Venice."[102]

---

[100] Ibid., 5.
[101] Ibid., 88–90.
[102] Ibid., 87.

Shepherd argued that a number of these people moved to America at about the time of the Revolution and settled along the North Carolina/South Carolina border. As local whites began to suspect that they were mulattoes and treated them accordingly, some moved across the mountains to present-day Hancock County, Tennessee.

Shepherd also explained that the Melungeons were mis-named.

> The term "Melungeon" is an East Tennessee provincialism; it was coined by the people of that country to apply to these people. It is derived from the French word "melange," meaning a mixture or medley, and has gotten into the modern dictionaries. It was applied to these people because it was at first supposed that they were of mixed blood—part white and part negro. This name is a misnomer, because it has been conclusively proven that they are not mixed with negro blood, but are pure-blooded Carthagenians, as much so as was Hannibal and the Moor of Venice and other pure-blooded descendants of the ancient Phoenicians.[103]

The court ruled that the girl was not a Negro, and that she was the heir apparent to her father's estate.[104] Lewis Shepherd went on to become a judge and a leader of the Chattanooga legal establishment. He told the story of the "Celebrated Melungeon Case" in *Watson's Magazine* in May of 1913, and in his own memoirs, published in 1915.

Although Shepherd said his theory of Carthaginian origin had been "conclusively proven," there is no evidence that anyone had ever suggested this origin prior to this particular court case. "Carthaginian" or "Phoenician" ancestry was not mentioned in any of the earlier writings of the Melungeons, nor is there any record of a Melungeon suggesting such an ancestry. Shepherd states in his memoirs, "It was proven by tradition amongst these people that they were descendants of the ancient Carthaginians...," yet there is no recorded oral tradition suggesting this. The *Littel's Living Age* article mentioned "Portuguese adventurers" as possible ancestors of the Melungeons, but did not mention Carthaginians. It seems quite likely that Shepherd combined a little history with a lot of imagination, making the Melungeons seem a noble relic of antiquity.

---

[103] Ibid., 82–90.
[104] Ibid., 90.

Some researchers, including Jack Goins, believe that much of Shepherd's argument originated with the argument given by Colonel John Netherland in his defense of Melungeons in the illegal voting trial of 1846. Although no record survives of Netherland's defense, it is quite possible that Shepherd knew of the case, and perhaps even had access to records of the trial. Shepherd cites no sources for any of his information.

A more prosaic—and more plausible—argument would have been to argue that the Melungeons were not Negro, but Indian. Shepherd could have presented his client as a modern-day "Indian princess" and evoked legends of Pocahontas. However, while many white American were sentimental about the "noble red man," the reality of free Indians was disturbing. In 1872, many western tribes were engaged in warfare with whites, and were successful often enough to preclude much sympathy from whites, especially following the victory of the Sioux and Cheyenne over George A. Custer's 7th Cavalry at Little Big Horn in June of 1876. Indians in the western United States were an impediment to American notions of "Manifest Destiny." At the same time, the remnants of eastern tribes which had not been removed to the west had roughly the same social status as blacks. This was largely because many (but not all) Indian groups accepted intermarriage with blacks, and the offspring of these unions were accepted in these Indian communities. (The offspring of white/black unions were, almost without exception, shunned by whites.) In the courtroom, the suggestion of Indian ancestry probably would not have had the desired effect. Shepherd had to totally refute the suggestion that his client had even a trace of African ancestry. "[O]ur Southern high-bred people," he wrote, "will never tolerate on equal terms any person who is even remotely tainted with negro blood, but they do not make the same objection to other brown or dark-skinned people, like the Spanish, the Cubans, the Italians, etc."[105]

Despite the fact that Shepherd provided no evidence whatsoever to back his claims, the "Celebrated Melungeon Case" provided a legal precedent in cases involving Melungeons for many years afterward. This court ruling would be cited in any case where the question of African ancestry among the Melungeons arose. The case also laid the foundation for the first of many legends that would be built around the Melungeons in the coming decades.

---

[105] Ibid., 88.

Moors, Nanticokes, and Wesorts

About 1875, after heavy rains had inundated their farmlands, a group of tri-racial people called the Moors moved from Woodland Beach, Delaware, to Chiswold, near Dover. Unlike most tri-racial groups, these Moors lived near a city and just west of a major thoroughfare. Other groups of Moors lived in more remote areas of Sussex County, Delaware, and southern New Jersey.

As with the Melungeons and other tri-racial groups, the Moors' origins were mysterious and the subject of much speculation and legend. One legend was that a colony of Spanish Moors settled on the Delmarva peninsula sometime prior to the American Revolution. After generations of intermarriage with local Indians, they became the group known as the Moors.

Another legend involves Spanish or Moorish pirates who shipwrecked along the coast and were taken in by Nanticoke Indians. Again, intermarriage with the Indians produced the people known as the Moors.

A third, more romantic legend, was said to be preferred by most of the Moors. This legend involved a wealthy woman, either Spanish or Irish, who bought a slave. The slave turned out to be a Spanish prince. They fell in love, married, and had children. The father and the children, however, had such swarthy complexions that the family was not accepted by local whites, and instead mixed with the Indians of southern Delaware.

Most scholars, and eventually most of the Moors themselves, came to believe that the Moors were the result of a mixture of Europeans and Indians (Nanticoke and Lenni Lenapi, or "Delaware"), and some unspecified African strain.[106]

The Nanticokes had been in conflict with the white settlers along the Chesapeake Bay almost from the time of the arrival of the latter. In 1642 and again in 1647, the Nanticokes were at war with the Maryland Colony. A peace treaty was signed in 1668, but war broke out again in 1677–78. The problem, as usual, was the theft of Indian land by whites. A reservation for the Nanticokes was proposed in 1698 and finally established in 1704. However, when the Nanticokes migrated to seasonal

---

[106] *The Moors of Delaware: A Look at a Tri-Racial Group*, http://www. mitsawokett.com/MoorsOfDelaware/trirace3.html

hunting grounds, whites took possession of tracts of land, claiming they had been abandoned. Finally, in 1742, the Nanticokes joined with the French in war against the English. After the failure of that effort, a large portion of the Nanticokes decided to leave Maryland for Pennsylvania. After the American Revolution, most of the Nanticokes fled to New York and Canada, while others joined their Lenni Lenape cousins, eventually being removed to Oklahoma. Not all the Nanticokes had left Maryland. The colony declared the Nanticoke reservation vacant in 1767. Nanticokes in Pennsylvania petitioned for help from the governor of that colony to help reunite the tribe, but learned that Maryland claimed to be unaware of any Nanticokes remaining in the colony.

A small group of Nanticokes did remain in Maryland, avoiding whites as much as possible. As whites began to encroach on the land occupied by the Nanticokes, the Indians quickly adapted to the ways of the whites. They worked as farmers and fishermen. Some sharecropped for white landowners until they could buy their own land, and many Nanticokes prospered in business.

The State of Delaware, fearing a slave uprising from neighboring Maryland, passed a law prohibiting the sale of firearms to anyone with "black blood." In 1856, a prominent shop owner named Levi Sockum was charged with selling ammunition to his son-in-law, Isaac Harmon. Delaware maintained that Sockum and Harmon both had "black blood," but the pair claimed that they were not black, but were Nanticoke Indians, a tribe whites believed extinct.

In Sussex County Delaware, Sockum and Harmon found Lydia Clark, an elderly Nanticoke woman who still spoke the original language and maintained many of the old traditions. Sockum and Harmon intended to use Lydia Clark's testimony to prove that they, too, were Nanticokes. Clark lived on the land of a prominent white family, however, and was coerced into testifying against Sockum and Harmon. Clark spun a story about a prince from the Congo who was a slave aboard a ship. The ship was stranded, and the slave married an Indian woman. However, in her testimony, Clark stated that both Harmon and Sockum were also Nanticoke Indians, and she identified other Nanticoke families as well. The Nanticokes were no longer "extinct."

In 1881, facing discriminatory Jim Crow laws, the Nanticoke community incorporated, and the Delaware General Assembly officially recognized the incorporated body—not as Indians, but as a "Special Class of Colored People."[107]

About 1880, according to researcher Brewton Berry, a woman known as Aunt Sallie Thompson began describing her community as "we sort" of people to distinguish them from "you sort," or African Americans.[108] From that time on, that tri-racial community was known as Wesorts.

The Wesorts, like other tri-racial people, strenuously objected to being considered black, preferring to claim an Indian ancestry. Early anthropologists, however, considered them tri-racial, with the Indian component most likely the extinct Piscataway tribe.

Unlike most tri-racial groups, who tended to be Protestant when they were religious at all, the Wesorts were Roman Catholic. At St. Ignatius Church in Charles County, Maryland, the parishioners were divided into three groups: whites sat in the front pews, Wesorts in the rear pews, and blacks in the balcony. Their social status in the community was ambiguous; while they apparently always had the right to vote, they attended black schools and were considered to be of lower status than whites. Family names included Butler, Harley, Linkins, Mason, Newman, Proctor, Queen, Savoy, Swan, and Thompson.[109]

Swan Burnett

Swan M. Burnett was born in New Market in east Tennessee in 1847. He became a doctor and practiced medicine in his hometown before moving to Washington, D.C., where he became widely known as an eye and ear specialist. He married Frances Hodgson, an English writer who spent part of her childhood in New Market and became famous as the author of several popular novels, including *Secret Garden* and *Little Lord Fauntleroy*. In 1889, Burnett reminisced about the Melungeons for a lecture, which he later adapted into a brief article for the *American Anthropologist*. Like many who grew up in east Tennessee, Burnett

---

[107] "The Nanticoke People," http://www.graydovetrading.com/Nanticoke. html#Fight.

[108] Berry, *Almost White*, 35.

[109] Leah C. Sims, "Unraveling a Deceptive Oral History: The Indian Ancestry Claims of Philip. S. Proctor and his Descendants," http://www.eskimo.com/~lcsims/ tayacfraud.ht~;Gilbert, "Memorandum," 446.

believe the Melungeons to be some sort of malicious fairy-tale, only later learning that they actually existed.[110]

> Legends of the Melungeons I first heard at my Father's knee as a child in the mountains of Eastern Tennessee, and the name had such ponderous and inhuman sound as to associate them in my mind with the giants and ogres of the wonder tales I listened to in the winter evenings before the crackling logs in the wide-mouth fireplace...I learned...that they were not only different from us, the white, but also from the negroes—slave or free—and from the Indian...They resented the appellation Melungeons, given to them by common consent by the whites, and proudly called themselves Portuguese. The current belief was that they were a mixture of the white, Indian, and negro...As a rule, they do not stand very high in the community, and their reputation for honesty and truthfulness is not to be envied.

Burnett suggested that the word "Melungeon" came from a corruption of the French *melangee*, and that the people who bore the name resented it greatly. Despite his suggestion that the Melungeons had some African ancestry, Burnett claimed that they did not intermarry with white, blacks, or Indians.[111]

Burnett's article appeared in a professional journal, and did not receive wide attention. It may, however, have been the source for a New York newspaper article read by an ambitious young woman who was hoping to make a name for herself as a journalist in Nashville. Will Allen Dromgoole visited Newman's Ridge in the summer of 1890 and gave the Melungeons a great deal of unwanted national publicity. Dromgoole's antipathy toward the Melungeons would be reflected in her articles, and would fill the Melungeons with resentment for generations to come.

---

[110] Bible, *The Melungeons*, 13.
[111] Burnett, "A Note on the Melungeons," 347–49.

3

WILL ALLEN DROMGOOLE
AND THE ARENA ARTICLES

In the summer of 1890, a young writer from Nashville made the journey of over 300 miles to Newman's Ridge in Hancock County. The writer was a woman with the masculine-sounding name of Will Allen Dromgoole. She was born William Ann Dromgoole on October 25, 1860 to John Easter Dromgoole and his second wife, Rebecca. She changed her name to William Allen when she was just six years old and was known as Will Allen for most of her life.[1]

Dromgoole was educated at home and at private schools. She graduated from Clarksville Female Academy in 1876. She later studied at the New England School of Expressionism in Boston.

Law was her first choice of careers; she studied with her father, but women were not permitted to practice law at the time, so she embarked on the twin careers of politics and writing. She worked as an engrossing clerk in the Tennessee Senate and wrote poetry and feature stories. Her first literary recognition came with an 1890 story entitled "Fiddling His Way To Fame," a story about Tennessee's fiddle-playing governor, Bob Taylor.

In the course of her Senate duties, Dromgoole very likely heard the term "Melungeon" used as a political and/or regional epithet. After reading about the Melungeons in the New York *World* in 1887, she began asking questions about them. She describes her search in her first *Arena* article, but never explains what piqued her curiosity to such a

---

[1] Biographical information in this chapter is drawn from a lecture delivered by Dr. Kathy Lyday-Lee at Third Union, Wise, Virginia, 20 May 2000.

degree, a curiosity strong enough to send her over 300 miles to one of the most remote corners of Tennessee.

Will Allen Dromgoole was 29 years old in the summer of 1890 when she made the trip to Hancock County. Accompanying Dromgoole were Nashville artist Thomas Sharp and an unnamed guide. She never stated how she actually got to Newman's Ridge. An unmarried woman traveling with two male companions would have been considered unconventional, if not improper, and she had to have been an object of intense curiosity when she arrived on the Ridge. She told her hosts she was traveling for her health and apparently never indicated that she was writing about them.

Dromgoole's first article, entitled "Land of the Malungeons," appeared in the Nashville *Sunday American* on 31 August 1890. In this article, she described how she became aware of the Melungeons. All she knew of these mysterious people was their reputation for making moonshine.

> How I chanced to go and how I first heard of the Malungeons was through a New York newspaper. Some three years since I noticed a short paragraph stating that such a people exist somewhere in Tennessee. It stated that they were rather wild, entirely unlettered and largely given to illicit distilling. It spoke of their dialect as something unheard of, but failed to locate the human curiosities. I had but one cue by which to trail them—voz: they were illicit distillers. After repeated inquiry, and no end of laughter at my expense, I went to Capt. Carter B. Harrison, who was once United States marshal and did a good deal of work in this district.
>
> "The Malungeons?" said Capt. Harrison. "O yes; you will find them in ———county [I will give the county later], and Senator J———, of the state senate, can tell you all about them."
>
> I trailed Senator J——— for six months, and with this result:
>
> "Go to ———," said he, "and take a horse forty miles across the country to ———, Tenn. There strike for ——— ridge, the stronghold of the Malungeons."[2]

---

[2] Will Allen Dromgoole, "Land of the Malungeons," *Nashville Sunday American*, 31 August 1890, 10.

Few of Dromgoole's friends shared her enthusiasm for the subject of the Melungeons or thought her capable of making the trip to Hancock County.

> When I started out upon my hunt for the Malungeons various opinions and vague whispers were afloat concerning my sanity. Mr friends were too kind to do more than shake their heads and declare they never heard of such a people. But the less intimate of my acquaintances cooly informed me that I was "going on a wild-goose chase" and were quite willing to "bet their ears" I would never get nearer a Malungeon than at that moment. One dear old lady with more faith in the existence of the Malungeons than in my ability to cope with them begged me to insure my life before starting and to carry a loaded pistol. Another, not so dear and not so precautious [sic], informed me that she "didn't believe in women gadding about the country alone, nohow."[3]

Dromgoole observed several Melungeons at a church service in Big Sycamore and noted that they were quite varied in appearance.

> I found here all colors—white women with white children and white husbands, Malungeon women with brown babies and white babies, and one, a young copper-colored woman with black eyes and straight Indian locks, had three black babies, negroes, at her heels and a third [sic] at her breast. She was not a negro. Her skin was red, a kind of reddish-yellow, as easily distinguishable from a mulatto as the white man from the negro. I saw an old colored man, black as the oft-quoted ace of spades, whose wife is a white woman.[4]

Dromgoole reported that the "old colored man" had faced prosecution for having a white wife, but that he claimed to be "Portyghee" and was not convicted. While noting that many Melungeons claimed Cherokee and Portuguese ancestry, she found the claim of "Portyghee" blood puzzling.

---

[3] Dromgoole, "Land of the Malungeons."
[4] Ibid.

Where they could have gotten their Portuguese blood is a mystery. The Cherokee is easily enough accounted for, as they claim to have come from North Carolina and to be a remnant of the tribe that refused to go when the Indians were ordered to the reservation. They are certainly very Indian-like in appearance. The men are tall, straight, clean-shaven, with small, sharp eyes, hooked noses and high cheek bones. They wear their hair long, a great many of them, and evidently enjoy their resemblance to the red man. This is doubtless due to the fact that a great many are disposed to believe them mulattos, and they are strongly opposed to being so classed. The women are small, graceful, dark and ugly.[5]

Not only did Dromgoole find the Melungeon women unattractive, but she described the Melungeons as a group as "exceedingly lazy. They live from hand to mouth in hovels too filthy for any human being. They do not cultivate the soil at all." Instead, according to Dromgoole, the main occupation of the Melungeons was working their apple and peach orchards for the purpose of distilling brandy. "They all drink, men, women and children, and they are all distillers; that is, the work of distilling is not confined to the men."

Describing a visit to the two-room home of a "Mrs. Gorvins," Dromgoole spared no adjectives in describing the ugliness of her hostess.

[T]he saints and hobgoblins! The witch of Endor calling dead Saul from sepulchral darkness would have calked her ears and fled forever at the sight of this living, breathing Malungeon witch. Shakespeare would have shrieked in agony and chucked his own weird sisters where neither "thunder, lightning nor rain" would ever have found them more. Even poor tipsy, turvy Tam O'Shanter would have drawn up his gray mare and forgotten to fly before this, mightier than Meg Merrilles herself. She was small, scant, raw-boned, sharp-ankled, barefoot, short frock literally hanging from the knee in rags. A dark jacket with great yellow patches on either breast, sleeves torn away above the

---

[5] Ibid.

elbow, black hair burnt to an unfashionable auburn long ago, and a corncob pipe wedged between the toothless gums...I never saw an uglier human creature, or one more gross-looking and unattractive...[6]

Dromgoole also related tales of the Melungeons' depredations during the Civil War.

> During the war they were a terror to the women of the valley, going in droves to their homes and helping themselves to food and clothing, even rifling the beds and closets while the defenseless wives of the absent soldiers stood by and witnessed the wholesale plundering, afraid to so much as offer a protest. After the war the women invaded their territory and recovered a great deal of their stolen property.[7]

Dromgoole failed to explain how the "defenseless" white women could have "invaded" Melungeon territory to recover their stolen property. If the Melungeons were that weak—or the white women so tough—they probably could not have stolen the property in the first place.

A second article appeared in the Nashville *Sunday American* two weeks after the first. Dromgoole expanded on her descriptions of the poor living conditions of the Melungeons, and claimed that "There are but three names among them—real Malungeon names—Collins, Mullins, Gorvens. Lately the name of Gibbins has found a way among them, but the first three are their real names."[8] When these *Sunday American* articles were rewritten for a national magazine, Dromgoole would acknowledge several other "real" Melungeon names. Since she only made one trip into Melungeon country, her expanded information almost certainly came from an uncredited source after the publication of the Nashville articles. As will be shown, her national articles contained other uncredited information supplied by readers.

---

[6] Ibid.

[7] Ibid.

[8] Will Allen Dromgoole, "A Strange People," *Nashville Sunday American*, 14 September 1890, 10.

Dromgoole closed her second newspaper article by deriding the hospitality of her hosts on Newman's Ridge.

> At one place I staid to dinner. No one ate with me except my own guide, and the food and shelter were given grudgingly, without that hearty willingness which characterizes the old Tennessee mountaineer, who bids you "light and hitch, feed your critter and be ter home." I was invited to eat, to be sure, but the family stood by and eyed me until my portion of bread and honey almost choked me. Corn bread, thick, black, crusted pones, steaming hot, and honey sweet enough and clean—aye, clean, for the wild bees made it from the wild flowers springing straight from God's planting. I paid 15 cents for my dinner. A mountaineer would have knocked you down had you offered money for dinner under such circumstances. Bah! The Malungeon is no more a mountaineer than am I, born in the heart of the old Volunteer state.[9]

Dromgoole, admittedly not a mountaineer herself, does not explain how she knows of the habits and characteristics of "the old Tennessee mountaineer" with whom the Melungeons compare so poorly. Food and shelter may have been given "grudgingly" by the Melungeons because those commodities were so obviously scarce. Among the many failings Dromgoole lists among the Melungeons—illiteracy, lack of hygiene, dishonesty—she seems most offended by the fact that she was charged 15 cents for her meal.

Several letters concerning the Melungeons were printed by the *Daily American* in the weeks following publication of Dromgoole's two articles. Some doubted the existence of such a people in Tennessee, while others insisted that the Melungeons were merely mulattoes. One letter from "C.H." related stories told by the family slaves before the Civil War.

> Since childhood I have been anxious to know if such a people really existed or not; have thought perhaps it was only a myth hatched in the very fertile brain our imaginative negro

---

[9] Ibid.

nurse who used to entertain us with stories of the Malungeons, ghosts, hobgoblins, Brer Rabbit, Brer Fox, etc. They would frighten us by saying "If you don't behave, the Malungeons will get you," and if angry with one another they would say, "You are as mean and low-lived as a Malungeon, and you are nothing but an old Ish[10] anyhow." When we asked who the Malungeons or Ishes were, they said they were runaway negroes, who had married Indians, and their children, and that the negroes belonging to quality folks would not associate with them. Most of the negroes, both blacks and mulattoes, held these Malungeons in contempt. These things come back to me after forty years, when I heard the negro slaves of my father tell stories of their meanness. They were always insulted if called a Malungeon.[11]

In a letter published beside Dromgoole's article of Sunday, September 14, "J.W.S." of Murfreesboro provided an odd bit of biological misinformation.

Now, Mr. Editor, a race of mulattoes cannot exist long like the Malungeons have. They go from mulattoes to quadroons and from these to octoroons. There the race stops. Who ever heard of an octoroon woman bearing children? There is not a case on record, so that if these people are or were mulattoes...the race would have been extinct long ago, as no children have been born of women springing from mulattoes beyond the quadroon mother, and it seems that some of these Malungeon women have as many as seventeen children, who, if they had come from mulatto parentage, would long ago have passed the octoroon stage.[12]

---

[10] "Ish," or "free issue" was a derogatory term used by slaves to describe free blacks, and sometimes tri-racials as well.

[11] *Nashville Sunday American*, 14 September 1890, 10. C. S. Everett maintains that the author of the letter, "C. H.," is from Hancock County, but there is no evidence from the letter that this is so. Everett, "Melungeon History and Myth," 378.

[12] "'Will Allen' Defended," *Nashville Sunday American*, 14 September 1890, 10.

Dromgoole would use this quote almost verbatim, without attribution, in her first *Arena* article:

> Yet if we will consider a moment, we shall see that a race of mulattoes cannot exist as these Malungeons have existed. The race goes from mulattoes to quadroons, from quadroons to octoroons, and there it stops. The octoroon women bear no children, but in every cabin of the Malungeons may be found mothers and grandmothers, and very often great-grandmothers.[13]

On Monday, 15 September 1890, the *Daily American* printed a letter from Dan W. Baird that seems to be the source for the information about John Sevier meeting supposed Melungeons in the 1780s.:

> At the time when John Sevier attempted to organize the "State of Franklin" there were living in the mountain section of East Tennessee a colony of dark-skinned people, evidently of African or Moorish descent, who did not affiliate either with the white, the Indian or the negro race. They called themselves "Malungeons" and claimed to be of Portuguese descent. Upon what reason they based their descent will probably never be known, but it is an established fact that they were refused affiliation with the whites and disdained intercourse with the Indians or the negroes. All the negroes ever brought to America came as slaves. The people called Malungeons were never slaves in this country and never have mixed with the negroes until since the war between the states.[14]

Baird's letter also details the actions of the Tennessee constitutional convention of 1834 which disfranchised "free persons of color," including, presumably, the Melungeons. Baird quoted Representative John McKinney of Hawkins County, who referred to the Melungeons as persons "doomed to live in the suburbs of society." This information ended up, without attribution, in Dromgoole's first *Arena* article published in 1891.

---

[13] Will Allen Dromgoole, "The Malungeons," *The Arena* 3 (March 1891): 472.

[14] Dan W. Baird, "A Backward Glance," *Nashville Daily American*, 15 September 1890, 2.

Not to be outdone by a Nashville newspaper, the Knoxville *Journal* featured a front-page Melungeon story on 28 September 1890. The unnamed "special correspondent" referred to the Dromgoole articles, and was even more contemptuous than Dromgoole in describing the Melungeons. "They are as a rule ignorant, uneducated and the knowledge and practice of virtue among them is woefully missing." The author suggested that they were of "mixed white and negro blood," and, referring to a Melungeon colony in Kentucky, stated "They are grossly ignorant, beastly in their habits and weak mentally and physically. The are nearly all afflicted with leprosy or some other disease equally loathsome and horrible..."[15]

Dromgoole's *American* articles offended several East Tennessee senators, who helped assure her failure to be re-elected to her post as engrossing clerk. In 1891 Dromgoole left Tennessee and went to Waco, Texas, to become a teacher. She remained active in journalism, and founded the Waco Women's Press Club, but soon returned to Nashville to care for ailing father and to re-write for national publication.

The *Arena* was a Boston-based magazine with national circulation. The loss of Dromgoole's Senate position at the hands of East Tennessee legislators may have embittered her and colored her feelings about her visit to Newman's Ridge. The *Arena* articles seem more malicious than their *American* counterparts. A notable difference is Dromgoole's implication that the Melungeons had African-American ancestry, something that was only vaguely implied in her *American* articles. Kathy Lyday-Lee, a professor of English at Elon College in North Carolina, has studied Dromgoole extensively, and believes that while Dromgoole offers us a fascinating look at the Melungeons at ths particular point in history, her prejudicial statements overshadowed the factual information offered about the Melugneons ."The real tragedy of the first *Arena* article," Lyday-Lee says, "is...that while it appears to be an historical and anthropological look at a culture, it is written by a person clearly biased against the culture as a whole."[16]

The *Arena* published the first Dromgoole article in March of 1891. For national publication, Dromgoole used her full name rather than the "Will Allen" *nom de plume* she had employed previously. She

---

[15] "The Melungeons: A Peculiar Race of People Living in Hancock County," *Knoxville Journal*, 28 September 1890, 1.

[16] Lyday-Lee, "The Dromgoole Articles."

appropriated Dan Baird's information concerning John Sevier's alleged encounter with the Melungeons in the late eighteenth century, and the Tennessee Constitutional Convention.

> When John Sevier attempted to organize the State of Franklin, there was living in the mountains of Eastern Tennessee a colony of dark-skinned, reddish-brown complexioned people, supposed to be of Moorish descent, who affiliated with neither whites nor blacks, and who called themselves Malungeons, and claimed to be of Portuguese descent. They lived to themselves exclusively, and were looked on as neither negroes nor Indians.
>
> All the negroes ever brought to America came as slaves; the Malungeons were never slaves, and until 1834 enjoyed all the rights of citizenship. Even in the Convention which disfranchised them, they were referred to as *"free persons of color"* or "Malungeons."
>
> Their condition from the organization of the State of Tennessee to the close of the civil war is most accurately described by John A. McKinney, of Hawkins County, who was chairman of the committee to which was referred all matters affecting these *"free persons of color."*
>
> Said he, speaking of free persons of color, "It means Malungeons if it means anything. Although 'fleecy locks and black complexion' do not forfeit Nature's claims, still it is true that those locks and that complexion mark every one of the African race, so long as he remains among the white race, as a person doomed to live in the suburbs of society.[17]

In the first *Arena* article, Dromgoole paints the Melungeons as outcasts, moonshiners, and a terror to society.

> In the farther valleys they were soon forgotten: only now and then and old slave-mammy would frighten her rebellious charge into subjection with the threat,—"The Malungeons will get you in you ain't pretty." But to the people of the foot hills and nearer valleys, they became a living terror; sweeping down

---

[17] Will Allen Dromgoole, "The Malungeons," 472.

upon them, stealing their cattle, their provisions, their very clothing, and household furniture.

They became shiftless, idle, thieving, and defiant of all law, distillers of brandy, almost to a man. The barren height upon which they located, offered hope of no other crop so much as fruit, and they were forced, it would appear, to utilize their one opportunity.

After the breaking out of the war, some few enlisted in the army, but the greater number remained with their stills, to pillage and plunder among the helpless women and children.

Their mountains became a terror to travelers; and not until within the last half decade has it been regarded as safe to cross Malungeon territory.[18]

Dromgoole describes for *Arena* readers her introduction to the Melungeons and the steps she took to track them down.

I saw in an old newspaper some slight mention of them. With this tiny clue I followed their trail for three years. The paper merely stated that "somewhere in the mountains of Tennessee there existed a remnant of people called Malungeons, having a distinct color, characteristics, and dialect. It seemed a very hopeless search, so utterly were the Malungeons forgotten, and I was laughed at no little for my "new crank." I was even called "a Malungeon" more than once, and was about to abandon my "crank" when a member of the Tennessee State Senate, of which I happened at that time to be engrossing clerk, spoke of a brother senator as being "tricky as a Malungeon."

I pounced on him the moment his speech was completed. "Senator," I said, "what is a Malungeon?"

"A dirty Indian sneak," said he. "Go over yonder and ask Senator ———; they live in his district."

I went at once.

"Senator, what is a Malungeon?" I asked again.

"A Portuguese nigger," was the reply. "Representative T____ can tell you all about them, they live in his county."

---

[18] Ibid.

From "district" to "county" was quick traveling. And into the House of Representatives I went, fast upon the lost trail of the forgotten Malungeons.

"Mr. ____," said I, "please tell me what is a Malungeon?"

"A Malungeon, said he, "isn't a nigger, and he isn't an Indian, and he isn't a white man. God only knows *what* he is. *I should call him a Democrat, only he always votes the Reublican ticket.*"[19]

Dromgoole's descriptions of the Melungeons were even more derogatory in the *Arena* than those contained in the Nashville *Sunday American* articles.

They are a great nuisance to the people of the county seat...The people of the town do not allow them to enter their dwellings, and even refuse to employ them as servants, owing to their filthy habit of chewing tobacco and spitting upon the floors, together with their ignorance or defiance of the difference between *meum* and *tuum*...They are exceedingly shiftless, and in most cases filthy. They care for nothing except their pipe, their liquor, and a tramp "ter town."... The Malungeons are filthy, their home is filthy. The are rogues, natural, "born rogues," close, suspicious, inhospitable, untruthful, cowardly, and to use their own word, "sneaky.".. .The most that can be said of one of them is, "He is a Malungeon," a synonym for all that is doubtful and mysterious—and unclean.[20]

Without actually coming out and saying so, Dromgoole repeatedly hints that the Melungeons are of at least partial African ancestry.

In many things they resemble the negro. They are exceedingly immoral, yet are great shouters and advocates of religion. They call themselves Baptists, although their mode of baptism is that of the Dunkard.

There are no churches on the Ridge, but the one I visited in Black Water Swamp was beyond question and inauguration of

---

[19] Ibid.
[20] Ibid.

the colored element. At this church I saw white women with negro babies at their breasts—Malungeon women with white or with black husbands, and some, indeed, having the trhree separate races represented in their children; showing thereby the gross immorality that is practised among them. I saw an old negro whose wife was a white woman, and who had been several times arrested, and released on his plea of "Portygee" blood, which he declared had colored his skin, not African.

The dialect of the Malungeons is a cross between that of the mountaineer and the negro—a corruption, perhaps, of both...The pure Malungeons, that is the old men and women, have no toleration for the negro, and nothing insults them so much as the suggestion of negro blood. Many pathetic stories are told of their battle against the black race, which they regard as the cause of their downfall, the annihilation, indeed, of the Malungeons, for when the races began to mix and to intermarry, and the expression, "A Malungeon nigger" came into use, the last barrier vanished, and all were regarded as somewhat upon a social level.[21]

The remainder of this initial *Arena* article consists of descriptions of the Melungeons and particularly their impoverished homes. In contrast, Dromgoole portrays the typical white mountaineers as "clean—cleanliness itself."[22] She also praises the white mountaineer for his honesty, courage, and generosity—all traits she found lacking in the Melungeons. And nowhere in Dromgoole's writing will one find any hint that white mountaineers engaged in the illegal distillation of alcohol; that activity is portrayed as the exclusive domain of Melungeons.

In her second *Arena* article, published in June, Dromgoole discusses the origin of the Melungeons. Her primary source for genealogical information was Calloway Collins, one of her hosts.

---

[21] Ibid.
[22] Ibid.

Somewhere in the eighteenth century, before the year 1797, there appeared in the eastern portion of Tennessee, at that time the Territory of North Carolina, two strange-looking men calling themselves "Collins" and "Gibson". They had a reddish brown complexion, long, straight, black hair, keen, black eyes, and sharp, clear-cut features. They spoke in broken English, a dialect distinct from anything ever heard in that section of the country.

They claimed to have come from Virginia and many years after emigrating, themselves told the story of their past.

These two, Vardy Collins and Buck Gibson, were the had and source of the Malungeons in Tennessee. With the cunning of their Cherokee ancestors, they planned and executed a scheme by which they were enabled to "set up for themselves" in the almost unbroken Territory of North Carolina.

Old Buck, as he was called, was disguised by a wash of some dark description, and taken to Virginia by Vardy where he was sold as a slave. He was a magnificent specimen of physical strength, and brought a fine price, a wagon and mules, a lot of goods, and three hundred dollars in money being paid to old Vardy for his "likely nigger." Once out of Richmond, Vardy turned his mules shoes and stuck out for the wilderness of North Carolina, as previously planned. Buck lost little time ridding himself of his negro disguise, swore he was not the man bought of Collins, and followed in the wake of his fellow thief to the Territory. The proceeds of the sale were divided and each chose his habitation; old Vardy choosing Newman's Ridge, where he was soon joined by others of his race, and so the Malungeons became a part of the inhabitants of Tennessee.[23]

Dromgoole attempts to trace the lineage of the Melungeons, and maintains that the original Melungeon inhabitants of Newman's Ridge all took the name "Collins" after Vardy Collins, described as "the main stem" of the Melungeon tree.

---

[23] Will Allen Dromgoole, "The Malungeon Tree and Its Four Branches," *The Arena* 3 (June 1891): 745–51.

The tree at last began to put forth branches, or rather three foreign shoots were grafted into the body of it; the English (or white), Portuguese, and African.

The English branch began with the *Mullins* tribe, a very powerful tribe, next indeed for a long time to the Collins tribe, and at present the strongest of all the several branches, as well as the most daring and obstinate.

Old Jim Mullins, the father of the branch, was an Englishman, a trader, it is supposed, with Indians...He stumbled upon the Ridge settlement, fell in with the Ridgemanites, and never left them. He took for a wife one of their women, a descendant of old Sol Collins, and reared a family known as the "*Mullins* tribe." This is said to be the first white blood that mingled with the blood of the dusky Ridgemanites...Mullins tribe became exceedingly strong, and remains today the head of the Ridge people...

The African branch was introduced by one Goins (I spell it as they do) who emigrated from North Carolina after the formation of the state of Tennessee. Goins was a negro, and did not settle upon the Ridge, but lower down the Big Sycamore Creek in Powell's Valley. He took a Malungeon woman for his wife (took up with her), and reared a family or tribe .The Goins family may be easily recognized by their kinky hair, flat nose and foot, thick lips, and a complexion totally unlike the Collins and Mullins tribes. They possess many negro traits, too, which are wanting to the other tribes.

The Malungeons repudiate the idea of negro blood, yet some of the shiftless stragglers among them have married among the Goins people. They evade slights, snubs, censure, *and the law*, by claiming to have married Portuguese, there really being a Portuguese branch among the tribes.

The Goins tribe, however, was always looked upon with touch of contempt, and was held in a kind of subjection, socially and politically, by the others...

The Portuguese branch was for a long time a riddle, the existence of it being stoutly denied. It has at last, however, been traced to one "Denhan," a Portuguese who married a Collins woman...Denhan, it is supposed, came from one of the Spanish

settlements lying further to the south. He settled on Mulberry
Creek, and married a sister of Old Sol Collins...

So we have the four races, or representatives, among, as
they then began to be called, the Malungeons; namely, the
Indians, the English, the Portuguese, and the African. Each is
clearly distinct and easily recognized even to the present day.

The Portuguese blood has been a misfortune to the first
Malungeons inasmuch as it has been a shield to the Goins clan
under which they have sought to shelter themselves and
repudiate the African streak...[24]

Dromgoole's obvious belief in white superiority reflected the
general attitude of Southern whites of her day. By 1890, "Jim Crow"
laws had almost completely overturned the rights guaranteed to African-
Americans by the Constitution and enjoyed by them, to at least some
degree, during Reconstruction following the Civil War. The "science" of
eugenics (which will be discussed in the next chapter) was beginning to
legitimize the racism of America's white majority. This school of
thought held that the white race was genetically superior to other races,
and that the "inferior" races posed a threat to the domination, and the
very existence, of the white race. Dromgoole may have been an
unconventional young woman by the standards of her day, but her racial
attitudes were solidly in the mainstream of white America.

In the South of 1890, African-Americans were portrayed in the
press as a threat to white society, and particularly to white women. A
review of Nashville *Daily American* articles for a five-day period
between the publication of Dromgoole's two articles reveals a number of
stories of racial conflict; if blame was assigned for the incidents, it was
invariably assigned to the blacks.

On Friday, 5September 1890, the story of a lynching was headed
"His Just Deserts: A Masked Mob's Speedy Vengeance on a Mississippi
Negro." The story describes the attempted rape of a white woman by "a
negro named Rogers." As was usual in lynchings, "The coronor's jury
could not ascertain the names of any of the parties engaged in the
hanging."[25]

---

[24] Dromgoole, "The Malungeon Tree," 745–51.
[25] "His Just Deserts," Nashville *Daily American*, 5 September 1890, 1.

"Don't Fraternize," read a headline from 6 September. The sub-head proclaims, "Race War Between White and Black School Children in Chattanooga." This article concerns a series of fights between black and white schoolchildren and asserts, "Many fights come off as a result of the blacks attacking the whites on their way to school..." No mention is made of any provocation whites may have offered.[26] On that same page of the 6 September *American* is a story certain to inflame the minds of white Southerners: "Two Colored Lovers: A White Girl Causes a Murder in Reading, Pa." A waitress named Katie Kunkel allegedly divided her affections between two black porters who worked with her. The men were jealous of each other, resulting on one man shooting and killing the other. Miss Kunkel was arrested along with the assailant, but the article fails to mention what charges had been placed against her. Her real crime, without doubt, was fraternizing with black men.[27]

Attacks on blacks were portrayed as humorous incidents, as this headline from 7 September demonstrates: "An Exciting Scene: A Drunken Negro Almost Brained by a Conductor; The Former Stones an Electric Car After Being Ejected, And Pays Dearly For It..." Not surprisingly, the article blames the "drunken Negro" for starting the altercation, and no charges were filed against the conductor.[28]

While an attack on a black man is portrayed as amusing, attacks on whites were seen as far more serious. "Race War Breaks Out," stated a headline in the 9 September issue. A farmer in Jackson named Young had threatened some blacks, who then allegedly drew guns, leading to their immediate arrest. The paper claimed that "nearly fifty negroes" fired several shots in to Young's home. Young "secured a posse of friends" who intended to "exterminate the negroes from the community."[29]

America was entering a period historian James Loewen calls "the nadir of race relations in America," the period between about 1890 and beyond 1920.[30] America was obsessed with race. The period between 1888 and 1893 saw more African-Americans lynched than any other period in history. The Supreme Court legitimized segregation in its 1896

[26] "Don't Fraternize," *Nashville Daily American*, 6 September 1890, 2.

[27] "Two Colored Lovers," *Nashville Daily American*, 6 September 1890, 2.

[28] "An Exciting Scene," *Nashville Sunday American*, 7 September 1890, 7.

[29] "Race War Breaks Out," *Nashville Daily American*, 9 September 1890, 1.

[30] James Loewen, *Lies Across America* (New York: The New Press, 1999) 427.

Plessy v. Ferguson decision. The Ku Klux Klan would be revived in 1915. Given the tone of race relations in general at that time, Dromgoole's attitude toward the Melungeons, while condescending, is rather mild. She obviously considered them inferior to whites, but the fact that she stayed in their homes and ate with them indicates a degree of tolerance that probably would not have been shown to blacks.

Dromgoole at times seemed to describe the Melungeons as Indians, using terms such as "Indian eyes," "half-breed," and "squaw." At other times, she clearly believed them to be "as black as the oft-quoted ace of spades."[31] Her general tone indicates she didn't think the distinction between black and Indian mattered much. Most of white America would have agreed.

To this day, many Hancock Countians resent the articles written by Will Allen Dromgoole. They believe that Dromgoole portrayed their ancestors unfairly; more than a few resent the implication of African ancestry among the Melungeons. Milum Bowen told a reporter in 1947 about a poem the people of Newman's Ridge made up about Dromgoole. "I can't remember the rest of the words," Bowen said, "but the last of it was 'Will Allen Damfool.'"[32]

Kathy Lyday-Lee points out, "The Melungeon stories helped to advance her career in one area, but ended it in another." Although Dromgoole wanted recognition as a reporter, the Melungeon stories pointed out her shortcomings in that field. Dromgoole continued to work in journalism; she started at the Nashville *Banner* in 1902, wrote editorials and began a column entitled "Song and Story" in 1903, and became widely known as a popular writer of fiction and poetry.

Upon America's entry in World War One in 1917, Dromgoole was recruited as a warrant officer with yeomanry rating in US Navy, perhaps the first woman in ever in this position. She continued her writing career. Her poem "The Bridge Builder" is still read at commencements and other occasions calling for an inspirational work. She never again, however, wrote of the Melungeons, and there is no record of her feelings about the people of Newman's Ridge other than the four articles presented in this chapter. Will Allen Dromgoole died in 1934.

---

[31] Dromgoole, "Land of the Malungeons," 10.

[32] William Worden, "Sons of the Legend," *Saturday Evening Post* (18 October 1947)

Dromgoole's articles were the foundation for most of what was written about the Melungeons for the next 100 years. Most writers have used her as a source, whether credited or not, and many have used her observations in lieu of traveling to Newman's Ridge to collect their own.

Lyday-Lee believes Dromgoole told the truth as she saw it, but based her report on information gathered from the stories of just a few families. Her racism is quite obvious, but Lyday-Lee points out that what we perceive as racist and sexist attitudes today were commonplace, acceptable, and perhaps even required in certain aspects of Southern Victorian society. In her writing, Dromgoole does seem to feel sympathy for the plight of the Melungeons, their sudden loss of civil rights after the 1834 Constitutional Convention and subsequent ostracism, and appreciates the physical beauty of some (but certainly not all) of the people. For the most part, however, she saw the Melungeons exactly as practically any other Caucasian of that period would: a product of racial mixing among the lowest classes of society, "a blot on our state,"[33] and certainly inferior to whites. In light of what was soon to come for Melungeons and other tri-racials, Dromgoole's attitude seems almost benign by comparison.

---

[33] Dromgoole, "Land of the Malungeons," 10.

4

SCIENTIFIC RACISM

Eugenics: A science which deals with improving the hereditary qualities of a race or breed through methods which include control of mating.[1]

As America entered the twentieth century, the position of non-whites in society had barely improved from the century before. The idea of "Manifest Destiny" had served white Americans well, providing a justification for the enslavement of one group of non-whites and the virtual annihilation of another.

African Americans, who had been freed from bondage and guaranteed their rights as American citizens at the end of the Civil War, found themselves effectively disfranchised and powerless, a position reinforced by the U. S. Supreme Court's *Plessy v. Ferguson* ruling which ruled that segregation was compatible with the ideals expressed in the Constitution. In the south, the former slave became a tenant farmer, or sharecropper, working on land owned by white men for a fraction of the proceeds of his labor. It was a system even more economical for the planter than slavery had been; the tenant farmers (many of whom were poor whites) found themselves with even less economic and physical security than that afforded to slaves.

The last significant conflict between whites and Native Americans, the "battle" of Wounded Knee in late 1890 was merely the massacre of the last remaining band of free Indians in the continental United States. All the tribes in America had by this time either been exterminated or confined to reservations. Even land "guaranteed" for Indians was being appropriated by whites. The largest concentration of "reservation"

---

[1] "Eugenics/Sterilization," http://member.aol.MRandDD/eugenics/htm.

Indians was in Indian Territory, which was soon to be opened to white settlement and renamed Oklahoma.

America was a white man's country. More than that, it was a country controlled by white men descended from Anglo-Saxon and Celtic forebears. These white men considered themselves the "real" Americans, the descendants of those who wrested the continent away from "savages" and created a potential Christian—or more precisely, Protestant—paradise. The "race question" however, was an obstacle to the realization of that paradise.

There were other problems facing white America besides race. The white Protestant vision of America as an agrarian paradise was rapidly transforming into something entirely different. After the Civil War, as American industries grew and American farms became mechanized, tremendous numbers of people left the farms and moved to the cities. These rural-to-urban migrants often felt they had left behind a purer, simpler life, and were uneasy in the cities with the strange people and strange ways of urban life. Immigration from eastern and southern Europe hit its peak in the late nineteenth and early twentieth centuries, and these newcomers brought religious beliefs and social ideals that were strange and disturbing to many Americans. Labor unions gained strength with the increase in the number of industrial workers and, as the economy endured a series of depressions, became more radical.

In 1859, Charles Darwin published *Origin of the Species*, and introduced the concept of "survival of the fittest." It was a comforting concept for the most wealthy and successful members of society; "social Darwinism" tended to explain away the glaring social and economic inequities in America, relieving them of any guilt they might feel over having so much when others had so little. Those who were successful in life, the reasoning went, were superior to those who were not successful. "However," as biologist Garland Allen writes, "by the turn of the century, this simplistic idea had been turned on its head. A declining birthrate among the wealthy and powerful indicated that the captains of industry were, in fact, losing the struggle for existence. The working class not only was organizing against them, but they were out-reproducing them."[2] To many, it was obvious that society—and mankind—needed better management.

The progressive movement was a response to the pressures brought on by a rapidly industrializing society. Progressives believed in an enlarged role for government and scientific management in economic and social issues. A scientific approach to the social ills of society was introduced by a half-cousin of Charles Darwin, Sir Francis Galton.

Galton was a geographer, meteorologist, tropical explorer, founder of differential psychology, inventor of fingerprint identification, pioneer of statistical correlation and regression, convinced hereditarian, proto-geneticist, and best-selling author. In his 1896 book *Hereditary Genius,* he presented strong evidence that talent is an inherited characteristic. His 1883 book *Inquiries into Human Faculty* introduced the term *eugenics.* Galton saw eugenics as moral philosophy, a means to improve the human race by encouraging the ablest and healthiest people to reproduce. This ideal is generally known as *positive eugenics.* However, the movement which grew in the United States, as well as Scandinavia and Germany, advocated the removal of the least able from the breeding population, and was known as *negative eugenics.*

Scientists had long been concerned about environmental factors that might influence heredity and cause poor health, insanity, and defective offspring. The "degeneracy theory" was established in the early 1700s, and by the mid-nineteenth century, most scientists accepted the idea that poor environments caused degenerate heredity. Sociologist Richard Dugdale believed good environments could transform degenerate families into productive citizens within three generations, and published a study of the Jukes, a family of petty criminals in Ulster County, New York, in 1877. Within a few years, however, the degeneracy theory was challenged by the work of August Weismann. Weismann argued that changes in the body tissue, or soma, had little or no effect on reproductive tissue, or the germ plasm. By the beginning of the twentieth century, degeneracy theorists had incorporated Weismann's position and

---

[2] Garland E. Allen, "Social Origins of Eugenics," *Image Archive on the American Eugenics Movement,* Dolan DNA Learning Center, Cold Spring Harbor Laboratory, http://vector.cshl.org/htmp/eugenics/essay1text.html, 1.

adopted the concept of negative eugenics.[3] America now had a scientific basis for its racism.

Garland Allen writes, "In an era troubled by rapid and seemingly chaotic change, eugenics offered the prospect of a planned, gradual, and smooth transition to a more harmonious future...Just as a new group of professional managers was making a place for itself in American economic life, eugenicists emerged as scientists with a special expertise in the solution of perennial social problems. Eugenics provided what seemed to offer an objective, scientific approach to problems that previously had been cast almost wholly in subjective, humanitarian terms. Whereas charity and state welfare had treated only symptoms, eugenics promised to attack social problems at their roots."[4]

Eugenics was promoted with the financial support of individuals and foundations. Breakfast cereal manufacturer J. H. Kellogg formed the Race Betterment Foundation in 1906, and in 1910 the Eugenics Record Office (ERO), a source of much eugenics propaganda, was created with funding from Mrs. E. H. Harriman, wife of the railroad magnate. The ERO, based at Cold Spring Harbor, New York, hosted seminars each summer to teach eugenics researchers how to conduct field work. The ERO publication *Eugenical News* published articles which supported the racist and anti-immigration aspects of eugenics research. By the 1920s, eugenics was firmly established in American intellectual life. The National Education Association formed the Committee on Racial Well-Being to help incorporate eugenic content into college courses. In 1928, eugenics was a topic in 376 separate college courses. The majority of high school science texts published between 1914 and 1948 treated eugenics as a legitimate science, and advocated segregation, immigration restriction, and even sterilization of the biologically unfit.[5]

---

[3] Elof Carlson, "Scientific Origins of Eugenics," *Image Archive on the American Eugenics Movement*, Dolan DNA Learning Center, Cold Spring Harbor Laboratory, http://vector.cshl.org/htmp/eugenics/essay1text.html, 1–2.

[4] Allen, "Social Origins of Eugenics," 3–4.

[5] Steve Selden, "Eugenics Popularization," *Image Archive on the American Eugenics Movement*, Dolan DNA Learning Center, Cold Spring Harbor Laboratory, http://vector.cshl.org/htmp/eugenics/essay6text.html, 1–3; David Miklos, "Eugenics Research Methods," *Image Archive on the American Eugenics Movement*, Dolan DNA Learning Center, Cold Spring Harbor Laboratory, http://vector.cshl.org/htmp/eugenics/essay3text.html, 2.

Eugenicists conducted interviews, collected medical histories, and constructed pedigrees of various "types" of people. The ERO created questionnaires which coordinated family genealogies with medical conditions. Information was also drawn from insane asylums, prisons, and orphanages, and studies were conducted on the ethnic makeup of these "societal dependents" and the cost of maintaining them. Harry Laughlin, the director of the ERO, testified before Congress that immigrants from southern and eastern European countries had disproportionately high rates of mental illness and criminal tendencies.[6]

According to David Miklos of the present-day Dolan DNA Learning Center, Cold Spring Harbor Laboratory, Laughlin's testimony used skewed data "to fit his bigoted view of America." The methods used by most eugenics researchers were seriously flawed by today's standards. Eugenicists used poor survey and statistical methods. Few researchers were able to conduct interviews with more than three generations of any given family. Medical records were rarely available, so information about a family's "pedigree" was generally obtained by second-hand reporting or hearsay. Laughlin and others based many studies on information of this nature.[7]

Eugenicists also believed that if a numerical value can be produced, such as a score on an intelligence test, the measure is valid. Today, it is widely recognized that standardized IQ tests often contain questions that are culturally biased, dependent upon cultural background and experience. Eugenicists, however, believed them to be an accurate measure of native intelligence. A set of IQ tests given to immigrants showed that 87 % of Russians, 83% of Jews, 80% of Hungarians, and 79% of Italians were "feebleminded." Some immigrants were returned to their country of origin as a result of low scores. Individuals were placed in mental institutions, sometimes even sterilized, on the basis of these "scientific" tests.[8]

The eugenicists provided a pseudo-scientific rationale for the ethnic hostility that was gaining momentum in the United States. White Americans felt their racial identity was in jeopardy, both from

---

[6] Miklos, "Eugenics Research Methods," 2.

[7] Ibid; Garland E. Allen, "Flaws in Eugenics Research,"*Image Archive on the American Eugenics Movement*, Dolan DNA Learning Center, Cold Spring Harbor Laboratory, http://vector.cshl.org/htmp/eugenics/essay5text.html, 1–3.

[8] Allen, "Flaws in Eugenics Research," 2.

immigrants of non-Anglo-Saxon stock, and from the threat of race mixing. Anti-immigration sentiment grew among "native-born" white Americans. In 1891, 11 Italian immigrants were lynched in New Orleans. As economic uncertainty increased, so did hostility toward immigrants. An economic depression caused widespread hardship in 1893, and in 1894, the Immigration Restriction League was formed. By 1921, Congress would impose quotas on immigration, favoring those who came from northern and western Europe.

While immigrants posed one threat to the "racial purity" of white Americans, race mixing, or miscegenation, was another. The Reconstruction era following the Civil War was an attempt, ultimately unsuccessful, to secure political rights for African-Americans in the South. Whites feared that political equality would be followed naturally by social equality, and that intermarriage between whites and blacks would doom the white race. As Thomas Dixon stated repeatedly in his popular novel *The Leopard's Spots*, "One drop of negro blood makes a negro," and "The future American must be a white man or a mulatto."[9]

"Jim Crow" laws restricting the rights of blacks and other non-whites were passed in all regions of the country in the closing years of the nineteenth century. Social equality would be avoided by eliminating all notions of political equality; black Americans were to be second-class citizens. The Ku Klux Klan was revived in 1915, symbolically drawing the line between white and black Americans. In the opening years of the twentieth century, there was no middle ground, no place in American society for people who were neither white nor black.

Tri-Racials in the Twentieth Century

As a new century dawned, Melungeons and other tri-racial groups were becoming better known, and experienced increased contact with outsiders. Some of those outsiders meant to help, and provided educational opportunities, health care, and sometimes even a sense of ethnic and cultural identity. Others had less beneficial intentions.

In 1897, author John Fox Jr. used a Melungeon character in his short story "Through The Gap," published in his book *"Hell Fer Sartain"and other stories.* Fox presented the Melungeons as mixed-Indian people. Fox was familiar with Melungeons; not only had he

---

[9] Thomas Dixon, *The Leopard's Spots* (New York: Doubleday, Page, & Co., 1902).

grown up near Melungeon communities in southwest Virginia, he later had business dealings with them. For a time, Fox worked for his brother securing mineral rights for coal companies from local landowners. According to Darlene Wilson, who has extensively researched both Melungeons and John Fox Jr., Melungeon landowners who were accepted as white by their neighbors were particularly vulnerable to Fox's methods of persuasion. He simply hinted to landowners that he knew of the landowners non-white ancestry; the unspoken implication was that word of that ancestry might spread if the landowner did not sell mineral rights to his property. In this era of heightened racial tensions, the threat was quite effective.[10]

In December of 1912, Paul Converse published "The Melungeons" in *Southern Collegian*. Converse describes the Brewer-Collins feud which occurred "at an election a few years ago" when Wiley Brewer, a justice of the peace, had a dispute with a member of the Collins family and was shot and wounded. Gunfire broke out and three men fell dead before Wiley's brother Will subdued the gathered men at gunpoint and continued the election. Later, the Brewer brothers were ambushed; Will was killed and Wiley was wounded again. At the time of the Converse article, Wiley Brewer was reportedly hiding in another part of the county and was afraid to return to his home.

Converse suggested that the Melungeons' fearsome reputation derived from their moonshining activities and the violence associated with that trade. "Up to two decades ago, whiskey flowed like water in the Blackwater country...A stranger who ventured into that region in those days did so at the risk of his life for he was at once taken for a detective or a 'revenue.'"[11]

Converse provided the first known written record of Mahala Mullins, who has become a legendary figure in Melungeon folklore. She was born Mahala Collins about 1825 and died in 1902. She was the daughter of Solomon Collins and Jincie Gwinn (or Goins). She married John Mullins, and bore fifteen children.[12] Like many Appalachian

---

[10] John Fox Jr., *"Hell Fer Sartain" and other stories* (New York: Garrett Publishing, 1969); Darlene Wilson, Wayne Walker, in-person interview, September 1997.

[11] Paul Converse, "The Melungeons," *Southern Collegian* (December 1912): 59–69.

[12] Jim Callahan, *Lest We Forget: The Melungeon Colony of Newman's Ridge* (Johnson City TN: Overmountain Press, 2000).

residents, Mahala maximized the profits to be made from small plots of corn by converting the grain into whiskey. Well into the late twentieth century, there were residents of the area who claimed, quite improbably, to have sampled her fabled liquor.[13]

Converse was shocked that this "queen of the blind tigresses"[14] plied her trade "within five miles of a county seat and a temple of justice." However, Mahala Mullins didn't have the option of mobility. Mahala was a large woman; people who knew her estimated her weight at 350 to 400 pounds, and photographs suggest that she suffered from elephantitis. Obviously relating some of the exaggerated tales that grew up after Mahala's death, Converse reported her weight at 500 pounds. Later legends would place her weight as high as 600 pounds. In any event, Mahala apparently grew so obese she could not get through her door, thereby thwarting any attempt to arrest her for moonshining. She was, as Hancock County sheriff Wash Eads said, "ketchable, but not fetchable."[15]

The *Southern Collegian* article suggested that Batey[16] Collins, a deputy sheriff described by Humble as the "chief" of the Melungeons, was "induced" to cooperate with revenue officers to bring an end to illicit distilling in the region, and "with his aid, moonshine stills became a thing of the past although blind tigers still inhabit some of the dense forests."[17]

Converse described the primitive farming techniques of the Melungeons and their log or rough lumber houses. He does not mention that the same farming techniques and rough houses could be found among many of the white inhabitants of the region as well. Whites also participated in feuding (the Hatfield-McCoy feud was well known to most Americans in 1912) and moonshining. Most of Converse's descriptions of Melungeon life would have applied to a large percentage of Appalachian whites of that era. If not for their "peculiar" ethnic

---

[13] Bible, *The Melungeons*, 100.

[14] The term "blind tiger" commonly refers to an establishment where moonshine or bootleg liquor is sold.

[15] Converse, "The Melungeons," 65; Vic Weals, "Home Folks," *Knoxville Journal*, 24 July 1953. Converse relates the quote from the lawman as "seeable and talkable but not bringable."

[16] Spelled "Beatty" in the original article and in subsequent writings; thanks to DruAnna Overbay for providing the correct spelling.

[17] Converse, "The Melungeons," 66.

heritage, it seems unlikely that the Melungeons would have attracted Converse's notice.

That ethnic heritage was, however, very significant to Converse."They are," he wrote, "as different from their neighbors, the mountain whites, who are the purest descendants of the Scotch Irish and English colonists known today on the American continent, as they are from the Pennsylvania Dutch or the Connecticut Yankee."[18]

Converse described the typical Melungeon physical characteristics, including prominent cheekbones, dark hair, and deep-set dark eyes, and commented on their resemblance to Indians. "Their lips are not noticeably thicker nor their feet broader than those of pure Caucasians, and although their hair is sometimes wavy, it is seldom, if ever, kinky. Some of the small boys look like young Indians fresh from their smoky wigwams." He notes the claim of some Melungeons to Portuguese ancestry, and cites the belief among some that they descended from survivors of the "Lost Colony." He relates that some theories connected the Melungeons with Venice or "Servia." He even cites the "Celebrated Melungeon Case" of 1872, in which Lewis Shepherd argued a Phoenician ancestry for the Melungeons, months before Shepherd's account appeared in *Watson's Magazine*.

Despite all these explanations for the Melungeons' dusky complexions, Converse clearly suggests the Melungeons had African ancestry. "[M]ost people...hold the Melungeons to be a mixed race, having Indian, Negro and Caucasian blood in their veins." He cites the Bureau of Ethnology classification of Melungeons as "a branch or offshoot of the Croatan Indians of North Carolina, who are a people of obscure and mixed descent in whose veins Indian blood predominates." Indian blood might predominate, but the "one drop" rule concerning African blood was certainly in force for tri-racials; most white Americans accorded them the same social status as mulattoes. Converse also mentioned, "They [the Melungeons] are very sensitive and become angry if accused of having negro blood in their veins."[19]

Virginia's remnant Indian tribes faced the same accusations. The Nansemonds had, with state aid, operated their own school until about 1900. The members of the tribe refused to send their children to a "colored" school; they petitioned the state and their own "Indian" school

---

[18] Ibid., 62.
[19] Ibid., 61–63.

was reopened. Author Helen Rountree writes, "A precedent in Virginia Indian affairs was set thereby: buck passing. Neither the attorney general nor anyone else wanted the responsibility of defining what 'Indians' were."

In 1919, anthropologist Frank Speck began working with Indian remnants in Virginia. "He came to Virginia," says Rountree, "with the intention already formed of organizing into tribes any "Indian" groups he found, rather than observing them at length and collecting documents about them before acting." Speck feared that these groups were under such pressure, they needed to be organized in order to survive. Fieldwork could be put off until later.

Working with the various remnants of the Powhatan empire—the Mattaponi, the Pamunkey, the Rappahannock, and others—Speck prevented the complete dissolution of their ethnic and cultural identities. As the individual tribal groups became organized, they encouraged other groups to do the same. The Rappahannocks, for example, were genuinely afraid of retaliation by neighboring whites if they organized. With encouragement from both Speck and the Pamunkeys, however, they took the risk.

Frank Speck gave the Powhatan groups an even greater pride in their Indian ancestry. He also gave the as-yet unorganized groups needed symbols of identity, namely tribal names and tribal organizations. Within a few years, the Indian identity of these groups would be invalidated by law.[20]

The Kingsport (Tennessee) *Times* of 7 August 1923, featured a story headlined "Distinct Race of People Inhabits the Mountains of East Tennessee; Is Different From All Other Races." The uncredited story describes "a race as different from all the others as the negro is different from the American Indian."

> Moreover, this species of the human family is found nowhere else in America. It is the sinister race of the Melungeons, a mysterious race, few in numbers, whose origin is open to speculation...They are of about the same color as

---

[20] Rountree, *Pocohontas's People*, 216.

mulattoes, but their hair is straight and they have intermarried with the Caucasian race to a limited extent.

The article retells Judge Shepherd's story of the "Celebrated Melungeon Case," and refers to Dromgoole's *Arena* articles. Nothing in this article suggests any reason the Melungeons should be described as "sinister" except for the inference that the Melungeons had African ancestry—a charge contradicted by the reference to Judge Shepherd's theories, then affirmed by the quotations from Dromgoole.

Although the article deals with people in east Tennessee, the story is datelined Nashville, which suggests the story originated with another newspaper or a news service. However, this article does not appear in any known bibliographies; if it appeared in other newspapers, it went largely unnoticed.[21]

The Vardy School—The Early Days

The Tennessee legislature provided funding for public schools in 1873. However, in Hancock County, Melungeons were expected to attend the Sandy Flats School on Newman's Ridge, a school reserved for Negroes. Melungeons refused to send their children there, a move which would have certainly destroyed their already fragile claim to being "white." Since Melungeon children were not permitted to attend schools with whites, they had no educational opportunities until missionaries from the "outside" provided those opportunities.

In 1897 a Presbyterian missionary named C. H. Humble published an account of a visit he and another missionary made to Blackwater Valley (also known as Vardy Valley). The missionaries felt the Melungeons were an essentially Indian people with "marked Indian resemblances in color, feature, hair, carriage, and disposition. They described Batey Collins as the "chief" of the "clan." Batey's son, a storekeeper and the local teacher, said that the people of Blackwater and Newman's Ridge resented the appellation "Melungeon," and asserted

---

[21] *Kingsport Times*, "Distinct Race of People Inhabits the Mountains of East Tennessee, Tuesday, 7 August 1923, 1.

that they were a "pure blood people." The article also suggested a Portuguese origin for at least some of the Melungeons.[22]

The Northern Presbyterian Church, headquartered in New York City, was involved in establishing mission schools, and soon had five operating in northeast Tennessee. The Presbyterian Church of Vardy opened on February 26, 1899, with 25 members. The first missionaries were two women, Margaret McCall of Topeka, Kansas, and Annie Breem Miller of Rogersville, Tennessee. Author Jim Callahan speculates that female missionaries had a better chance of survival in Hancock County during that period. Illegal distillation and sale of whiskey was still rampant in the region, and male missionaries almost certainly would have been suspected of being either revenue agents or potential competitors. And although the region had a reputation for violence, there was little perceived danger to the female missionaries; as Callahan wrote, "Anybody known to force themselves on a woman could be shot by vigilantes or unknown assailants and thrown into the tall weeds." The two missionaries boarded with Batey and Cynthia Collins, who had also donated the land for the new church.[23]

The first permanent minister at the Vardy Presbyterian Church was the Reverend J. H. Wallin, who arrived at the end of 1901. Records do not indicate whether he lived in the Valley. Several different ministers served the church during its early years, coming from Presbyterian churches in east Tennessee and western North Carolina.[24]

A one-room log cabin had served as a schoolhouse and meeting place for Vardy Valley since soon after the Civil War. In 1902, the Presbyterians built a new schoolhouse and began offering classes. The missionaries served as teachers and were paid by the Presbyterian Board of Missions.[25]

Mary Rankin joined the staff of the Vardy Church and School in 1910 after transferring from a school in Ozone, Tennessee, south of Knoxville. Rankin, originally from Scotland, was the first teacher in the

---

[22] C. H. Humble, "A Visit To The Melungeons," *Home Mission Monthly* 2 (1897): 243–46.

[23] DruAnna Overbay, ed., *Windows on the Past* (Sneedville TN: Vardy Community Historical Society, 2002) 21, 25; DruAnna Overbay, "Museum's Contents Reflect Vardy's Past," *The Vardy Voice* (May 2002); Callahan, *Lest We Forget*, 209–10.

[24] Overbay, *Windows on the Past*, 27–28.

[25] Ibid., 86–87.

Valley to have a college degree. "Miss Rankin," as her students affectionately remember her, served the community as a nurse, midwife, and teacher until her retirement in 1946. She held classes for students of all ages during the week, and taught Sunday School to both parents and children on Sundays. She established a night school for adults, teaching many to read and write. She also established a school lunch program to insure each child would have at least one hot, nutritious meal each day.[26]

Since there was no other school on the north side of Newman's Ridge, the Hancock County Board of Education supplemented Miss Rankin's salary from the Presbyterian Board of Missions, and allotted her six dollars and a box of crayons for supplies. The school began attracting students from the entire eight-mile length of the valley. The Vardy school was open to anyone; it was not exclusively a Melungeon school. Indeed, few if any of the students would have considered themselves Melungeons unless called such by an outsider. The missionaries realized the word "Melungeon" was offensive and did not use it.[27]

After the arrival of the Reverend Chester Leonard, of Kenosha, Wisconsin, in 1920, he and Mary Rankin introduced innovative educational techniques such as maps, pictures, and slides, visual aids which were state of the art for any school in America, not to mention a rural school in an isolated valley. Claude Collins recalled that the Vardy school implemented methods that would be considered progressive many years later. "When I was going to the University of Tennessee to get my Master's degree, I studied individualized instruction and open-space schools. That's just what I grew up in [at Vardy]...they had slides to illustrate [lessons]; they had filmstrips...You traveled at your own pace."[28]

By the late 1920s, the popularity of the progressive school had swelled the ranks of students beyond the capacity of the small schoolhouse built in 1902. The Reverend Leonard opened the church for classes and began planning a new school building. He persuaded members of the community to donate 60,000 feet of lumber, all of which

---

[26] Ibid., 33–35, 87; *The Vardy Voice* (January 2002).

[27] William Paul Grohse papers (Microfilm Roll # 7) East Tennessee State University; *The Vardy Voice* (January 2002).

[28] W.C. "Claude" Collins, Wayne Winkler, in-person interview, January 2002; Sneedville, TN.

had to be cut by the donor, brought to the sawmill, then hauled to the construction site. Supplies such as desks, chairs, and blackboards were hauled by wagon from the nearest railroad station at Ben Hur, Virginia.[29]

Although the building wasn't quite completed, the Vardy Presbyterian Community School opened for classes in the summer of 1929. The building was finally completed and dedicated on Thanksgiving Day. The impressive three-story structure was unique in a rural area where one-room schoolhouses were typical. Ninety-six windows encircled the building, providing solar heat in the winter and cross-ventilation in the summer.[30]

The first level contained a library, along with a woodworking shop. "Almost everything for the school was made there," according to Vardy alumnus Charles Sizemore. "Tables, bookcases, shelves, and all this other stuff." Classrooms on the first floor also served as an adult education center where local women were taught basic nursing skills.

Three classrooms were located on the second floor, along with an assembly room. "The first thing we did when we went to school in the morning, we met in the assembly room for Bible reading and prayer." recalled Sizemore. "Then we went on to our classes." One classroom held first and second grades, another held third and fourth grades, and the remaining classroom was for grades five through eight. "I was wondering about why they had so many grades in that room," Sizemore recalled in a presentation on the Vardy School. "I talked to DruAnna [Overbay] this morning, and she said when kids got older, they dropped out of school, and they had less kids in that room, even though they had four grades."

The third floor held the cafeteria and kitchen, which was also used for teaching home economics. An infirmary, a museum, an apartment for the Reverend and Mrs. Leonard, and rooms for visiting teachers were also on the third floor. A carriage house was located on the west side of the building. "In that carriage house, they had a blacksmith shop," recalled Sizemore. "The men in the community could go there and use that shop. They also taught metalwork... I remember my Dad going and he made some things there." Privies for boys and girls were located

---

[29] Overbay, *Windows on the Past*, 92–93.

[30] Ibid., 95–96.

outside near the carriage house, and nearby was a large willow tree which provided switches for use on misbehaving students.[31]

The seven-acre campus boasted a three-level playground on the hill behind the school., with outdoor restrooms at the edge of the lower level. The lower level was reserved for younger students and contained swings and seesaws. The second level was for older students and featured pits for horseshoe pitching, a favorite pastime of the Reverend Leonard. The third level of the playground contained ballfields as well as rope swings and a device known as the trolley. "The trolley was a heavy wire with a pulley tied to one big tree and coming down a decline over a little ravine and onto another tree," recalled Dave Swartz, a ministerial intern at Vardy during the 1940s. "That was a source of a lot of pleasure as well as a few accidents."[32]

The impact of the Presbyterian mission school at Vardy is immeasurable. The Reverend Chester Leonard, along with the multi-talented Miss Mary Rankin, would continue to provide Vardy students with educational opportunities which allowed many to escape the pattern of poverty and ignorance that was prevalent in many rural communities of that time. During the 1930s, the Vardy School worked with other Presbyterian institutions to provide promising students the opportunity to be educated beyond the eighth grade. As Claude Collins put it many years after his Vardy days, "Had it not been for the Vardy Community School and Church, I would never have been able to see the need of an education. I owe my life to the great institutions of Vardy Community School and Church."[33]

Missionaries and Monacans

The Monacan Indian community at Bear Mountain in Amherst County, Virginia, entered the twentieth century in much the same circumstances as the Melungeons. Most were farmers, growing tobacco, corn, and oats on the hillsides and bottom lands. Some of the Monacans owned their land; most were tenant farmers. Most of the locals recognized their Indian heritage, but focused more attention on their real or suspected

---

[31] Charles Sizemore, "The Vardy School," presentation at Fourth Union, 21 June 2002.

[32] Overbay, *Windows on the Past*, 102–103.

[33] Ibid., 98.

Negro ancestry. They were called "Issues," a variant of "free issues," a derogatory term used by slaves prior to the Civil war to describe free blacks.

An 1896 article in the Richmond *Times* drew attention to the Monacan group, although the paper called them "Amherst County Indians" and maintained (without offering proof) that the group was actually an offshoot of the Cherokees. The article suggested that several of the young people in this group were bright and would benefit from educational opportunities. More than a quarter-century later, Arthur Estabrook and Ivan McDougal wrote that the Monacans were not permitted in the white schools, and that the county had started a school for them in 1895. This school likely served only a portion of the Monacan community; it was taught by a Mr. Hamlet, a white citizen of the county who had a low opinion of the educational potential of his students.[34]

The Reverend Arthur Gray established an Episcopal mission in Amherst County in 1907. He acknowledged a suspicion among the neighboring whites that the Monacans were not "pure" Indians when he wrote "...they call themselves 'Indian men' and 'Indian women'...The white people have usually judged the whole tribe from the lowest element among them, as these are the most conspicuous, and so fair treatment has not always been accorded them."

Gray began conducting services once a month in a log cabin schoolhouse. A local resident, J.J. Ambler, purchased a quarter-acre next to the schoolhouse and by the summer of 1908, the mission had a new chapel. The chapel cost $1,500 to build, and contributions came from several parts of the country to pay for it. The chapel was consecrated on October 15, 1908.

Cornelia Packard, the daughter of the dean of the Virginia Theological seminary, was the first mission worker besides the Rev. Gray to arrive at Bear Mountain. A "Miss Spencer" assisted with teaching duties, and the two women lived together until Miss Packard's health failed in 1912. The Church sent Lucy Bloxton to take her place.

Lucy Bloxton taught day school and Sunday school. The state paid her for teaching half the year; for the other half, she worked for free, or for nothing more than the support given her by the Church. Bloxton

---

[34] Wood and Shields, *The Monacan Indians*, 20–25; Arthur H. Estabrook and Ivan E. McDougal, *Mongrel Virginians* (Baltimore: Williams & Wilkins, 1926) 159.

worked diligently with the people of the community, and became very close to them. In 1916, Bloxton married one of the community, a member of the Adcock family. The couple was shunned by the whites of the community, and eventually forced to leave. Eventually, Sweet Briar College built a mission house for the new deaconesses at the mission, to house them together and, conceivably, to help keep them from forming too close relationships with the Monacans. Students from the college, calling themselves "Bum Chums," sometimes visited the mission and organized activities.[35]

While most tri-racials denied having any black ancestry, nearly all the groups had African-American members, and some families had obvious Negroid features. That is not to say that all members of these groups shared that ancestry, but as a group, they were often considered on the same social level as blacks.

Some tri-racial families assimilated into nearby black communities, and their descendants would consider themselves black—often without any knowledge of any other ethnic background. Others maintained their Indian identities and struggled to rebuild their cultures. Still others, like the core family groups of Newman's Ridge, Blackwater, and other Melungeon communities, considered themselves white, or white and Indian. By the 1920s, most of these individuals were genetically more white than anything else, for as Converse wrote, "many whites have already intermingled and intermarried with them..."[36] In that era of "scientific" racism, however, "mostly white" was not white enough; "mostly white" or even "Indian" meant "colored" and were the equivalent of "black."

At least, that's how W. A. Plecker saw it. And he had the power and ability to make others see it that way as well.

Racial Integrity in Virginia

The "one-drop" rule—"one drop of negro blood makes a negro," in the words of novelist Thomas Dixon—had been a standard of racial measurement in the southern United States for generations, but it was not the legal formula for determining who was a "negro." The various states had different legal definitions for both blacks and Indians. In just about

---

[35] Wood and Shields, *The Monacan Indians*, 20–25.
[36] Converse, "The Melungeons,"69.

every state, a family could "become white," or at least meet that state's definition of "whiteness," simply by marrying whites for enough generations to meet the requirements. Many black, Indian, and tri-racial families were doing just that. In a racially segregated society, those who could "pass for white" sometimes sought white spouses as a matter of practical survival. If an individual in the late nineteenth or early twentieth centuries had a choice between living as a white person or living as a non-white, chances are that he or she would choose the former, with all the rights and legal protection afforded to white Americans and *only* white Americans.

The head of Virginia's Bureau of Vital Statistics, Walter Ashby Plecker, didn't think this was a healthy trend at all. He believed "there is a danger of the ultimate disappearance of the white race in Virginia, and the country, and the substitution therefor of another brown skin, as has occurred in every other country where the two races have lived together." This "mongrelization," in Plecker's view, caused the downfall of several earlier civilizations. He was determined to prevent this in America, or at least in Virginia.[37]

Born in Augusta County, Virginia in 1861, Plecker graduated from the University of Maryland Medical School in 1885, and practiced medicine in Virginia and Alabama. He claimed to have studied Indians in some unnamed location "in the west," and was appointed registrar of the Bureau of Vital Statistics in Virginia in 1912.[38] The following year, his fellow Virginian, President Woodrow Wilson, segregated the Federal workforce. It was a time for drawing lines between black and white; "Jim Crow" laws had been passed in most southern states, as well as in many areas above the Mason-Dixon line. The Ku Klux Klan, revived in 1915, was by the early 1920s a potent political force across the United States.

By 1920, most serious scholars had abandoned the doctrine of eugenics, primarily because the study of human genetics was proving far more complex than originally thought. The movement was still extremely popular among others, primarily laymen who were pessimistic about mankind and felt that "inferior" types had to be controlled. The eugenics movement was also attractive to racists, who wanted to maintain political control for the "superior" type, and who wanted

---

[37] Walter Ashby Plecker, *Report of the Bureau of Vital Statistics*, Richmond VA: 10.

[38] Rountree, *Pocahontas's People*, 218.

neutralization—or elimination—of "inferior" types. Both pessimistic laymen and racists were to be found in various positions of power in the local, state, and federal governments. Proponents of eugenics policies turned to that part of the "scientific" community that agreed with them, and these academics gave legitimacy to the movement by "proving" that the "inferior" types exhibited more negative traits—crime, illegitimacy, lower scores on intelligence tests—than did whites. This reasoning held that if an individual had an "inferior" ancestor, that individual was also "inferior." "The "one-drop rule" now had a pseudoscientific basis and was ready to be passed into law. And in Virginia, Registrar Plecker stood ready to enforce the law."[39]

Plecker became involved in the eugenics movement after taking office, and lobbied hard for the passage of the Racial Integrity Act. His background as a physician no doubt influenced many of Virginia's legislators. When the new law went into effect in 1924, Arthur Estabrook and Ivan McDougal spoke for many in praising the Act as a means of preserving the 'purity" of the white race.

> [Virginia's Racial Integrity Law of 1924] provides not only for the registration of the people of Virginia by color, but makes an entirely new definition of the colored race. Section five reads in part as follows: "For the purposes of this act, the term 'white person' shall apply only to the person who has *no trace whatsoever* of any blood other than Caucasian; but persons who have one-sixteenth or less of the blood of the American Indian and have no other non-Caucasic blood shall be deemed to be white persons." By inference then *any* trace of negro blood is sufficient to classify one as colored…It also provides that whites may marry only with whites or a person with no other admixture than American Indian. If this law can be enforced, it will preserve racial integrity.[40]

While no modern anthropologist has been able to establish the existence of a "pure" Caucasian, the official position of the Commonwealth of Virginia was that its citizens, or at least those that mattered, were exactly that. For those of mixed racial heritage, as Helen

---

[39] Rountree, *Pocahontas's People*, 220.
[40] Estabrook and McDougal, *Mongrel Virginians*, 180.

Rountree writes, "It was now very difficult to be 'white' in Virginia and very easy to be 'colored.'" Many of Virginia's Indians had long been thought to have, in Thomas Jefferson's words, "more negro than Indian blood in them."[41] By the 1920s, whites in Virginia assumed that nearly all Indians in the state had at least some degree of African ancestry. In the interest of racial purity, to prevent these mixed-race people from mixing with "pure" whites, the Racial Integrity Act of 1924 categorized *all* non-whites as "colored.

As far as most white Virginians were concerned, there was only one problem with categorizing all Virginia's Indians as "colored." Many of Virginia's elite took pride in their descent, actual or otherwise, from Pocahontas. Under the Racial Integrity Act, therefore, a person with one-sixteenth or less "Indian blood," and no other non-white admixture, was considered white. In this way, Virginia's prominent citizens could boast of their kinship to the non-Caucasian "Indian princess" and still be considered "pure."

Needless to say, most of those who suddenly found themselves "colored" were not pleased. Virginia, like most southern states, was segregated in all aspects of life. Public facilities for "colored" people, such as schools and hospitals, were inferior to those set aside for whites. Employment opportunities were limited to the least desirable jobs, and a strict code of social conduct provided a daily reminder of one's lower status. The "Pocahontas rule" provided the only loophole through which individuals and families of Indian ancestry could avoid being categorized as "colored." This was a loophole Walter Plecker guarded zealously, determined to eliminate what Rountree called the "way-station to whiteness."[42]

After taking office in 1912, Plecker decreed that all babies born in state would receive birth certificates. Until 1924, the state took the midwife's word for the race of the child and of the parents. The Racial Integrity Act set out the guidelines for racial designations, and the certificates required the recording of the race of all known ancestors. For those born before 1912, who otherwise would have had no official birth

---

[41] Rountree, *Pocahontas's People*, 221; Thomas Jefferson, *Notes on the State of Virginia, 1787*, William Peden, editor, (Chapel Hill University of North Carolina Press, 1954) 96. Jefferson, at that time Governor of Virginia, was speaking of a group of Mattaponi. Other Indians, he noted, were "tolerably pure of mixture with other colours."

[42] Rountree, *Pocahontas's People*, 222.

certificates of any kind; "registration" to receive a certificate from the Vital Statistics Bureau was voluntary. However, these birth certificates were required when enrolling in a school, registering for the draft, and so forth. Thus, in a real sense, "registration" was not voluntary at all. Further, the law made it a felony to falsify one's race on a certificate. In time, "falsification" came to mean disagreement with the classification made by the Vital Statistics Bureau.[43]

Plecker set out to define all of Virginia's Indians and tri-racials as "colored." He collected old county and federal records on Virginia's Indians to justify this position. Most of these records listed the Indians as "persons of color." Plecker did not take into account the conditions under which these records were made or how the meaning of words had changed. "To him," writes Rountree, "'color' in 1830 meant the same thing as 'color' did in 1930, and if the term appeared in an old document, the negritude of the person so designated was 'proved.'" Plecker expected all county records, past and present, to conform to this standard. He would tolerate no "Indian" classification. Any state records dealing with Indians were to indicate that they were "colored." The birth certificates issued to Indians after 1924 listed them as such. These birth certificates were filed with county clerks, and often the individuals so named did not know of their designation until years later, particularly when they were drafted.[44]

Officially classifying Virginia's Indians as "colored" was not enough for Plecker; he wanted all the white people of the state to consider them "colored" as well. Plecker worked diligently to portray Indian groups as Negroes illegally trying to become "white." He delivered lectures and wrote pamphlets on the subject of the dangers of race mixing. In one pamphlet, *Eugenics in Relation to the New Family*, he urged adults to marry within their own race and only with "healthy stock." Plecker claimed racial mixtures made for degraded stock and endangered society. He concluded that there were no Indians in Virginia unmixed with Negro blood, therefore there were no "true" Indians in the state. This pamphlet accompanied each birth and marriage certificate issued by the bureau.[45]

---

[43] Ibid., 219, 21.
[44] Ibid., 222–23.
[45] Ibid., 223.

Mongrel Virginians

Plecker's campaign against mixed race people in Virginia was reinforced in 1926 with the publication of *Mongrel Virginians*, a study of the Monacan community of Amherst County, by Arthur Estabrook and Ivan McDougal. Many years after publication, Estabrook wrote:

> The main studies in *Mongrel Virginians* were made in Amherst and nearby counties in Virginia and North Carolina, in the areas south of Fayetteville. We secured some information about triple mixtures in Southern Maryland, the river areas in Virginia along the Potomac River, a section east of Columbia, S.C., and two areas in Tennessee, one in the eastern part, the other west of Asheville. There is a small group in Eastern Long Island and another near Plymouth, Mass.[46]

Mongrel Virginians focused on the Amherst County Monacans, known locally as "Issues." Arthur H. Estabrook worked for the Carnegie Institute of Washington's Eugenics records Office in Cold Spring Harbor, Long Island, New York. His approach to the study of the "Issues" was similar to that taken by Richard Dugdale for his study of the Jukes family.

While inspecting county jails for the New York Prison Association, Dugdale developed data for his famous study. *The Jukes: A Study in Crime, Pauperism, Disease, and Heredity* was published in 1877. "Jukes" was a fictitious name for a real family whose history Dugdale traced for seven generations to a single couple in upstate New York. The early eugenics movement seized onto Dugdale's study as evidence that "bad genes" were transmitted from generation to generation, causing lower intelligence, promiscuity, and criminal behavior. Dugdale actually recognized that much of the Jukes' behavior was more the result of adverse social conditions than inherited traits, but that conclusion was ignored by most of the eugenicists who cited the "Jukes" as "proof" of several questionable eugenics theories. These theories were later used as justification for incarceration and even sterilization of individuals

---

[46] Arthur Estabrook, letter to Christine Jones, librarian at Tennessee Polytechnical Institute, 2 June 1957, attached to copy of *Mongrel Virginians* in library at Tennessee Technical University, Cookeville, Tennessee.

thought to be from "poor stock." When Dugdale's original manuscripts were discovered in 1911, Arthur Estabrook was able to learn the real names of the "Jukes" and publish a follow-up, *The Jukes in 1915*.[47]

Estabrook and McDougal's study of the Issues was coordinated through Sweet Briar College, which had long worked with the Bear Mountain mission. Fieldwork began in January 1923 and lasted about two years. Estabrook and McDougal "protected" the identities of their subjects by not only giving them fictitious names, but designating their county as "Ab" County. Neighboring whites called this group "Issues," but for *Mongrel Virginians* Estabrook and McDougal named them "the WIN tribe," "WIN" being an acronym for "White-Indian-Negro." However, this designation did not fool the individuals who were portrayed in the book, who knew exactly to whom Estabrook and McDougal referred.[48]

> They are described variously as "low down" yellow negroes, as Indians, as "mixed." No one, however, speaks of them as white. The Win's themselves in general claim Indian descent although most of them realize they are "mixed," preferring to speak of the "Indian" rather than of a possibility of negro mixture in them. A few claim to be white. The term by which they have been known locally for many years is that used to designate the negro slaves who were given their freedom by their masters before the Civil War. This term clung to these freed negroes. These freed negroes mated with themselves or the half-breed Indians in the county. Because the freed ones were looked down upon by other negroes, having no masters, and also were unable to associate with the whites, this group necessarily remained separate and the name of the freed negroes clung to the whole. Hence this group described had come to be called such in earlier days. The term Wins, however, in Ab County, has remained only attached to this mixed group, most of the mixture having taken place previous to the Civil War.[49]

---

[47] www.encyclopedia.com entry for Dugdale; http://www.galafilm.com/afterdarwin/english/timelines/eug_1877_jukes.html.

[48] Estabrook letter to Jones; Estabrook and McDougal, *Mongrel Virginians*, 13; Wood and Shields, *The Monacan Indians*, 27.

[49] Estabrook and McDougal, *Mongrel Virginians*, 14–15.

The authors acknowledged that the Monacans displayed many traits associated with Indians. However, they obviously accepted many common racial stereotypes in assigning traits to various ethnic groups.

> The persistency of Indian traits among the Wins appears remarkable when the remoteness of pure Indian blood is taken into consideration. When one sees a group of men walking along the county road they will always be found parading in single file and for the most part noncommunicative...there is practically no music among them and they have no sense of rhythm even in the lighter mulatto mixtures. As is well known, the negro is "full" of music...It would seem from these and many other observations that the negro temperamental characteristics are completely dominated by the Indian.[50]

That so-called "scientists" could accept folklore as fact is appalling. A true scientist would not write "As is well known, the negro is 'full' of music;" the statement was as ridiculous in 1926 as it is today. Even more appalling is the fact that many whites cited works such as *Mongrel Virginians* as scientific justification for racist policies and practices.

The Monacans, whose number Estabrook estimated as 658, were portrayed as an inbred and promiscuous group.

> ... approximately half of the matings have been into the family itself...The social barrier erected in earlier times and still continued against the Wins by the whites and negroes of Ab County has been to a great extent the chief factor in forcing the Wins into mating with their own folks. This social barrier is not due to their own choosing as many of them consider it a desirable social asset to be married to a white person or one lighter than themselves. Hence matings on the part of the Wins into the white is much desired.[51]

Those whites who married into Monacan families suffered the same rejection as the missionary Lucy Bloxton, who married a Monacan in

---

[50] Ibid., 201–202.
[51] Ibid., 148–50.

1916. Estabrook and McDougal described whites who married Monacans as "low class white families," "a low grade white family." "Practically all of the out matings have been into poor stocks mentally. The consanguineous matings into the group are likewise of poor stock into itself."[52] The authors also portrayed the Monacan girls as very sexually active.

> The girls become "boy-crazy" at the age of nine, ten and eleven...The young girls at eleven and twelve are sexually active while the boys of thirteen are distinctly adolescent. In the case of the young girl, the period of adolescence is almost simultaneous with her leaving school, the latter follows the former. The child in the next few years becomes more or less promiscuous, generally with the younger boys of the vicinity. Pregnancy is generally followed by marriage unless the girl has been too promiscuous... The sexual relations of the Wins are on a very low plane, almost that of the animal in their freedom.[53]

If the Monacans were indeed as promiscuous as portrayed by Estabrook and McDougal, they somehow managed to avoid one of the usual consequences. "The physicians in Ab county report little or no venereal disease among the Wins...If gonorrhea is present it has never come to the attention of the physicians."[54]

The Commonwealth of Virginia had never spent much on educational facilities for non-whites, but Estabrook and McDougal believed that what little was spent was being wasted.

> After the Civil War the Wins were given a chance to attend the schools for the negroes when these were started but they were denied admission to the white schools. As the Wins refused to attend the negro schools, claiming Indian blood and declining to associate with the colored race, the result was that they remained without schooling. Beginning about 1895, the county started a school for the "Indians" with Mr. Hamlet, a white citizen of the county, as teacher... Mr. Hamlet states that none of

---

[52] Ibid., 150.
[53] Ibid., 157.
[54] Ibid., 158.

the Wins was able to do average work in school or progress sufficiently to make his training of any value.[55]

This school was still in operation at the time the authors made their study. The average level of education of the "Wins" in the 1890s was third grade; it was the same in 1923. "In the course of the thirty years of schooling," they write, "not one of the Wins have been sufficiently educated to become a teacher and take on the position of a leader of his own people."[56]

Estabrook and McDougal also examined several other tri-racial groups in Virginia, North Carolina, and Tennessee. Although they wrote very little about these groups, they maintained their format of disguising the names of peoples and places, even when those people and places were well-known and the pseudonyms were confusing. "Robin County" is obviously Robeson County, and the "Rivers" are the Lumbee, or Croatans as they were widely (and unpopularly) known. "Cremo" Island is Roanoke Island, home of the "Lost Colony."

> The Robin County, North Carolina, region is the home of approximately 10,000 "Indians" called the "Rivers." Their history is in doubt, but they claim to be descended from the Captain John White colony left on Cremo Island... White went back to England for supplies leaving 120 people under 90 family names in the colony. There were friendly Indians "50 miles up into the main" called Rivers Indians who wanted the whites to move to their country. It was arranged by White that if these people went to the Rivers country they were to leave the word "Rivers" carved on a tree so that he would know where there [sic] were when he returned. In 1590 when White returned the word "Rivers" was found carved as directed... Apparently at this time no attempt was made to find them...
>
> A River is very sensitive of the fact that there has been some negro admixture and hedges away from an enquiry into the matter. They resent questioning as to the probability of the negro having come into their blood and cooperation so far with them has been impossible. Suggestions furnished by white people in

---

[55] Ibid., 159–160.
[56] Ibid., 161.

Swenson point to the mixture with the negro taking place about the year 1835 when by act of the legislature these Indians were classed as colored.[57]

Estabrook and McDougal also wrote a very brief entry on the Melungeons: "In southwest Virginia and in eastern Tennessee are the Meros, a mixed group of people generally dark in color, some with straight hair, some curly, and 'dark' skin color. It is said that this special group which is quite numerous, is an offshoot of the Rivers, and it is considered a triple mixture."[58]

Mongrel Virginians provided a "scientific" justification, albeit after the fact, for the Racial Integrity Act. Using the Amherst County Monacans as examples, *Mongrel Virginians* warned that race-mixing meant the degradation of the white race.

It is evident from this study that the intellectual levels of the negro and the Indian race as now found is below the average for the white race. In the Wins the early white stock was probably at least of normal ability, i.e., for the white. After the mating of this white… stock with the Indian, the general level of the white was lowered in the mixture… The whole Win tribe is below the average, mentally and socially. They are lacking in academic ability, industrious to a very limited degree and capable of taking little training…

Unquestionably the people covered by this study represent an ever increasing social problem in the South. Social consciousness has only begun to be awakened. Amidst the furor of newspaper and pamphlet publicity on miscegenation which has appeared since the passage of the Virginia Racial Integrity Law of 1924 this study is presented not as theory or as representing a prejudiced point of view but as a careful summary of the facts of history.[59]

Almost immediately, the findings of Estabrook and McDougal were challenged. In 1928, a University of Virginia graduate student named

---

[57] Ibid., 188–190

[58] Ibid., 197.

[59] Ibid., 199, 202.

Bertha Wailes refuted their conclusions. Wailes had worked with the Monacans of Amherst County, and wrote about the poverty and lack of opportunities they faced, their unfair treatment and low pay by white landlords. Nonetheless, the Commonwealth of Virginia accepted the view of Estabrook and McDougal toward its non-white citizens; the Racial Integrity Law would remain in effect until 1971.[60]

Prior to the enactment of the Racial Integrity Act in 1924, non-whites, bi-racials, tri-racials and others with dark skin in Virginia had lived along a sort of racial continuum; they weren't considered completely white, but had some of the privileges accorded whites. While an individual might have been subject to Jim Crow laws when away from home, in his or her home county, that same individual might have a higher status among familiar people. The Racial Integrity Act eliminated those considerations. Anything other than "pure" white was "colored," and "colored" was the same as "black" in the eyes of the law.

Some of these "colored" people shared with the whites strong prejudices against African-Americans. A number of the Powhatan Indian groups practiced their own version of the "one-drop" rule and shunned contact with blacks. To this day, many individuals among the Melungeons and other mixed race groups vehemently deny that their ancestors intermarried with blacks, and consider Walter Plecker to be an unreasoning tyrant for imposing that status on their ancestors.

These people miss the point. In Plecker's view, *it did not matter* whether these individuals actually had an African ancestor or not. They were not white; whatever else they might be was of no consequence. *Partly white* or *mostly white* were simply not sufficient to meet Plecker's definition of a white person.

Racism was certainly not the only motivation for denying black ancestry. Many, if not most, of the people classified as tri-racial in the early twentieth century actually did have at least some African ancestry. Given a more tolerant social climate, they might well have acknowledged or even celebrated their diverse heritages. However, to accept the status of "colored" meant accepting a future with little chance for improvement. It meant being restricted to "colored" public facilities which were invariably far below the standards enjoyed by whites. Educational opportunities were almost non-existent. Employment was

---

[60] Rountree, *Pocahontas's People*, 351; Wood and Shields, *The Monacan Indians*, 27.

limited to the most menial jobs. No rational person would choose such a status if a choice were possible. Black people in the southern United States had tasted at least some of fruits of full American citizenship during the all-too-brief years of Reconstruction following the Civil War, only to watch their citizenship vanish with the last of the Federal troops in 1876. The Indians of Virginia saw whatever social and legal status they possessed disappear with the passage of the Racial Integrity Act of 1924.

The right of self-definition was reserved for whites. If a white Virginian wanted to claim kinship to Pocahontas, the claim was accepted and the claimant was not penalized for his or her non-white ancestry. However, an individual with seven white great-grandparents and one Indian great-grandparent, but who was deemed "colored" under the law, did not have the right to claim the rights and privileges of a white person. Moreover, that person was automatically presumed to have African ancestry as well as Indian, and was relegated to the lowest social status.

Walter Plecker had effectively classified all non-whites in Virginia as "colored." In his view, he was saving the citizens of the Commonwealth of Virginia, or at least those Virginians he considered worth anyone's attention. Saving Virginia was not the same as saving America, and Plecker's next challenge was to get the Federal government to accept his classifications.

The 1930 Census

Virginia's 1924 Racial Integrity Law allowed the Bureau of Vital Statistics to make determinations of who was white and who was not, and therefore granted the Bureau the power to decide who could marry whom. County clerks had the right to deny marriage licenses to those who could not prove that they were of the same race. Plecker's Bureau was more than willing to share its files with whites who were contemplating marriage to one of Virginia's "mongrels," and even to help dissolve such a marriage after it had taken place. "[The Bureau of Vital Statistics] furnished information upon which to base annulments of interracial marriages, and... perhaps prevented other similar marriages by giving out facts to inquiring young people whose suspicions were aroused."[61]

Plecker was determined that Indians and mixed-race people in Virginia would be counted as "colored" in the Federal census of 1930. The Virginia tribes were not recognized by the Federal government, and had no protection against arbitrary classifications by state officials. If such a precedent could be set in Virginia, non-whites could be easily and effectively categorized (and segregated) across America. Plecker began his campaign early, writing to the director of the Census in 1925 to argue that the Indians of Virginia were actually "mulattoes."[62]

The Indians and tri-racials were not pleased. Anthropologist and Indian advocate Frank Speck urged the tribes to collect affidavits from neighboring whites, testifying to their Indian status. Speck intended to use these affidavits to argue in their favor. In retaliation, Plecker attempted to have all Speck's books, including his 1925 work on the Rappahannocks and his 1928 book on all the Powhatan people, banned from Virginia's public libraries. Speck was embarrassed by this action and concentrated his fieldwork elsewhere for a while. The Indians were on their own.[63]

Plecker kept up the pressure on the census bureau, alleging that the Indians' claims were false, and that their reservations should be closed on the grounds that the residents were mulattoes. The Census Bureau gave in to many of Plecker's demands, and instructed enumerators that persons of mixed Negro and Indian blood should be counted as Negro unless the Indian blood predominated or the person in question was accepted in the community as an Indian. Thus the enumerators were responsible for determining the validity of the claims of the persons enumerated. The Census Bureau pointed out that the classification on the census did not establish their legal racial status. As Rountree writes, "Perhaps that did not happen in the District of Columbia, but status in the census mattered very much in Virginia at the time."[64]

Plecker's victory was incomplete, but he managed to win many of his points. He sent a list to the Census Bureau of names of families he

---

[61] Rountree, *Pocahontas's People*, 224; W.A. Plecker, *Report of the Bureau of Vital Statistics*, Richmond VA: 1926, 7.

[62] Rountree, *Pocahontas's People*, 226–27.

[63] Ibid., 224.

[64] Ibid., 226–28.

accused of "passing as white," and asked that they be counted as "colored." The bureau refused to make those changes. However, for some listings, they added an asterisk and a footnote to the effect that the Indian status of these persons was questioned.[65]

Amherst County's Monacan community was initially deemed "colored". The enumerator for Amherst County, Ernest Duff, wrote to Washington to protest the "colored" classification, and the Monacans were listed as "Indian*."[66]

Frank Speck returned to Virginia in 1939 with a group of graduate students. This fieldwork produced a great deal of material on the Virginia tribes. Speck worked to gain federal recognition for the Eastern Chickahominies, who were more organized than the other tribes, but his effort was unsuccessful.

The Census Bureau eventually gave in to most of Plecker's demands, and for the 1940 census, most of the enumerators listed people the way Plecker instructed them. The result was that the 1940 census showed far fewer Indians in Virginia than did the 1930 census.[67]

By then, Plecker's Bureau of Vital Statistics had been issuing birth certificates for 28 years. Since 1924 the question of an individual's race was decided by Plecker's office: either white or colored. In the late 1930s Plecker's office began "correcting" birth certificates issued prior to 1924. Many of the people defined as "colored" by Plecker's Bureau either had not received copies of their birth certificates, or hadn't paid close attention to what those certificates said. When America entered World War II and began conscripting young men, these birth certificates—and the opinions of the white men on draft boards—would again consign tri-racial people to an inferior status, this time within the segregated American military.

Tri-Racials and the Military

At the time of America's entry into World War II, many tri-racials still lived in relatively isolated areas and had experienced only limited contact with whites. Most of that contact was with whites who lived close to the tri-racial community, and were accustomed to their ethnic backgrounds.

---

[65] Ibid., 228.

[66] Wood and Shields, *The Monacan Indians*, 28.

[67] Rountree, *Pocahontas's People*, 229–30.

These whites generally granted the tri-racials a unique social status—not quite as high as that of whites, nor as low as that of blacks. Whites familiar with the tri-racials knew that the suggestion of African ancestry was offensive to then, and even those whites who were convinced of that ancestry avoided saying so unless offense was intended.

The Selective Service established draft boards across America, typically manned by prominent white men in the community. In areas inhabited by tri-racials, the men on the draft boards were usually aware of their unique racial status. The military, however, recognized only two races: white and black. Indians from federally-recognized tribes were permitted to serve with whites. Tri-racials were another matter entirely. Those who maintained a semblance of tribal identity—the Lumbees, the Powhatans, the Monacans, and others—had a better-than-even chance of being considered Indian, even if the members of the draft board believed them to have at least some African ancestry. Other groups, however, had no tribal identity to claim. For Melungeons, Brass Ankles, and others, their racial status would be determined by their local draft boards.

For the white men on the draft boards, establishing a racial classification for their tri-racial neighbors was sometimes a daunting task. They were often influenced by local prejudices, but just as often sympathetic to the young men from their counties who were facing military service. It was difficult enough to send these men away from their homes without subjecting them to the indignities faced by black soldiers in the Jim Crow Army. The simplest answer was often to accept the draftee's own classification and let the Army sort it out later. "When they say they are white, I put them down as white," said one draft board member. "It's not our business to argue with people about their race. I just let them worry about that at the induction center."[68]

Those induction centers were generally staffed by soldiers from other parts of the country, men who were unfamiliar with tri-racials and were often astounded that such people existed. "A major up here at Fort Jackson called me one day and said 'What do you mean by sending us a nigger with that white contingent?'" recalled a member of a South Carolina draft board. "I just told him that he wasn't a nigger and he wasn't white either. I explained as best I could that down here they have

---

[68] Berry, *Almost White*, 100.

their own school and church, and they don't associate with niggers at all. The major just said, 'Well, I'll be damned,' and he hung up."[69]

Tri-racial men were willing to serve in the military—but only if they could do so with the status of white men. When that status was not granted, these men often refused to be inducted at all. In 1943, six men from a community of Waccamaw Indians near Wilmington, North Carolina, were drafted and classified as Negroes. Their request to be classified as Indians was refused, and they fled to the swamps near their home. They were apprehended and charged with violation of the Selective Service Act. An understanding judge dismissed the charges, and thereafter the local draft board classified all Waccamaws as 4–F. Many tri-racial men requested assistance from local politicians in establishing their racial status in the military. If the individuals in question were considered white enough to vote in their home districts, their local representatives were likely to argue in their favor. These efforts, however, were not always successful.[70]

In Virginia, one local draft board held an "Indian Day," and drafted the local Nansemond men as whites. This tactic was repeated, after some initial resistance, for ten men of the Upper Mattaponi group. Most of the Powhatan groups were granted "white" status in the military, but ten Western Chickahominy men were inducted as blacks and protested their classifications. Walter Plecker provided evidence that these men were considered "colored" in Virginia, and the Army considered the case closed. However, the chief of the tribe wrote to President Roosevelt, and the Western Chickahominy men eventually served as white men.

A member of the Eastern Chickahominy tribe was drafted and deemed "colored." A resident of Hampton, this individual was one of several who had been removed from white schools through the efforts of Walter Plecker; the draft board considered that satisfactory evidence of his racial status. The resulting protest was so violent that board members went into hiding. After promising not to shoot anyone, the man was classified as "nationality unknown" and served with whites.[71]

Twenty-three members of the Rappahannock tribe served in the military, but four men were prosecuted for refusing to serve with blacks. One of these men, Oliver Fortune, insisted on serving with whites, but

---

[69] Ibid.

[70] Ibid., 100–102.

[71] Rountree, *Pocahontas's People*, 233.

records from Caroline County listed his family as "colored" and revealed that Fortune had attended schools and churches for blacks. Appeals from Frank Speck and even the governor of Virginia to the Selective Service were fruitless; Fortune and two others were convicted and served two years in a federal penitentiary in Richmond.[72]

In Amherst County, Virginia, the Monacans challenged the drafting of their men into black regiments. Two 1943 court cases were settled in the Monacans' favor, and the draft board agreed to accept the stated race of each Monacan draftee.[73]

In Tennessee, some dark-skinned Melungeons were classified as Negroes by white military authorities and had to get county officials to sign affidavits asserting that they were considered white in their home community. While Tennessee Melungeons were usually able to sort our their classification problems with the draft board, Melungeons in southwestern Virginia had to contend with county and state records which categorized them as "colored." In 1942 and 1943, as America and her allies desperately fought for freedom, Walter Plecker was busily attempting to curtail the civil rights of still more Virginians.

Racial Classification Continues

In the late 1930s and early 1940s, Plecker began "correcting" the birth certificates issued before 1924, negating any "Indian" designation. At first, he merely wrote on the backs of the birth certificates and issued copies of both the front and back when copies were requested. A member of one of the Virginia tribes received a copy of his birth certificate with the "warning" attached, and protested to Plecker that he was an Indian. Plecker replied, "The early records of this State show this group of people are descendants of free Negroes." Other protests met the same fate; Plecker would not budge on his classifications.[74]

Later, Plecker added a printed "warning" to the backs of certificates issued by his Bureau. The "warning" was as big as the certificates

---

[72] Ibid.

[73] Wood and Shields, *The Monacan Indians*, 29.

[74] W. A. Plecker letter, 27 February 1942, cited in Rountree, *Pocahontas's People*,

themselves, 728 words long, and cited references to eastern tribal Indians as well as mixed blood groups such as the Melungeons.[75]

Plecker looked to neighboring Tennessee for help in classifying the Melungeons. In a letter dated 5 August 1942, Plecker queried the Secretary of State in Nashville in an attempt to further research the murky origins of the Melungeons.

> Dear Sir:
> Our bureau is the only one in any state making an intensive study of the population of its citizens by race.
> We have in some of the counties of southwestern Virginia a number of so-called Melungeons who came into that section from Newman's Ridge, Hancock County, Tennessee, and who are classified by us as of negro origin though they make various claims, such as Portuguese, Indians, etc.
> The law of Virginia says that any one with any ascertainable degree of negro is to be classified as colored and we are endeavoring to so classify those who apply for birth, death and marriage registrations.
> We have a list of the free negroes, by counties, of the 1830 U. S. Census in which we find the racial origin of most of these Melungeons classified as mulattoes. In that period, 1830, we do not find the name of Hancock County, but presume that it was made up from portions of other counties, possibly Grainger and Hawkins, where we find considerable numbers of these Melungeon families listed.
> Will you please advise us as to that point and particularly which of these original counties Newman's Ridge was in.
> Thanking you in advance and with kindest regards, I am
> Very truly yours,
> W. A. Plecker, M.D.
> State Registrar

On 12 August, Tennessee's State Librarian and Archivist replied to Plecker.

---

[75] Ibid., 232.

My dear Sir:

The Secretary of State has sent your letter to my desk.

You have asked us a hard question.

The origin of the Melungeons has been a disputed question in Tennessee ever since we can remember.

Hancock County was established by an Act of the General Assembly passed January 7th, 1844 and was formed from parts of Claiborne and Hawkins counties.

Newman's Ridge, which runs through Hancock county north of Sneedville, is parallel with Clinch River and just south of Powell Mountain. The only map on which we find it located is edited by H. C. Amick and S. J. Folmsbee of the University of Tennessee in 1941 published by Denoyer-Geppert Co., 5235 Ravenswood Ave., Chicago, listed as [TN 7S]* TENNESSEE. On this map is shown Newman's Ridge as I have sketched it on this little scrap of paper, inclosed. But we do not have the early surveys showing which county it as originally in. It appears that it may have been in Claiborne according to the Morris Gazetteer of Tennessee 1834 which includes this statement: "Newman's Ridge, one of the spurs of Cumberland Mountain, in East Tennessee, lying in the north east angle of Claiborne County, west of Clinch River, and east of Powell's Mountain. It took its name from a Mr. Newman who discovered it in 1761."

Early historians of East Tennessee who lived in that section and knew the older members of this race refer to Newman's Ridge as "quite a high mountain, extending through the entire length of Hancock County, and into Claiborne County on the west. It is between Powell Mountain on the north and Clinch River on the south." Capt. L. M. Jarvis, an old citizen of Sneedville wrote in his 82nd year: "I have lived here at the base of Newman's Ridge, Blackwater, being on the opposite side, for the last 71 years and well know the history of these people on Newman's Ridge and Blackwater enquired about as Melungeons. These people were friendly to the Cherokees who came west with the white immigration from New River and Cumberland, Virginia, about the year 1790... The name Melungeon was given them on account of their color. I have seen the oldest and first settlers of this tribe who first occupied

Newman's Ridge and Blackwater and I have owned much of the lands on which they settled. They obtained their land grants from North Carolina. I personally knew Vardy Collins, Solomon D. Collins, Shepard Gibson, Paul Bunch and Benjamin Bunch and many of the Goodmans, Moores, Williams and Sullivans, all of the very first settlers and noted men of these friendly Indians. They took their names from white people of that name with whom they came here. They were reliable, truthful and faithful to anything they promised. In the Civil War most of the Melungeons went into the Union army and made good soldiers. Their Indian blood has about run out. They are growing white... They have been misrepresented by many writers. In former writings I have given their stations and stops on their way as they emigrated to this country with white people, one of which places was at the mouth of Stony Creek on Clinch river in Scott County, Virginia, where they built fort and called it Ft. Blackamore [sic] after Col. Blackamore who was with them... When Daniel Boone was here hunting 1763–1767, these Melungeons were not here."

The late Judge Lewis Shepherd, prominent jurist of Chattanooga, went further in his statements in his "Personal Memoirs", and contended that this mysterious racial group descended from the Phoenicians of Ancient Carthage. This was his judgment after investigations he made in trying a case featuring the complaint that they were of mixed negro blood, which attempt failed, and which brought out the facts that many of their ancestors had settled early in South Carolina when they migrated from Portugal to America about the time of the Revolutionary war, and later moved into Tennessee. At the time of this trial covered by Judge Shepherd charges that Negro blood contaminated the Melungeons and barred their intermarriage with Caucasians created much indignation among families of Phoenician descent in this section.

But I imagine if the United States Census listed them as mulattoes their listing will remain. But it is a terrible claim to place on people if they do not have negro blood. I often have wondered just how deeply the census takers went into an intelligent study of it at that early period.

I have gone into some detail in this reply to explain the mooted question and why it is not possible for me to give you a definite answer. I hope this may assist you to some extent.
Sincerely,
Mrs. John Trotwood Moore
State Librarian and Archivist

Mrs. Moore obviously recognized the hardship that Plecker intended to impose on Melungeons in southwest Virginia, pointing out that "it is a terrible claim to place on people if they do not have negro blood." However, as a later letter showed, she was sympathetic to Plecker's overall goals. On 20 August Plecker replied:

Dear Mrs. Moore:
We thank you very much for your informative letter of August 12 in reply to our inquiry, addressed to the Secretary of State, as to the original counties from which Hancock County, Tennessee, was formed.
We are particularly interested in tracing back, as far as possible, to their ultimate origin the melungeons [*sic*] of the Newmans Ridge section, especially as enumerated in the free negro list by counties of the states in the U. S. 1830 census. This group appears to be in many respects of the same type as a number of groups in Virginia, some of which are known as "free issues," or descendants of slaves freed by their masters before the War Between the States. In one case in particular which we have traced back to its origin, and which we believe to be typical of the others, a slave woman was freed with her two mulatto sons and colonized in Amherst County in connection with a group of similar freed negroes. These sons were presumably the children of the woman's owner, and this seemed to be the most satisfactory way of disposing of them. One of those sons became the head of one of the larger families of that group. All of these groups have the same desire, which Captain L. M. Jarvis says the melungeons have, to become friends of Indians and to be classed as Indians. He referred to the effort which the melungeon group made to be accepted by the Cherokees, apparently without great success. It is interesting also to know the opinion expressed by

Captain Jarvis that these freed negroes migrated into that section with the white people. That is perfectly natural as they have always endeavored to tie themselves up as closely as possible either with the whites or Indians and are striving to break away from the true negro type.

We have a book, compiled by Carter G. Woodson, a negro, entitled "Free Negro Heads of Families in the United States in 1830," listing all of the free negroes of the 1830 census by counties. Of the names that Captain Jarvis gave, we find included in that list in Hawkins County, Solomon Collins, Vardy Collins, and Sherod (probably Shepard) Gibson. We find also Zachariah Minor, probably the head of the family in which we are especially interested at this time. We find also the names of James Moore (two families by this name) and Jordan and Edmund Goodman. In the list for Grainger County we find at least twelve Collins and Collens heads of families. This shows that they were evidently considered locally as free negroes by the enumerators of the 1830 census.

One of the most interesting parts of your letter is that relating to the opinion of the Judge in his "Personal Memoirs," seemed to have accepted as satisfactory certain evidence which was presented to him that these people are of Phoenician descent from ancient Carthage, which was totally destroyed by Rome. We have in Virginia white people, descendants of Pocahontas, who married John Rolfe about 1616. About twelve generations have passed since then, and we figured out that there was about 1/4000th of 1% of Pocahontas blood now in their veins, though they seem to be quite proud of that. If you go back to the destruction of Carthage in 146 B. C., or to the destruction of Tyre by Pompey in 64 B. C., when all characteristic features of national life became extinct and with it racial identity, you will see that the fraction of 1% of Phoenician blood would reach astronomical proportions and be totally lost in the various mixtures of North Africans, with which the Carthaginians afterwards mixed. The Judge also speaks of the inclusion of Portuguese blood with this imaginary Phoenician blood. It is a historical fact, well known to those who have investigated, that at one time there were many African slaves in Portugal. Today there are no true negroes there but their blood shows in the color and racial characteristics of a large part of the Portuguese population of the present day. That mixture, even if it could be shown, would be far from constituting these people white. We are very much afraid that the Judge followed the same course pursued by one of our Virginia judges in hearing a similar case, when he accepted the hearsay evidence of people who testified that they had always understood that the claimants were of Indian origin, regardless of the documentary evidence reaching back in some cases to or near to the Revolutionary War, showing them to be descendants of freed negroes.

We will require other evidence than that of Captain Jarvis and His Honor before classifying members of the group who are now causing trouble in Virginia by their claims of Indian descent, with the privilege of inter-marrying into the white race, permissible when a person can show his racial composition to be one-sixteenth or less Indian, the remainder white with no negro intermixture. We have found after very laborious and painstaking study of records of various sorts that none of our Virginia people now claiming to be Indian are free from negro admixture, and they are, therefore, according to our law classified as colored. In that class we include the melungeons of Tennessee.

We again thank you for your care in passing on this information and would be delighted if you ever visit in Virginia and in Richmond if you will come into our office. Miss Kelley and I would be greatly pleased to talk with you on this and kindred subjects and to show you the work which Miss Kelley is doing in properly classifying the population of Virginia by racial origin. She is doing work which, so far as I know, has never before been attempted.

Very sincerely yours,
W. A. Plecker, M.D.
State Registrar

Despite the misgivings of Tennessee's Archivist as to whether the Melungeons should actually be classified as Negroes, her 20 September reply left little doubt that she agreed with Plecker's aims. "Virginia is fortunate to have you and Miss Kelly doing such an important piece of research. I wish Tennessee could borrow you. Anyhow, what you are doing will be, in effect, for all the Southern States and there was never a time when it was more needed."[76]

In January of 1943, Plecker sent a circular to all public health and county officials in Virginia, listing, county by county, the surnames of all families suspected of having African ancestry. The cover letter stated that they were "mongrels" and were now trying to register as white. The names listed in the southwestern Virginia counties included Collins, Gibson, Moore, Goins, Bunch, Freeman, Bolin, Mullins, and others described as "Chiefly Tennessee Melungeons."

In his letter to county officials, Plecker referred to an earlier letter warning of "groups of 'free issues' or descendants of 'free mulattoes'" who were making a "determined effort to escape from the negro race."

Now that these people are playing up the advantages gained by being permitted to give "Indian" as the race of the child's parents on birth certificates, we see the great mistake made in not stopping earlier the organized propagation of this racial falsehood. They have been using the advantage thus gained as an aid to intermarriage into the white race and to attend white schools and now for some time, they have been refusing to register with war draft boards as negroes...

Some of these mongrels, finding that they have been able to sneak in their birth certificates unchallenged as Indians are now making a rush to register as white... Those attempting this fraud should be warned that they are liable to a penalty of one year in the penitentiary (Section 5099 of the Code). Several clerks have likewise been actually granting them licenses to marry whites, or at least marry amongst themselves as Indian or white. The danger of this error always confronts the clerk who does not inquire carefully as to the residence of the woman when he does not have positive information...

Please report all known or suspicious cases to the Bureau of Vital Statistics, giving names, ages, parents and as much other

---

[76] Correspondence located by S. J. Arthur in Tennessee State Library and Archives, Nashville, posted at http://www.geocities.com/bourbonstreet/inn/1024/plecker.html.

information as possible. All certificates of these people showing "Indian" or "white" are now being rejected and returned to the physician or midwife, but local registrars hereafter must not permit them to pass their hands uncorrected or unchallenged and without a note of warning to us. One hundred and fifty thousand other mulattoes in Virginia are watching eagerly the attempt of their pseudo-Indian brethren, ready to follow in a rush when the first have made a break in the dike.[77]

Plecker's campaign against the tri-racials of Virginia affected not only their draft status, but their educational opportunities and access to public facilities and services as well. His activities against tri-racial draftees and their families while America was at war with the racist Nazi regime seem ironic on the surface. However, Plecker's sympathies with Hitler's racial policies were deeper than the obvious parallels would indicate. Earlier, he had joined with Richmond realtor Earnest Cox to found the Anglo-Saxon Clubs of America. In the 1930s, Cox began a correspondence with Wilhelm Frick, the Nazi secretary of the interior, and spoke of the "common Teutonic heritage" of southern whites and Germans. Frick was later executed for his participation in the Holocaust. After the war, Cox corresponded with several former Nazi officials, some living in Argentina.[78]

Plecker and Cox were not alone among Virginians (and other Americans) in their admiration for Hitler's policies. In 1943, a eugenics student at the University of Virginia wrote admiringly of Hitler's policy of sterilizing "undesirables:" "This is a great step in eliminating the racial deficients." Virginia adopted a sterilization law in 1924, the same year as the Racial Integrity Act, and "Mr. Jefferson's University" became a hotbed of eugenics study. The University was proposed as a national center for eugenics by noted eugenicist Dr. Harry Laughlin; the proposal was unsuccessful, but Laughlin later received an honorary degree from Nazi-controlled Heidelberg University for achievements in the "science of racial cleansing."[79]

---

[77] Ibid., 234; W.A. Plecker, Virginia State Registrar, letter to various county officials, January 1943, cited in Elder, *Melungeons*, 190–92.

[78] Peter Hardin, "Eugenics in Virginia," Richmond *Times-Dispatch*, 26 November 2000, online edition.

[79] Ibid.

Virginia was not the only state pursuing eugenics policies, but with Plecker's guidance, was certainly the most active, particularly in regard to tri-racial groups. Plecker served as Virginia's Registrar of Vital Statistics until his retirement in 1946. He stated that he intended to spend his retirement studying Virginia's Indians, but never got the opportunity; he was killed by a truck as he crossed a street without looking for traffic. His successor continued Plecker's policies, although not as vigorously, until her retirement in 1959. The next registrar destroyed the Racial Integrity File, and years later another registrar permitted Indians to change their birth certificates to read "Indian." However, Virginia's Racial Integrity Act would not be officially repealed until the US Supreme Court struck it down in its 1971 *Loving v. Virginia* ruling.[80]

To reiterate a point made earlier, the refusal of tri-racials to accept classification as "colored" cannot be seen as a reflection of their personal racial attitudes. While many of these individuals undoubtedly shared the prevailing biases against blacks, the issue was not entirely one of pride or social status. To accept the status of "colored" meant accepting substandard educational and employment opportunities, limited access public facilities and services; in short, second-class citizenship. Such a status was difficult enough for blacks to accept, even though they had been born with it. For tri-racial people to be "demoted" in status in mid-life was certainly even more difficult to accept. As long as there was a possibility of being classified "Indian" or even "white," tri-racial people naturally tried to be identified as such.

Many of today's tri-racial descendants see Plecker as a villain who arbitrarily persecuted their parents and grandparents. However, in the view of Plecker and most Virginians (if not most Americans), these individuals were *not* white, and only whites were entitled to the full range of rights and privileges guaranteed to all American citizens. Race-mixing was unacceptable to the majority of white Americans. Plecker took the logical steps to prevent further mixing and to segregate those with mixed ancestry, and there was never any serious (white) opposition to his policies. Those who mourn the injustice done to tri-racials during Plecker's reign should expand their sympathies to *all* persons of color who suffered under America's repressive racial laws and attitudes.

---

[80] Rountree, *Pocahontas's People*, 237.

Walter Plecker's efforts had at least one positive effect on tri-racial communities. Many of them organized to fight Plecker's efforts to influence the Census Bureau and the Selective Service. These organizational efforts often involved research into the Indian identity of their respective groups, and a feeling of community among others. Within a generation or two, many of these groups would reject the labels and attitudes imposed on them by neighboring whites, and establish their own identities.

5

A TIME OF TRANSITION

During the late 1930s and 1940s, the Melungeons were featured in several newspaper and magazine articles. Virtually all of these articles assumed, accurately in most cases, that the reader had never heard of such people. Few of these pieces added any significant new information about the Melungeons; instead, most presented folk tales and increasingly fantastic theories of origin. While journalists found the Melungeons a source for interesting feature articles, scientists began the first serious academic research of the Melungeons and other tri-racials.

Nashville journalist James Aswell wrote about the Melungeons for the Nashville *Banner*. "Lost Tribes of Tennessee's Mountains" appeared in the *Banner* on August 22, 1937. The story mixed facts with folklore, with more emphasis on the latter. Aswell later compiled a collection of Tennessee folk tales, many of which he collected personally, into a volume entitled *God Bless The Devil! Liar's Bench Tales*, published under the supervision of the Federal Writer's Project by the University of North Carolina Press in 1940. Four of Aswell's stories were based on the Melungeons. The first, "Old Horny's Own," dealt with the origin and history of the Melungeons; portions of this story were quoted in Chapter Two.

The Federal Writer's Project was part of one of President Franklin Roosevelt's "New Deal" programs. Supervised by the Works Progress Administration, the Federal Writer's Project hired unemployed authors to assemble the 48–volume *Guide To The States*. Two writers on the Tennessee project, O. N. Walraven and Leo Zuber, wrote about Melungeons, but only Walraven's brief entry made it into the *Guide*, in a section about Oakdale, near Harriman: "In the village is a small colony of Melungeons, a dark-skinned people found only in the mountainous regions of East Tennessee and western North Carolina."[1]

Bonnie Ball, a schoolteacher and historian in southwestern Virginia, wrote several articles about the Melungeons in the 1940s. Ball's father had grown up near Newman's Ridge in Tennessee, and later invited two Melungeon families to live on his farm near Stickleyville, Virginia, where they worked the land and the livestock. Bonnie Ball later taught their children, and those of other Melungeon families, in the local elementary school.

Ball's first article on the Melungeons, "America's Mystery Race," appeared in *Read* magazine in May 1944. With minor variations, the article appeared in *Negro Digest* ("Mystery Men of the Mountains") in January 1945, the Virginia State Highway Bulletin ("Virginia's Mystery Race") in April 1945, and *Southern Literary Messenger* ("Who Are The Melungeons") in June 1945.

The 18 October 1947 issue of *Saturday Evening Post* gave the Melungeons their first national exposure since Will Allen Dromgoole's articles in *The Arena* in 1891. Like Dromgoole's articles, "Sons of the Legend" was resented by the people of Hancock County and Sneedville, Melungeon and white alike, for its portrayal of the area and its people. Early in the article, Worden brings up a bit of recent county history most would have preferred forgotten.

> Only once did the town ever get its name into newspapers farther away than Knoxville, when once some years before the war, Charlie Johns, a lank mountaineer, married Eunice Winstead, who was certainly not more than thirteen years old and was variously reported as being only nine. Their pictures and story made most of the United States newspapers in a dull news period.
>
> Charlie and Eunice still live near Sneedville, but nothing has been written about them for a long time. They do not want anything more written.[2]

---

[1] *Tennessee: A Guide to the State*, Federal Writer's Project, Works Progress Administration (New York: The Viking Press, 1939) 362.

[2] W. L. Worden, "Sons of the Legend," *Saturday Evening Post* (18 October 1947).

Obviously relying on the work of previous writers, Worden perpetuated the myth that the Melungeons were on Newman's Ridge when the first white settlers arrived.

> When the first Yankee and Scotch-Irish mountain men drifted down the Clinch River from its sources in Virginia toward the place where it meets the Holston to make the Tennessee River, they found in the rich farmland of the Clinch valley a strange people already settled. They were dark, tall, not exactly like Indians, certainly not at all like the escaped Negroes lurking on the outskirts of white slave-holding settlements. Even then they kept to themselves, had little to do with Andy Jackson's men and the others, the trappers, adventurers and farmers who came down the line of the river... Certainly they must have been there fairly early in the eighteenth century. Hale and Merritt's *History of Tennessee and Tennesseans* says a census of the settlements in 1795 listed 975 "free persons" in the East Tennessee mountain area, distinguishing between them and the white settlers. As there never was any considerable number of Negroes in the mountains, these must have been the strange people of the Clinch Valley.

Like Dromgoole, Worden stopped short of asserting that the Melungeons had African ancestry. However, he certainly suggests that others thought that was the case.

> But the other settlers apparently were unwilling to admit that they dark people were Caucasians, and the dividing line between "whites" and "Malungeons" began to be drawn—by the whites. Forty years later the division became serious. In the Tennessee Constitutional Convention of 1834, East Tennesseans succeeded in having the Malungeons officially classified as "free persons of color." This classification was equivalent to declaring them of Negro blood and preventing them from suing or even testifying in court in any case involving a Caucasian. The purpose was fairly obvious and the effect immediate. Other settlers simply moved onto what good bottom land the Malungeons had, and the dark people had no recourse except to

retire with what they could take with them to the higher ridge land which no other settlers wanted and where no court cases could arise. Some may have been on Newman's Ridge previously, but now the rest climbed the slopes to live, taking with them their families, a few household possessions, some stock and a burning resentment of this and other injustices, such as the fact that their children were not welcome in the settler's schools, only in Negro schools, which they declined to attend.[3]

Worden acknowledged the work of Will Allen Dromgoole, and the resentment that work engendered among Hancock Countians.

But her final estimate of the Malungeons did not please them, and they had a sort of revenge. Milum Bowen remembers that the ridge people created a jingle about the poetess and repeated it endlessly to each other. "I can't remember the rest of the words," he says, "but the last of it was 'Will Allen Damfool.'"[4]

Worden's "Sons of the Legend" recounted many of the legends and theories that had grown up around the Melungeons over the years, including the tales of Mahala Mullins, the "Celebrated Melungeon Case," moonshining, counterfeiting, and so on. The article also touched on some of the more recent problems faced by Melungeons.

The descendants are still farmers, for the most part, still have occasional trouble about their color. Within the last dozen years, disputes flared briefly in certain Hancock County districts about whether Malungeon children should go to white or Negro schools and during both wars of this century, Malungeons have had color trouble upon reporting to Southern cantonments. They still make a certain amount of tax-evading whiskey somewhere up the dim ravines, and now and then are hauled into court for it. Generally, they still avoid schools, except for the mission at Vardy, from which the Rev. Chester F. Leonard sends a few on to the University of Tennessee or to church colleges. One such

---

[3] Ibid.
[4] Ibid.

college, Maryville, has records of half a dozen entered, none graduated. Mr. Leonard, incidentally, says "The group is so intermingled that one cannot be sure of a typical specimen."[5]

Worden concluded "Sons of the Legend" with an accurate account of the reluctance of Hancock Countians to discuss the Melungeons, or to even speak the name.

> In the small Tennessee hill towns, now and then, a dark man will talk to a stranger, tell a few incidents heard or seen on Newman's Ridge or advise him, "See ___. If anybody knows, he will." Only ___ never does. A lovely woman may even, looking straight at the visitor with gray eyes, say, "My own grandfather had some Indian blood and perhaps some Spanish. We don't know much about the family, but there is a story that some of De Soto's men..."
> The lady may have small hands and feet, high cheekbones, straight hair and olive skin, and a regal carriage. She may talk for some time and tell much that is written in no books, some hearsay, some the most fanciful legend. But one word she will never say. She will never say, "Malungeon."[6]

In Hancock County, the reaction to the *Saturday Evening Post* article was more vehement that to Dromgoole's articles a half-century before. One reason for this reaction is that more Hancock Countians could read—thanks in large part to the work of the Vardy School. Another is the stature of the magazine itself; *Saturday Evening Post* was one of the most popular magazines in America, with a huge circulation. People all over America—even the world—read what Worden had to say about the Melungeons. And the people of Hancock County were not happy with what he had to say.

Of course, the biggest problem was the suggestion that the Melungeons had Negro ancestry. Worden, like Dromgoole, never actually comes out and says one way or the other. However, the frequent mention of that belief among many (including the state legislature)

---

[5] Ibid.
[6] Ibid.

suggests that there is at least some substance to the belief; as the old adage says, "where there's smoke, there's fire."

Non-Melungeons from Hancock County were displeased with the article's unflattering portrayal of Sneedville, which many outsiders consider a charming, if quite small, community. Locals did not welcome the retelling of the old scandal about Charlie and Eunice Johns. But most humiliating to non-Melungeons was the stigma of mixed race that now seemed attached to *all* Hancock Countians. Residents who traveled to Knoxville, Kingsport, or beyond were sometimes embarrassed to claim their home county for fear of being seen as one of "those" people. Years later, Charles Turner, the mayor of Sneedville and owner of the town's only drugstore, recalled that "college girls from Sneedville were called 'Melungeon.' It ruined college for them, and one of the girls came home in tears and never returned to get her degree."[7]

Claude Collins, then a student at the University of Tennessee in Knoxville, had never thought of himself as a Melungeon before reading Worden's article; in fact, he had never heard the word "Melungeon" before. There was no question, however, about who Worden was talking about. "[Those were] my relatives, my people in there," Collins recalled. "When I read the article, I was coming home to tell Mother about the story in the magazine... I don't guess I took time to look up the word to see what it meant." While the word "Melungeon" had no particular meaning to Claude, he quickly learned that it was a powerful epithet. "She looked at me and said 'Claude, don't you name that word any more!'"[8]

William Grohse, a Hancock County historian, believed that Worden never set foot in Melungeon territory, but relied on information gathered by his photographer, Dillon Ferris.[9] Nowhere in the article does Worden state that he personally visited Newman's Ridge or Blackwater, or that he himself spoke with anyone. He certainly seems confused about the geography of the area: "Newman's Ridge lies beyond Blackwater Swamp, and Blackwater lies beyond Sneedville."[10] Newman's Ridge

---

[7] Louise Davis, "Why Are They Vanishing?," Nashville *Tennesseean Sunday Magazine* (29 September 1963): 11.

[8] Collins interview, January 2002.

[9] William Paul Grohse, 15 August 1971, papers (Microfilm Roll # 7) East Tennessee State University.

[10] Worden, "Sons of the Legend."

actually begins its rise on the north side of Sneedville, about a block from the courthouse. One crosses the Ridge to go from Sneedville to Blackwater. Yet Worden seems determined to place Blackwater Swamp between Sneedville and Newman's Ridge: "From Sneedville, a few small roads lead northward toward the swamp and the ridge." And again he states, "The small roads lead up out of Sneedville across the swamp and end at the base of Newman's Ridge..."[11]

Although Worden claimed "Today, even the legend is in the process of being forgotten," "Sons of the Legend" was at least the fifth article published on the Melungeons in little over three years, and Worden's own article in a widely-circulated national magazine insured that the legend wouldn't be forgotten soon. He did acknowledge, however, the migration of Hancock Countians to cities, which was just beginning in 1947. Within the next ten years, hundreds of thousands of Appalachians would move to northern cities to escape the kind of poverty and isolation described by Worden. When Hancock Countians moved away, they left the label "Melungeon" behind; their children and grandchildren would never hear it. It was not the legend, but the reality that was in the process of being forgotten.

Worden suggested that the early Melungeons faced discrimination in the county schools: "Their children were not welcome in the settler's schools, only in Negro schools, which they declined to attend."[12] The problem with that statement is that there, at the time of the "settlers," there were no schools for blacks in the county. Brewton Berry pointed out that prior to Civil War, southern states took no responsibility for the education of its citizens. When they did assume responsibility, they made sharp distinctions between their responsibilities toward whites and non-whites.[13] Schools for white children were rare in that time and place; the likelihood that the early settlers in what is now Hancock County established schools for blacks—many, if not most, of whom were slaves—is slim indeed.

Many years later, schools for black children were established in the county. Claude Collins, who served as a county school administrator, recalled three black schools in the county. The Simpson School, named after the family that provided most of the students, was located on

---

[11] Ibid.
[12] Ibid.
[13] Berry, *Almost White*, 113.

Newman's Ridge above Sneedville. Two others were in Mulberry Valley."You could have a black school—or you could have a white school—with just ten students at that time, " recalled Collins. Black students who finished eighth grade and desired further education were sent to Morristown at county expense.[14]

Worden provided little information that hadn't already been published, but one original item was Kyle's Ford storekeeper Milum Bowen's quote concerning "Will Allen Damfool." However, it is remarkable that Bowen and the Reverend Chester Leonard are the only Hancock Countians quoted directly. The dark man and lovely woman quoted in the last two paragraphs are not named, and may well be composite characters. The article featured photographs of Elsie Gibson and her children, Laura Mullins and her children, Asa Gibson and his granddaughter Jewel, and Morgan Manis, Georgia Irene Manis, and Dr. Roy Doty—but none of them are quoted in the article. Worden's lack of direct, attributed quotes suggests either the author had little, if any, personal contact with county residents, or that practically none of those residents chose to speak about Melungeons to an outsider. A combination of both seems most likely.

"Melungeon" was still an epithet to those relatively few people who had ever heard the word. The people of Newman's Ridge, Blackwater, and Vardy certainly didn't use it themselves; as researcher Edward Price noted four years later, "There is no group of people who call themselves Melungeons or who would recognize themselves as thus separated from the rest of the country population."[15] "Melungeon" was a term used, when it was used at all, to describe *someone else*, usually in a derogatory manner. As such, it was not often used in polite company, or by those who were friendly with their dark-skinned neighbors. Worden acknowledged as much at the end of his article: "But one word she will never say. She will never say, "Malungeon.""[16] An outsider who ventured into Hancock County and started asking questions about Melungeons would get a cold reception at best from most residents. It seems likely that Worden never took that risk.

Worden's article in the *Saturday Evening Post* engendered a resentment toward the press and other outsiders who came to ask

---

[14] Collins interview, January 2002.

[15] Price, "The Melungeons," 258.

[16] Worden, "Sons of the Legend."

questions about this group of mixed-race people. This development was unfortunate because the first truly scientific studies of tri-racial people were about to be undertaken. After feeling humiliated by writers like Dromgoole, Estabrook, and Worden, few tri-racials were willing to cooperate with these new researchers. They still lived in the segregated South, and the last thing they needed was yet another writer claiming that they were Negroes.

From Folklore to Fact

As the pseudo-science of eugenics lost favor in the academic community, in large part due to its association with the Nazis, more reputable scientists began studying the phenomenon of the tri-racial groups scattered across the eastern United States. One of the first to publish his findings was William Gilbert, a researcher with the Library of Congress. In 1946, he compiled information on the ten largest groups of tri-racial groups (also listed in Chapter One): Brass Ankles, Cajans and Creoles, Croatans, Guineas, Issues, Jackson Whites, Melungeons, Moors and Nanticokes, Red Bones, and Wesorts.[17]

Gilbert described these groups as "racial islands...complex mixtures in varying degrees of white, Indian, and Negro blood...mixed outcasts from both the white and Negro castes of America." Gilbert felt that these groups deserved more study and hoped to generate interest by compiling a survey of these groups, noting population numbers, common surnames, physical characteristics, social status ("near white," "between that of whites and Negroes," "regarded as 'colored'"), environment and economy, and social organization.[18]

While Gilbert included some groups with a varying degrees of Indian self-identity, including the Nanticokes, the Croatans (later known as Lumbee), and Issues (Monacans), he did not include Virginia's Powhatan groups—even though the Pamunkey, Rapahannock, and especially the Chickahominy were still struggling with the legacy of Plecker and the "colored" classification.

In 1950, Edward Price of the University of California at Berkeley completed his doctoral dissertation on eastern "mixed-blood populations." As a professor of geography at the University of Cincinatti,

---

[17] Gilbert, "Memorandum," 438–77.
[18] Ibid.

he concentrated on the Melungeons for a 1951 article in the *Geographical Review*. Price acknowledged that folklore made up much of what people "knew" about Melungeons.

> In the native vocabulary of East Tennessee and adjacent parts of neighboring states the word "Melungeon" is widely used. To some people it is only a general derogatory term to be bestowed on anyone who momentarily arouses their antagonism. Middle Tennesseans are said to have applied it to their former East Tennessee enemies in the bitter period after the Civil War. And at times the Melungeons have had to fill the place of the bogeyman in holding children in the straight and narrow path—"The Melungeons will get you!"
>
> The persistent folk tale, however, insists that the Melungeons are unusual racially; it defines them as a dark-skinned mixed-blood group of uncertain origin whose center is on Newman's Ridge in Hancock County. An oriental appearance is attributed to them, but they are most commonly thought to be at least partly of Portuguese descent. The peculiarity of the mixture, however, is its supposed inability to blend color in crosses with whites; the Melungeon appearance may be lost for a generation or two, only to show up again in full strength.[19]

Price recounts some of the traditional Melungeon legends but noted that the "core of reality within the legend is not easily discovered."

> There is no group of people who call themselves Melungeons or who would recognize themselves as thus separated from the rest of the country population. Non-Melungeons, however, are in general agreement as to who are Melungeons. Identification centers about several localized concentrations. These Melungeons are considered to be mixed in race; it is noteworthy that they comprise a rather small number of families as known by their surnames, prominent among which are Collins, Mullins, Gibson, Goins, Freeman, and Sexton.[20]

---

[19] Edward Price, "Melungeons: A Mixed-Blood Strain of the Southern Appalachians," *Geographical Review* 41/2 (1951): 256.

[20] Ibid., 258.

Price observes that most of the Melungeons were "indistinguishable from other white farmers; many of them would not even be called brunet."

> Many of the dark-skinned group belong to families all or some of whose other members lack such a trait. Thus, though an unusual strain is indicated, the Melungeons evidently do not exist as a physically separate community; nor is their social separation official, for they attend white schools rather than the school for the few Negroes of the area...The recognition of Melungeons in this area is tacit; no strong lines are drawn. Parents may warn their daughters against entanglement with people of this strain. Some members of the community may regret to see a lax society allow a Melungeon to rise to a position of influence, but to others this is a matter of small concern. Though the separation of the Melungeons is not sharp, and though there is considerable intermarriage, it will probably take more than one generation to wipe out such a deep-seated caste distinction in this quiescent rural society.[21]

Although he was naturally curious about *who* the Melungeons were, as a geographer Price was primarily concerned with *where* the Melungeons were. Hancock County was the center of the population; Price estimated the number of Melungeons in the county at 1,000. Melungeon populations were also noted in Bristol and Kingsport, Tennessee, Dungannon (Scott County), Virginia, and Wise County, Virginia. In addition, a group of Melungeons was cited in the eastern Kentucky counties of Letcher and Knott; while not identified locally as Melungeons, many of this group of a few hundred had the names Collins, Gibson, and Sexton.[22]

South of Hancock County, Graysville in Rhea County, Tennessee, at the base of Walden's Ridge, was a concentrated Melungeon community; Price estimated the Melungeons made up thirty to forty percent of the population of 800. This community was dominated by a single surname: Goins. Another group of about two dozen families in

---

[21] Ibid., 259–60
[22] Ibid., 260–63.

Bazeltown, near Harriman, Tennessee, was also dominated by the Goins surname, and was the only Melungeon group to be "socially classified as colored." Other Melungeon communities were found near Nashville and in Bell's Bend on the Cumberland River.[23]

Price traced the migration of Melungeon families from the boundary region of Virginia and North Carolina to northeastern Tennessee, spreading as far as Magoffin County, Kentucky, and Highland County, Ohio. He also suggests that the original Melungeons came from a "general society of mixed-bloods in Virginia and the Carolinas consisting of certain loci of concentration and a floating population that connected them. Evidence from studies of other mixed-blood groups indicates that the Redbones of southwestern Louisiana and a colored group in Darke County, Ohio, also sprang from this society."[24]

In June of 1953, Price, by then a professor at Los Angeles State College, published "A Geographic Analysis of White-Negro-Indian Racial Mixtures in Eastern United States" in the *Annals* of the Association of American Geographers. This article covered nearly all the groups listed in Gilbert's 1946 "memorandum:" the Melungeons, the Croatans, the Redbones, the Cajans, the Issues, the Guineas, the Wesorts, the Moors and Nanticolkes, and the Jackson Whites. The Brass Ankles of South Carolina were the only group listed by Gilbert that were not covered in the section entitled "Larger Mixed-Blood Strains," but they were included in a section on smaller groups.[25].

Price concluded that the tri-racials arose from diverse sources, but that the name "Goins" seemed to be a "peculiar marker of these mixed-bloods," associated with the Melungeons, Redbones, and others. The name "Chavis" was also noted in several groups, primarily among the Croatans but also the Melungeons and Redbones. On the other hand, many of these groups "seem unrelated or unimportantly related one to the other." Most lived in the Coastal Plain or in Appalachia, primarily in the south and often near state lines or on the borders between hills and plains.

---

[23] Ibid., 263–64.

[24] Ibid., 270–71.

[25] Edward T. Price, "A Geographic Analysis of White-Negro-Indian Racial Mixtures in the Eastern United States," Association of American Geographers, *Annals* 43 (June 1953): 138–55.

Price cited research indicating that the first of these mixed-race people descended from free blacks, or blacks who had been indentured rather than permanently enslaved. He suggested that the tri-racial groups represented "similar responses to similar social conditions, each in a different area... The social attitude of these mixed-bloods must have been such that they found it congenial to take up with others of their own kind. They seem to have persisted in the static societies of rural areas stimulated perhaps by tradition of Indian blood or pride of early freedom."[26]

In 1957, Calvin Beale coined the term "triracial isolates" to describe "a class more numerous than the Indians remaining in the East, more obscure than those in the West, less assured than the white man or negro who regards his link of Indian descent as a touch of the heroic or romantic." A demographer for the Agricultural Marketing Service of the US Department of Agriculture, Beale published "American Triracial Isolates" in the December 1957 issue of *Eugenics Quarterly*.[27]

Beale, a Washington, DC native, began working for the U. S. Census Bureau in 1946 in preparation for the 1950 census. "There was at least one person there [at the Census Bureau] in authority who knew of William Gilbert's work," Beale recalled, "and who knew that... many of these groups [Gilbert] had looked at had been counted in the Census inconsistently, say, from one census to another as to their race, or that different enumerators would treat them differently within the same census." Census officials had an idea which Beale later conceded was "a little bit misbegotten." Census officials would pay close attention to the counties listed by Gilbert in his survey of "racial islands;" any persons listed as "Indian" would be placed in a separate "other" category. This would separate these tri-racial people from federally-recognized Indians.

After the 1950 Census was taken, Beale, who was working on a different project, had access to every portfolio of Census returns. "Any of them that were in these counties had a little stamp on it; I think it said 'Mixed Stock.' Then, pretty much using the surnames that Gilbert had, I went through to see how these people were counted."[28]

---

[26] Ibid., 149–55.

[27] Calvin L. Beale, "American Triracial Isolates: Their Status and Pertinence to Genetic Research," *Eugenics Quarterly* 4/4 (December 1957): 187–96.

[28] Calvin Beale, Wayne Winkler, in-person interview, 22 June 2002, Kingsport, Tennessee.

The study of tri-racial people interested Beale enough to continue studying them on his own, from the records and later from field work. He was particularly interested in groups that Gilbert had missed or had little information about. He visited the Gointown group in Rockingham County, North Carolina in 1954, and other groups over the years, including the Alabama Creeks, the Carmel, Ohio, Melungeons and the Robeson County Smilings. When the Census Bureau cut back personnel in the 1950s, Beale went to work for the US Department of Agriculture, and by 1957 had compiled enough information on tri-racial groups to publish an article in a magazine with an unfortunate name.

> Today, I wish that I didn't have to say it was in *Eugenics Quarterly*—not because *Eugenics Quarterly* was a bad journal. It was a very reputable journal. [The editor] heard me give a talk at the Population Association of America, which is the professional association of demographers, in 1953. They were going to publish the lists, the estimates, county by county, which the *Rural Sociology* magazine didn't want to do, and when they didn't want to do that, I just said "Thank you very much, I won't publish.' But "eugenics" had become a bad word, particularly after World War II, and it wasn't more than a couple more years before the journal took a different name.[29]

The term "tri-racial isolates" was, in part, borrowed from a term common among anthropologists, "racial isolates." "I wondered what to call these people *collectively*. Because I wasn't interested in an individual group, but in providing, as [Gilbert] had done, a synoptic of all of these groups. And I limited myself only to those who had, either by self-identity or local ascription, three races—whether or not any individuals in [those groups] were necessarily of tri-racial descent."[30]

Beale estimated the tri-racial population as at least 77,000, distributed in over 100 counties in 17 states, in groups ranging from 50 persons to more than 20,000. His explanation for the origin of these groups is simple:

---

[29] Ibid.
[30] Ibid.

...[T]hey seem to have formed through miscegenation between Indians, whites, and Negroes—slave or free—in the Colonial and early Federal periods. In places the offspring of such unions—many of which were illegitimate under the law—tended to marry among themselves. Within a generation or so this practice created a distinctly new racial element in society, living apart from other races. The forces tending to perpetuate such groups, and the strength of these forces, differed from place to place. Some groups subsequently dispersed or were assimilated during the nineteenth century. Some waxed in numbers; others waned. Most have persisted to the present day.

Beale excluded from his study Indian groups such as the Narragansett, Shinnecock, and Pamunkey because, even though they had "absorbed both white and Negro blood," they had "retained their tribal identity and historical continuity." Other Indian groups, such as the Lumbees, the Mattaponi, the Monacans, the Potomac, the Nanticokes, and the Rappahannocks, were counted as "triracial isolates."[31].
    Beale points out that "the designation of these groups as tri-racial is often the conclusion of the investigator rather than a reflection of public opinion in the area concerned."

In general all local informants will agree that the mixed population is partly white. (Blue eyes are commonly in evidence to validate this.) The white informant will insist that the mixed-blood people are partly Negro. Perhaps he will agree that they are partly Indian, perhaps not. The mixed-blood individual will usually insist—with vehemence, if necessary—that there is no Negro ancestry in his family (although he may not make this claim for all other families in the settlement) but that he is partly Indian. In a minority of communities unmistakable elements of Indian culture have been found. Presence of Negro ancestry may or may not be evident in some families from the occurrence of Negro hair forms or facial features. If evident, it tends to jeopardize claims of the group to non-Negro status. In sum, the groups described are with few exceptions considered only of

---

[31] Beale, "American Triracial Isolates," 187, 193, 194–95.

white and Indian descent by their members but are regarded to be partly Negro by neighboring whites or Negroes.[32]

Social and physical isolation, both imposed and voluntary, limited the choice of marriage partners, and Beale noted that inbreeding had led to genetic defects among some of the groups. The Jackson Whites of New York and New Jersey, for example, were well-known for albinism and polydactylism (extra fingers), while tri-racials in West Virginia reported hereditary deformities of the joints.

The Wesorts of southern Maryland were especially noted for both consanguinity and hereditary deficiencies. The Wesorts were predominantly Roman Catholic, and ecclesiastical dispensation is required for marriages between first or second cousins. One-sixth of the Wesort marriages performed in a particular parish over a century required such dispensation. The National Institute of Health studied the hereditary diseases among the Wesorts, particularly the exceptionally high incidences of albinism and a dental defect called dentinogenesis imperfecta, which generally caused its victims to lose all their teeth in early adulthood. Other genetic conditions under study among the Wesorts included lop ears, polycystic kidneys, deaf mutism, glaucoma, syndactylism, polydactylism, congenital cataracts, convergent and divergent strabismus (nonparalytic eye squint), and hyperstatic bone disease.[33]

Beale includes a table which enumerated all the groups and sub-groups listed in Gilbert's 1945 study. He used the 1950 Census records to determine the tri-racial population. For that Census, enumerators were instructed to list people of mixed white, Negro, and Indian ancestry by the names they were known by locally; these people would then be classified for publication as "other nonwhite races." However, of the estimated 77, 000 tri-racials enumerated in 116 counties, only 1,000 were listed under colloquial terms or with the race entry left blank. Beale acknowledges that the colloquial names were offensive to the people so termed, and that common courtesy or an instinct for self-preservation led many enumerators to lists groups as Indian or white. 33,000 were counted as Indian, 29,000 as white, and 14,000 as Negro, and more than

---

[32] Ibid., 188.
[33] Ibid., 189–90.

40 percent of the total—over 32,000—lived in North Carolina, with the vast majority being listed as "Indian."[34]

Over time, Beale notes, the groups that experienced change in their social status tended to go a "lighter classification." The Melungeons, for example, were commonly listed as "mulatto" prior to the Civil War. By 1950, nearly all were listed as white.[35]

In citing the high fertility rates among tri-racials, Beale asserts that if these rates continued, the tri-racial population would increase two-and-a-half times in each generation, forcing a wider distribution of that population. However, he also notes that as these groups dispersed geographically, marriage outside the group would become more common. In the meantime, Beale contends, these groups offer a unique opportunity for study by geneticists.[36]

Although his article was aimed at geneticists, Beale was a demographer who studied the geographic distribution of these populations. He accepted the racial classifications of the US Census Bureau at face value, and had no way of knowing whether the groups listed as "triracial," or individuals within those groups, actually had African ancestry. As he acknowledged, that judgement was "often the conclusion of the investigator." Yet, by classifying these groups as "triracial," he added a scientific legitimacy to long-standing assumptions which had social and legal ramifications.

At the time Beale's article was published, in late 1957, the modern civil rights movement in America was beginning to take shape following the bus boycott in Montgomery, Alabama, which began two years earlier. All over the south, segregation laws and practices were being challenged, and African-Americans were asserting their rights as citizens of the United States.

However, those segregation laws and practices were still in effect in the 1950s, and tri-racial people were doing all they could to avoid being categorized as black. Scientists like Price and Beale unintentionally reinforced many long-standing racial assumptions about tri-racial groups. After hearing that point made in a lecture in 2002, Beale commented, "I have to admit that I never thought of that before." In recent years, the term "triracial isolate" has become offensive to some, primarily because

---

[34] Ibid., 190–191, 194.

[35] Ibid., 191.

[36] Ibid., 192.

some individuals feel the term "isolates" suggests that they are inbred—an implication that was not intended by Beale, who says, "I don't really know what has happened to that term... Over time, certain words get rejected, their meaning changes."[37]

As the conflict between blacks and whites gathered momentum, those whose status was somewhere in between often found life extremely complicated. For many groups, the simplest solution was to stress their Indian heritage and culture, and become officially recognized as a tribe.

Tribal Identification

The first tri-racial group to gain official recognition as a tribe was the southeastern North Carolina group known as the Croatans. Most of the 40,000 or so Croatans lived in Robeson County. Their Indian ancestry is unknown, though some researchers suspect that the Croatans descended from the Cheraw tribe. The Croatans were also widely believed to be descendants of the Lost Colony. They never fought against whites until the Civil War, when they were drafted by Confederates as laborers along with Negroes. Many deserted, while others were suspected of aiding Union troops. In 1864, Home Guards captured and shot three members of the Lowry family. Henry Berry Lowry witnessed the incident, and soon led a band of "desperadoes." This group included Indians, deserters from the Union army and several blacks, and they terrorized the region for eight years before Lowry disappeared.

As Brewton Berry wrote, "All agree, friend and foe alike, that Henry Berry Lowry was the making of the Indians. He focused attention on their grievances. He let the white man know that they would never accept classification as Negroes. To his people, he gave courage, hope, and determination."[38]

Hamilton McMillan, a white man, spearheaded an effort to officially recognize the Croatans as a tribe, and in 1885 the North Carolina state legislature passed an act recognizing the group as the Croatan Indians. This act established segregated schools specifically for Croatans. Tribal recognition had a positive effect on the community; the Croatans built schools and churches, and in 1887 established Croatan Normal School, later renamed Pembroke State College for Indians.

---

[37] Beale interview, June 2002.
[38] Berry, *Almost White*, 154–55.

Eventually, however, the Croatans became dissatisfied with their name. "Croatan" had gradually become an epithet, especially when shortened to "Cro." Even the dictionary definition of "Croatan" became "people of mixed Indian, white, and Negro blood living in North Carolina." In 1911, they succeeded in removing the name "Croatan" from their official state title, and became "Indians of Robeson County." This title was apparently too vague to suit either the Indians or the legislature, and in 1913 the legislature declared them Cherokees. That designation seemed to please everyone except the federally-recognized Eastern Band of Cherokees who lived on a reservation in Jackson, Swain, and Graham counties in the mountains of western North Carolina. The tribe protested that there was no historical, linguistic, or cultural connection between the two groups. The former Croatans tried to get federal recognition as "The Siouan Tribes of the Lumber River," but failed.[39]

A major stumbling block in gaining any sort of federal recognition as a tribe was the fact that the Croatans had no native language or cultural tradition. They had, in the words of a reporter, "adopted the white man's language, lifestyle and Baptist and Methodist religions so long ago that no one remembers when anything was different." In 1914, Indian agent O. M. McPherson declared that the Croatans were "an amalgamation of the Hatteras Indians with Gov. White's Lost Colony."[40]

In 1953, the state legislature formally designated the tribe Lumbee Indians. On June 7, 1956, the US Congress officially designated them the "Lumbee Indians of North Carolina," but did not make them eligible for any federal services or a reservation.[41]

The Nanticokes of Delaware also struggled for years to gain Indian status. A court case in 1855 established that the Nanticokes were a mix of white, black, and Indian. An 1875 law taxed Negroes for support of their schools, and Nanticokes were included. The Nanticokes challenged this in court, and in 1881 Delaware's legislature authorized them to establish their own school and exempted them from the tax. In 1902, Nanticoke representatives appeared before the legislature demanding recognition as Indians rather than "colored persons." The result was "An

---

[39] Ibid.

[40] Bryce Nelson, "Lumbee Indians of N.C. Think They Have Answer," *Atlanta Journal and Constitution*, Sunday, 15 May 1977, online edition.

[41] Berry, *Almost White*, 159.

Act to Better Establish the Identity of a Race of People Known as the Offspring of the Nanticoke Indians," a legislative action officially recognizing the Nanticokes as Indians.

In 1916, the Delaware legislature, in appropriating funds for a new Nanticoke school, offended the tribe by referring to them as "Moors" and assigning a black teacher to the school. This act reflected the fact that most white people in Delaware believed the Nanticokes to be mulattoes. The Nanticokes withdrew their children and started their own school. Later, Nanticoke children were accepted in the Haskell Indian Institute in Lawrence, Kansas.[42]

During World War II, Nanticokes faced challenges to their racial status when they entered the military. After the war, the Nanticokes continued to emphasize their Indian heritage, wearing feathered headdresses for tourists and participating in Thanksgiving festivities. However, as Brewton Berry points out, even some of the Nanticokes themselves questioned their Indian identity.

> Many of them take inordinate pride in their Indian ancestry, vigorously dispute every hint of Negro blood, and carefully avoid contacts with those they regard as an inferior race. But there are others who say, "This Indian business is a lot of foolishness," who are indifferent to the issue of racial purity, and who accept philosophically the colored status which their society ascribes to them.[43]

In Rhode Island, the Narragansetts organized as tribe in 1935 and held periodic "powwows" for tourists. Both whites and blacks questioned the authenticity of the tribe. One white resident told Berry, "I can remember when Chief Red Owl was just a colored man name of Packard, working at the college in Kingston," while a black community leader commented, "Why don't those people quit playing Indian?... I've got more Indian blood in me than any of them."[44]

Gilbert identified several "mixed Indian peoples" in his 1945 survey, including the Mashpee, Pequot, and Wampanoag in

---

[42] Gilbert's 1945 study considered the Nanticokes and the Moors to be two separate groups, with only a few family names in common. Gilbert, "Memorandum," 445.

[43] Berry, *Almost White*, 136–42, 166.

[44] Ibid., 28–29.

Massachusetts, the Mohegan and Pequot in Connecticut, the Shinnecock and Poosepatuck in New York, the Machepunga in North Carolina, and of course the Virginia tribes—the Chickahominy, Mattaponi, Nansemond, Pamunkey, Potomac, Rappahannock, and Monacan (Issues). To that list, Brewton Berry added other Indian groups who were suspected of having little Indian blood, having retained almost nothing of their language and customs. These included the Matinecock of Long Island, New York, the Waccamaws of North Carolina, and the Wicocomico, Accohannock, and Werowocomo of Virginia.[45]

Official recognition was not forthcoming for most of these groups; North Carolina granted official Indian status to the Croatans in 1885, and the state of Delaware officially recognized the Nanticokes in 1902, but other "mixed Indian people" failed to gain such recognition. Even when local and state governments identified these people as "Indians," local residents, both black and white, were skeptical of their claims and considered them the equivalent of mulattoes. As one attorney told Berry, "Around here, these Brass Ankles will tell you they are Indians, descended from Pocahontas. Pocahontas? Why, poky nigger would be more like it." The registrar in Amherst County, Virginia, asserted, "Their ambition seems to be limited to securing recognition first as whites, and, if that fails, as Indians." An official with the National Association for the Advancement of Colored People felt that these "Indians" would be better off confronting the racial issue head-on: "They think they can solve their problems with feathers... They ought to forget all that foolishness and join with us. We could do more for them than anybody else."[46]

Most tri-racials, whether they claimed Indian status or not, were subject to the same social and legal restrictions faced by blacks. Those who chose to live apart from whites were generally left alone. Those who chose to consider themselves white—or at least to assert the same civil rights as whites—were in for a harder time.

---

[45] Gilbert, "Memorandum," 447; Berry, *Almost White*, 32.
[46] Berry, *Almost White*, 57, 62, 71.

Tri-Racials in the Civil Rights Era

On January 18, 1958, a hundred or so members of the Ku Klux Klan gathered for a rally near Maxton, in Robeson County, North Carolina. The population of the county was evenly divided between whites, blacks, and Lumbee Indians, and the Lumbees were the focus of this particular rally. According to the Klan, the Lumbees were "forgetting their place;" it was rumored that a Lumbee woman was dating a white man, and a Lumbee family had moved into a white neighborhood. The Klan burned a few crosses and publicized their rally across the county.

> At eight o'clock the Klansmen began to assemble, shotguns in hand. The Grand Wizard was present in full regalia. A huge banner emblazoned with the letters KKK was unfurled. A public address system was installed, and above the microphone there flickered a single electric light bulb. There were frequent flashes from newsmen's cameras.
>
> Across the road some five hundred Lumbees had gathered, also bearing arms. Except for their pungent jibes and raucous hoots, they were calm and orderly. The Klansmen ignored them.
>
> At a given signal the Indians fanned out and crossed the highway, shouting war cries and firing into the air. The Klansmen dropped their guns and made for their cars, leaving all their paraphernalia behind. The Indians smashed the loudspeaker, proudly grabbed the Klan banner, and bore aloft the rag-draped cross which the Klansmen, in their haste, failed to set afire.
>
> At this moment sixteen members of the highway patrol arrived on the scene, escorted the terrified Klansmen to safety, and proceeded to disarm the Indians, who offered no resistance.
>
> No one was hurt, despite the thousands of rounds of ammunition that had been fired...Only one arrest was made—a Klansman who was charged with drunkenness. The whole affair lasted barely thirty minutes.[47]

Newspapers across America told of the "Battle of Maxton," and the Lumbees were widely praised for routing the Klan. Few of the

---

[47] Berry, *Almost White*, 10–11.

newspapers took any notice of the three-way system of segregation in effect in Robeson County. There were three different county school systems—one for whites, one for blacks, and one for Lumbees. The courthouse had three sets of washrooms, and the movie theatre had three different seating areas.[48]

For nearly all the tri-racial groups, particularly those in the southern states, segregation was a daily reminder of their social status. There were exceptions; despite a few squabbles over whether Melungeons and whites should attend the same schools, most Melungeons were legally considered white. Legal acceptance is one thing; however, social acceptance is quite another. Even where tri-racials were considered black, the local customs and mores often differentiated between the two groups, granting the tri-racials a marginally higher status than blacks—but certainly lower than that of whites.

Brewton Berry cited instances of discrimination against tri-racials in hospital wards, libraries, jails, even in 4–H clubs and Home Demonstration Club meetings. A Red Cross official told Berry, "We conduct all kinds of classes—nutrition, first aid, and all kinds of things… No, we haven't done anything among the Melungeons. You see, we conduct classes only where they are asked for, and the Melungeons haven't asked us for any."[49]

Local attitudes toward tri-racials, particularly the belief that they had Negro ancestry, influenced the level of service they received from social and governmental agencies. A Farm Security Administration agent told Berry, "Morally those Brass Ankles are very low. *This is because of the Negro blood.* I would not say they are immoral; they are nonmoral; they just don't have any moral codes." Most whites considered tri-racials to be a burden to the community. A citizen of Hillsboro, Ohio, referring to Carmel Melungeons, said, "Lately these Carmelites have been moving to Dayton and Akron and Springfield and Columbus. We hope the rest of them will move. You can't do anything to improve those people. We've

---

[48] Nelson, "Lumbee Indians." Calvin Beale notes that there were actually *four* separate elementary school systems in Robeson County. "The Lumbees wouldn't accept the Smilings, who had a Goins base to them, just as the Lumbees do," Beale recalled, referring to a tiny tri-racial group that lived near the Lumbees. Beale interview, June 202.

[49] Berry, *Almost White*, 104–111.

had 'em long enough. It's time some other community had them on their hands."[50]

Old superstitions died hard, even among educated whites. Some foresaw dire consequences in permitting tri-racials to marry whites. One college-educated housewife remarked, "They will get by with it for a while, but what if a black child is born to them?" As Berry writes, "This 'black baby' is no myth to the vast majority of those with whom I talked, but instead is solid, scientific fact, amply supported by second- and third-hand reports of actual instances.[51]

Many, if not most, southern whites believed that marriage to a tri-racial was equivalent to marriage to an African-American—in other words, socially unacceptable. An attorney in Summerville, South Carolina, related the story of a Brass Ankle who went to college and got a good job in Raleigh. The young man became engaged to the daughter of a prominent attorney. The attorney wrote to the narrator asking about the young man's background. "I hated to be the obstacle in the way of this boy's progress. At the same time, I did have some responsibility to the girl and her family—and responsibility to the truth, too. So I wrote and told him this was a fine boy and had done well, but he came from a class of people suspected of not being pure white. I didn't say he had nigger blood. You have to be careful about that. Well, the wedding didn't come off... I've always felt a little guilty about what I did, but I had to do it."[52]

However, racial etiquette in the south allowed some leeway. One of the strongest southern taboos was addressing non-whites as "Mister" or "Ma'am." Berry asked a dentist's receptionist if she referred to Croatans as "Mr." or "Mrs."

"That all depends," she replied.

"Depends on what?" asked Berry

"Well," she said with a wink, "some Croatans have money."[53]

---

[50] Ibid., 55–56, 136.
[51] Ibid., 135.
[52] Ibid., 178–79.
[53] Ibid., 82.

Tri-Racials and Education

Many tri-racial groups, such as the Melungeons, had achieved a "near-white" status in their home communities by the 1950s. The question of education, however, became a major issue as tri-racials attempted to take full advantage of their local schools. Though Melungeons in Hancock County, Tennessee, were accorded nearly all the legal rights enjoyed by whites, some white parents argued that Melungeon children should not attend school with whites.[54] The school issue was a sore spot among tri-racials, most of whom refused to send their children to Negro schools. However, they were not welcome at white schools.

In Graysville, Tennessee, where Melungeons were also treated more or less as white, researcher Brewton Berry reported in 1963 that local teachers considered Melungeon children apathetic and stupid. Sixteen years later, another report commented on the generally "apathetic" attitude of the Graysville Melungeons, "noticable even in the children, [which] irritates their teachers... Melungeon children receive little to no encouragement from their parents in regard to their school work." Some Melungeon families in southeastern Tennessee were not apathetic, however, about the prospect of sending their children to school with black children. When the school system outside Rhea County tried to force Melungeon children to attend a Negro school, parents kept the children out of school or moved to neighboring districts. One mother told Berry, "I'd sooner my chilluns grow up ig'nant like monkeys than send 'em to that nigger school."[55]

Schools for tri-racial children—with the notable exception of the Vardy School in Hancock County—were generally far below the standard of nearby schools for white children. Most of the education of tri-racials was conducted in primitive schoolhouses—one reason for their high rates of illiteracy. Many of the schools were designated "Indian schools" to mollify resentful parents.[56]

When tri-racials did attend school with whites, their home environments often left them unprepared to compete with more advantaged students. One teacher observed, "We have a good many [tri-racial children] in this school. As a rule they are somewhat backward.

---

[54] Worden, "Sons of the Legend."

[55] Berry, *Almost White*, 19; Evans, "The Graysville Melungeons," 7, 15.

[56] Berry, *Almost White*, 114.

Their intelligence is all right, but they come from such poor backgrounds that they cannot keep up with the other pupils. They seem to feel that they are inferior." However, tri-racial children were generally unwelcome in white schools. One school principal said, "A few Melungeon families live in this district, but I don't encourage them to send their children here. We don't have any of them in school now. Had some a few years ago, but they weren't very happy. I don't believe in going out of my way to hunt for trouble. I don't want any of them in my school if I can help it."[57]

School boards generally treated these "Indian schools" as they did schools for black children: they ignored them and gave them only enough support to keep their doors open. The teachers assigned to these schools were often those considered the least qualified, and were sometimes licensed with temporary permits which were renewed yearly. One school trustee told Berry, "That teacher they've got down there—he's no good, and everybody knows it. The other trustees say he's good enough for the Croatans."[58]

Teachers did not consider these schools to be plum assignments, either. One teacher in South Carolina recalled,

> After my freshman year in college I had to drop out and make some money before going on with my education. So I accepted an appointment as teacher of that Brass Ankle school. When I got there I found out that they had arranged for me to board at the home of one of the school families, about a half a mile from the school. When I saw the family, I had the shock of my life. Some of them looked all right, but a few of them were pretty dark. I felt like I was living in a house with niggers... They did everything they could to make me comfortable. My room was clean, and they fed me fine. But I couldn't enjoy ny meals, setting there at the table with some of those people...After a couple of days, I knew I couldn't stand living there all year... So, the first chance I got, I went to town, five miles away, and found a place to live. Had to arrange to get out to school every morning and back in the afternoon, and it cost me some money. Then I told those people I had found a good

---

[57] Ibid., 129–30.
[58] Ibid., 128.

friend in town, and he wanted me to live with him. I guess they figured out the trouble, but they never let on, and I tried to be as nice to them as I could. I hated to do 'em that way, but I couldn't have lived in that house eight months.[59]

Like all parents, tri-racial people wanted the best education possible for their children. Often that involved moving away from regions where one's family was known and considered "not white." Those who moved to northern urban and industrial areas were generally successful in escaping the stigma and limitations they faced at home; these cities were full of swarthy Caucasians from various ethnic backgrounds, and in most areas, the schools were integrated anyway. Those who remained in the south often found that their new community was even more color-conscious than their former home. In the wake of the U. S. Supreme Court's 1955 *Brown vs. Board of Education* decision, which led to the eventual integration of southern schools, many southern communities were more determined than ever to keep the races separate. They weren't about to permit children of "questionable" race to integrate their schools.

In the mid-1950s, Allen and Laura Platt moved from Holly Hill, South Carolina to Mount Dora, located in central Florida's Lake County. The family consisted of Mr. and Mrs. Platt, a six-year-old niece, named Violet, and six children, ages 9–19. (Three older children did not accompany the family to Florida.) When children began school, some local parents complained about their skin color. Sheriff Willis McCall, an avowed white supremacist, began investigating. He lined the children up for photographs to aid him in determining if they were, indeed, black. As he worked, he made disparaging comments in front of the parents and children, including, "You know, he favors a nigger," and "I don't like the shape of that one's nose." Sheriff McCall determined the Platts were Negroes and advised them to stay out of school pending further investigation.

Allen Platt tried to present proof to the sheriff that his children were not Negroes, but to no avail. A local newspaper, *The Topic*, picked up the story. The editor, Mrs. Mabel Norris Reese, printed statements from Allen Platt that he was not a Negro, but was a mixture of Irish and Indian. Platt said "If the children never see the inside of another school,

---

[59] Ibid., 126–27.

they will not go to a Negro school." The case caused considerable controversy in Lake County; locals vandalized the newspaper offices, burned crosses on Mrs. Reese's lawn, and poisoned her dog. A rival newspaper was started, and local merchants filled the first issue with advertising to show support for its position—which was that the Platt children belonged in a Negro school.

However, the Platts also had their own supporters who contributed money for lawyers. The case dragged on for seven months. The Platts testified that they never associated with blacks, never worshiped in black churches, and that Allen Platt's grandfather had served in the Confederate army (as had Mrs. Platt's grandfather). Furthermore, Platt's attorney established that the Platt children had always attended white schools, that the Platts' marriage license stated they were white, and they had always voted in the Democratic primary elections—which, in most southern states after the Civil War, were only open to white voters.

The only evidence that the Platts were not white was that on some documents, the family were listed as Croatan, and the dictionary definition of that term was a mixture of white, black, and Indian. On October 18, 1955—one year after the Platt children were expelled from Mount Dora school—the court declared that the Platt children were white. A few nights later, a mob set fire to the Platts' home. Some time later, Sheriff McCall told a Lion's Club meeting, "In my book they're still mulattoes...This only proves that there are some people who will stoop to integrate our schools."[60]

For most tri-racial families, segregated education remained a problem until public schools were integrated—a process that continued through the 1970s and beyond in some locations. Until public schools integrated, tri-racial children generally attended schools that were poorer than those attended by local white children. In Hancock County, Tennessee, however, Melungeon children continued to benefit from the Vardy School.

The Vardy School—The Later Years

With the support of the Presbyterian Church, the Reverend Chester Leonard and Miss Mary Rankin continued to serve the students and parents at the Vardy Community School in Hancock County. The school

---

[60] Ibid., 179–83.

itself remained a model for progressive education and provided life-changing opportunities for its students. As vardy alumnus Claude Collins put it, "I owe my life to Vardy."[61]

Collins attended the Vardy School for eight years in the 1930s and 1940s. "I'm always happy to tell this," Collins said. "I only missed four days of school in eight years, walking off the Ridge, two miles and a half." At the time Collins attended Vardy, the teachers "were imported in; there were no local people [who] taught school there."

The school nurse, Miss Rankin, kept track of all the students, 125 of them during Claude Collins' days there. "She was there before the minister [the Reverend Charles Leonard] was. She kind of set the pace when he arrived. She already had the fires burning."

Even before the arrival of the Reverend Leonard, Miss Rankin looked after the health of her students, and those with special needs got individualized attention. "To show you how closely they monitored each student," says Collins, "every morning on my way to school, I had to stop at one of the houses [on the way to school] and drink two glasses of milk." Claude evidently seemed more in need of milk than his seven brothers and sisters. "None of them had to stop and drink the milk. They were always laughing at me." Several other students stopped at various houses on the way to school for some sort of breakfast.[62]

The hot lunch program at Vardy was the main meal of the day for many Vardy students. Vardy alumnus Troy Williams recalls that "I looked forward to really getting all I wanted to eat from the Vardy lunch program... it was started by donations from the people who lived in the community, [who] donated potatoes, sweet potatoes, Irish potatoes, and any other canned vegetable that they had...They donated it to the school so that we could have a hot lunch program." Parents canned extra food to contribute to the school, and donated time and labor in return for the lunches for their children.[63]

Vardy alumna DruAnna Overbay recalls the school's emphasis on health care. "One of the things we needed to do every morning before we went into school... we would go the clinic. Mr. Leonard had gone to

[61] Claude Collins, "The Vardy School," presentation at Fourth Union, 21 June 2002.

[62] Collins interview, January 2002.

[63] Troy Williams, "The Vardy School," presentation at Fourth Union, 21 June 2002.

Johns Hopkins Medical School to learn how to treat the people. Miss Rankin was a registered nurse. She had her Master's degree from Columbia University. Mr. Leonard and Miss Rankin took care of our medical needs as far as their expertise would allow them to. I know that I got my smallpox inoculation in the clinic."[64]

The Vardy Clinic was located in a small building behind the Reverend Leonard's house. The clinic served the health care needs of the valley, treating such ailments as Leonard and Rankin could handle, and offering educational seminars on the prevention of worms and trachoma. Dental clinics were also held, and inoculations were given to students and adults alike. The Reverend Leonard brought doctors into the valley for some of these clinics and attempted to persuade some of them to stay in the area, but without success. For the people of Vardy Valley and Newman's Ridge, the Vardy Clinic provided the only available access to medical care.[65]

Students at the Vardy school learned reading and writing in the early grades; by the third grade, most had mastered the multiplication tables. In addition to history, geography, and mathematics classes, students at Vardy also learned agriculture and vocational skills. Physical education was a part of the curriculum, and students took advantage of Vardy's well-stocked library.[66]

In addition to standard school subjects (which were taught utilizing audio-visual and participatory techniques that were far ahead of their time), religion and morality were also a part of the curriculum at the Presbyterian-operated school. "We had devotions every morning at the school, Bible reading and prayer," recalls Overbay, who now teaches at Jefferson County (Tennessee) High School. "We also, each of us in different classes, were responsible for putting on an assembly program. Sometimes we would get to read the Bible or sometimes we'd get to pray, but a lot of times we would perform in little one-act plays."[67]

Students attended the Vardy Community School from all over the valley and Newman's Ridge, as well as from nearby Lee County, Virginia. "We had students that rode horses to school," Collins

---

[64] DruAnna Overbay, "The Vardy School," presentation at Fourth Union, 21 June 2002.

[65] Overbay, *Windows on the Past*, 55.

[66] Ibid., 111.

[67] Overbay, "The Vardy School."

remembers. "There was a shed there that had been built by the manual training [class] where the horses were hooked every day."[68] The Vardy Community School was the only school available to students on the north side of Newman's Ridge, so even though it was a church-operated school, it received some state funding for teacher salaries. After repeated attempts by county officials to deny state funding to Vardy, the Reverend Leonard journeyed to Nashville in 1934 to argue the school's case. Not only was Leonard able to secure state funding, he received *carte blanche* from state education officials to continue his progressive educational techniques, with no restrictions concerning textbooks or techniques and no requirement for Vardy students to take countywide tests.[69]

Night classes for adults had begun in 1930. In 1935, the Berea Extension School of Berea, Kentucky, began offering educational programs at the Vardy Community School. Groups from nearby colleges brought plays, concerts, and other entertainment to Vardy Valley. "[Leonard] was very, very innovative," asserts Collins. "He kept something going. I think his philosophy was, 'If I keep the people busy and happy, they'll support my work.'"[70]

After completing eighth grade, students could catch a bus to make the trip on the winding, treacherous ride across Newman's Ridge, where they could attend Hancock County High School. However, some promising students were sent for high school classes to Berea College in Berea, Kentucky, or to Warren Wilson, a Presbyterian institution near Asheville, North Carolina which was both a high school and a junior college. Most of these students hadn't been more than a few miles from home in their lives. It is a testament to the faith parents had in the Reverend Leonard and the Vardy staff that these students had an opportunity to travel and receive an education. The reaction of Claude Collins' mother was typical. "The minister and the teachers... said to my mother, 'Claude needs to go to Warren Wilson.' I went to Warren Wilson. It would have been no different if they had said 'Europe,' 'cause Mother would have said 'yes,' no matter what it was. The minister and the teacher instilled into the parents, 'We may have the answer, if you'll just listen and do what we ask you to do.'"[71]

---

[68] Collins interview, January 2002, Bible, *The Melungeons*, 57–58.

[69] Overbay, *Windows on the Past*, 111–112.

[70] Ibid., 123; Collins interview, January 2002.

[71] Overbay, *Windows on the Past*, 110; Collins, "The Vardy School."

During World War Two, the Reverend Leonard kept a large map of the world on the wall with which he kept track of every county serviceman. Each week, Hancock Countians came by the mission to check the whereabouts of friends and family members and to discuss the latest war news. Leonard also had slides made from photographs of the Hancock County servicemen which were shown during these weekly gatherings.[72]

The Vardy School even made sure the children had gifts at Christmas time. "We got our Christmas gifts shipped in from the New Jersey Presbyterian Association that supported our church and school," says Troy Williams. "Some of the people there in Vardy knew our needs and distributed those products they sent—clothing, some toys. Of course, the very poor families received clothes and never got any toys. I don't know that there *were* toys, so you know where I was! That started Christmas for us. If you went to church at Vardy [or] went to school there, you got your Christmas gift from the Vardy Church. You got a box of hard candy and you got clothing."[73]

Vardy's "Hard Candy Christmases" are remembered fondly today by alumni of the school. R.C. Mullins reminisces about Christmas of 1947.

> Troy [Williams] and I continued on to the church. As we opened the door and stepped into the foyer we could smell Christmas. The big old cedar tree was being warmed by the Christmas lights and putting off a smell that was wonderful.
>
> We both was so excited as we stepped inside the church, our eyes fastened onto the huge tree. It went from the floor to the ceiling. It had lots of bright colored lights, decorations, little toys and boxes of candy. It was a sight that has always stayed with me.
>
> On this day, Preacher Leonard would tell the Christmas story and we would have other programs done by the children. I could hardly wait till it was over so we could get our Christmas.

---

[72] Louise Davis, "Why Are They Vanishing?," Nashville *Tennesseean Sunday Magazine*, 29 September 1963, 11; Bible, *The Melungeons*, 46; Collins interview, January 2002.

[73] Troy Williams, "The Vardy School."

The little box of hard candy was what I had waited for. I had not had any candy since last Christmas...

I always had to share my bed with my two brothers and most of the time wear hand-me-down clothes. But this little box of candy was all mine.[74]

The Reverend Chester Leonard began his tenure as minister of the Vardy Church in 1920, and served as principal of the new Vardy School when it was built in 1929. He continued as minister of the church after Drew Williams (DruAnna Overbay's father) took over as principal of the school in 1942. For the 1944–45 school year, Mossie Kate Overton was the principal, and Elmer Turner took the position in 1945–46. Elizabeth Horton Davidson, Harriet Stewart Mullins, and Drew Williams (again) served as principal at various times through the 1940s and 1950s. Meanwhile, the Reverend Leonard attempted, for health reasons, to resign his pulpit in 1947 and again in 1948. The church members would not permit him to resign. With occasional help from the Reverend Fitzhugh Dotson, the Vardy Church members took over most of the Rev. Leonard's duties, and the Leonards spent some time away from Vardy. In February of 1949, Leonard returned to the pulpit of the Vardy Church, but his health problems finally forced him to submit his resignation in September 1951.[75]

School attendance declined, due in large part to the outmigration of Hancock Countians to the Midwest and other areas. The teaching staff was reduced to two, and in the 1960s the Vardy School was incorporated into the Hancock County school system. The county lacked adequate funds to maintain the building, which quickly deteriorated, and the Vardy School was closed in 1973. The county auctioned the property back to the descendants of Batey Collins, who had originally granted the property to the Presbyterian mission. The three-story Vardy School building, once the pride of the community, is a ruin today. The Vardy Church is now a museum.

---

[74] R. C. Mullins and Macie Mullins, "My Hard Candy Christmas, " *The Vardy Voice* (December 2001).

[75] DruAnna Overbay, "Museum's Contents Reflect Vardy's Past, Part Two," *The Vardy Voice* (June 2002).

Despite the many successes of the Presbyterian mission at Vardy, they had one notable failure: as Henry Price noted, "the Presbyterian doctrine has never been widely accepted by the Melungeon families." "The Presbyterians are not here anymore," says Claude Collins. "There's not a Presbyterian church [in Hancock County]." Collins has pondered the question of why the Presbyterian doctrine did not catch on with the people of Vardy. "This area of the country—they've got to go to a Baptist church. Otherwise they're going to hell. That's just what they believe, so there's no use fighting a losing battle. I don't think a Presbyterian church—I don't think you could get the doors opened today." Despite a few successful conversions in its early days, the Presbyterian church at Vardy was attended primarily by faculty and staff at the mission.[76]

Providing a strong moral foundation for its students and giving students a sense of their own self-worth and potential were the ways in which Leonard and the staff at Vardy helped to steer their students away from the cycle of poverty that had ensnared so many of their neighbors. A 1934 report prepared for a Tennessee Valley Authority-sponsored project observed that Melungeons became sexually active "as soon as they are old enough... marry at an early age, bring into the world as many children as nature allows them, and in the end die no better off than their parents who lived the same kind of life as was led before them."[77]

In fairness, the same thing could have been written about people in countless rural American communities. Early marriage and numerous children have guaranteed poverty for generations of white, black, and brown people all over the world. The people of Newman's Ridge and Vardy Valley, however, had a resource that allowed many of its children to escape that cycle of poverty.

The Vardy Community School was unique among schools that served tri-racial children. In most areas, these children received

---

[76] Henry Price, "Melungeons: The Vanishing Colony of Newman's Ridge," lecture presented at the Spring Meeting of the American Studies Association of Kentucky and Tennessee, 25–26 March 1966, Tennessee Technical University, Cookeville TN transcript from Grohse Papers, Roll 7, Johnson City TN: East Tennessee State University,; Collins interview, January 2002.

[77] William E. Cole and Joe Stephenson Looney, *The Melungeons of Hancock County*, TVA-CWA Project, unpublished manuscript, cited in Evans, "The Graysville Melungeons," 13.

substandard instruction in inadequate facilities. The Vardy School was a progressive institution utilizing state-of-the-art techniques and provided its students with a quality education. It was not a "Melungeon school;" many of the students were Melungeons, and many were not. Many tri-racial children in segregated school systems attended run-down, under-supplied facilities. The children of Vardy attended the best school in the county. That fact certainly contributed to what many former students remember most about the Vardy Community School: the sense of self-worth that was instilled in each and every child. Decades after attending Vardy, R. C. Mullins fought back tears as he remembered the school that "cared about this little Melungeon boy," provided him with a strong moral foundation, and gave him the tools to succeed in life.[78] The self-esteem instilled in Vardy alumni would be a major factor in the celebration of Melungeon heritage that began in the mid-1960s.

"Vardy students had access to the finer things in life," Claude Collins concludes. The president of Sneedville's bank for fifty years, Miss Martha Collins, once told Claude that when she picked up a young person walking along the road, she could always tell within five minutes whether that person was a Vardy student. "She said, 'I can tell by their manners, by the way they talk, and the intellect they have. They're just different.'"[79]

Outmigration and Assimilation

As white Americans came to terms with the civil rights movement, most of the tri-racial groups had established or were in the process of establishing their respective identities as either white, black, or Indian. Neighboring whites often disputed the identity adopted by each respective group, but racial attitudes were softening. At the same time, tri-racial communities were rapidly disappearing. Educational and occupational opportunities drew individuals away from their traditional homes to urban areas, where few questioned their ethnic backgrounds. Intermarriage with whites also led to the gradual assimilation of many tri-racials into white society. Other tri-racials found acceptance in black communities or among Indian tribes. One way or another, the tri-racial

---

[78] R. C. Mullins, "The Vardy School."
[79] Collins interview, January 2002.

people were establishing themselves in recognized racial categories, and identifying themselves as either white, black, or Indian.

The Melungeons had nearly established themselves as white. Many did so by moving away from Hancock and surrounding counties to Michigan and Maryland, Illinois and Indiana, places where their heritage would be forgotten and their children would never hear the hated name "Melungeon." Even in Hancock County, the word "Melungeon" was rarely spoken. The Melungeon families had largely intermarried with whites, leading many to predict the complete dissolution of the Melungeons as an identifiable people within a couple of generations.

Between 1940 and 1970, more than 2,300 people moved away from Hancock County. The county had fewer inhabitants in 1963 than it had in 1863. While this pattern of outmigration was common all over the south, Hancock County (commonly ranked as one of the poorest counties in America) was particularly hard hit, as many of the "best and brightest" left for better opportunities elsewhere.[80]

Many migrants from Hancock and surrounding counties were escaping not only poverty and lack of opportunity, but the stigma attached to their Melungeon heritage. A 1963 article in the Nashville *Tennesseean Sunday Magazine* examined the gradual disappearance of the Melungeons. Louise Davis wrote, "Melungeons, like many of the other citizens of Hancock County, have broken out of the rigid trap of a region that has never had a railroad and had few highways to lift them over the fierce barrier of the mountains until recent years. One theory is that, with more travel to outside areas, they are intermarrying with whites so frequently that their distinctive characteristics are vanishing, and the Melungeons will soon be a relic of the history books."[81]

A 1964 United Press International article echoed this view with the headline "Melungeon Line Almost Extinct." John Gamble wrote, "It has been the mixing—and intermarriage—of Melungeon youths with the young people of Sneedville... that has brought the 'true' Melungeons to the point of extinction." Gamble also observed that while the Melungeons still avoided contact with outsiders, they "have taken to

---

[80] US Department of Commerce, *Hancock County Comprehensive Development Program*, 1970; Davis, "Why Are They Vanishing?," 12.
[81] Davis, "Why Are They Vanishing?," 11.

many modern gadgets. Most all of them have television sets, and many of the farmers drive tractors."[82]

By the mid-1960s, the Melungeons seemed destined to disappear into the realm of legend. As Davis wrote, "The Melungeons who used to sit on the fence around the courthouse square in Sneedville are no longer there." As one county resident said, "They have more or less just died out. The families have just eroded." A former teacher asserted that education also played a part in the disappearance of the Melungeons: "Once they get a college education, they seldom come back. They go to Chicago, or other distant places where they can get good jobs and nobody will ever call them Melungeon."[83]

Lincoln Memorial University in nearby Harrogate, Tennessee, offered many Melungeons the opportunity to earn a college degree by allowing students to work to pay their tuition. Appropriately, it was an LMU alumnus who helped many of these Melungeons learn to take pride in their unique heritage.

Daughter of the Legend

Kentucky author Jesse Stuart entered LMU in 1926, graduating three years later. He met several Melungeon students, and even fell in love with a young lady from Hancock County. According to a frequently-told tale, Stuart abandoned his Melungeon sweetheart due to family pressures, an incident that possibly led to the creation of his novel *Daughter of the Legend*, which incorporated stories he heard he learned from fellow students. Stuart later stated that he wrote the novel in 1942, but it was not published until 1965.[84]

Daughter of the Legend tells the story of a Virginia lumberman, Dave Stoneking, who travels to Oak Hill (a pseudonym for Sneedville) in 1940. There he meets a beautiful dark-skinned woman, Deutsia Huntoon, who lives on Sanctuary Mountain (Newman's Ridge). Dave falls in love with Deutsia, but can't understand why the "better" people of Oak Hill, as well as his friend and partner Ben Dewberry, look down upon Deutsia and others who live on the mountain.

---

[82] John Gamble, "Melungeon Line Almost Extinct," *Kingsport Times*, 26 November 1964, 9–C.

[83] Davis, "Why Are They Vanishing?," 12.

[84] Bible, *The Melungeons*, 100.

While exploring Sanctuary Mountain on his own, Stoneking meets with a mountain resident, Don Praytor, who tells Stoneking: "We're Melungeons. Did you ever hear of us Melungeons?"

"Melungeons don't get justice in the courts," he said. "We're hated! Despised. We're a lost people."...

"We're called Sons and Daughters of the Legend," Don said. We don't know who we are. There are so many theories about where we come from that we don't know what to believe. We've heard we're a white, Indian and Negro mixture. You'll never know what kind of blood Deutsia has in her veins."[85]

Later, Stoneking returns to the shanty he shares with Ben Dewberry and two other lumbermen, Hezzy and Mort.

"Did you ever hear of the Melungeons?" I asked Ben, as we sat around the breakfast table, smoking.

"I've just been a-waitin' for you to ask me that question, Dave," Ben said. "I'm glad you're a-gettin' your eyes open at last. So you've found out about 'em."

"Yes, I've found out about the Melungeons."

"I've left that up to you," he said. "I didn't want you to think I was puttin' my jib on where I didn't have any business. I didn't want to come between you and the girl you thought you loved."

"I asked you what you know about the Melungeons, and not about Deutsia," I said.

"You know she's a Melungeon, don't you?" Ben took another draw from his cigarette.

Mort and Hezzy sat silently on the other side of the table, smoking their pipes and listening.

"Yes, I know she's a Melungeon."

"Did you know it when you had that first date with her?"

"No, I'd never heard of the Melungeons then."

"You're not the first man that's been fooled by the beauty of the Melungeon women," Ben said. "They're so pretty while they're young that white strangers who have come into these

---

[85] Jesse Stuart, *Daughter of the Legend* (New York: McGraw Hill, 1965) 69–70.

parts have fallen for 'em before. But they've been smart enough to find out and to break away. I'm glad you're findin' out... They're not our equals," Ben said. "I don't care if they are a strong, good-looking race of people... You don't want to go with a Melungeon," Ben said. "It's disgraceful."

"Why is it disgraceful."

"You know about the blood in the Melungeons, don't you?"

"I don't know about their blood," I said. "But my guess is, their blood is red. It's not blue blood like the people in the valley think they have in their veins."

"If you'll listen, Dave," Ben said, dropping his cigarette stub in his coffee cup, "I'll tell you what I've heard about the blood in the Melungeons... Many of the people believe the Melungeon is a mixture of poor mountain whites, Indians and Negroes," Ben continued, "And here is what they say. That during the Civil War, Cantwell County fought for the Union almost to a man, and that many escaped mulattoes from the Deep South were smuggled to Cantwell County where they found refuge upon Sanctuary Mountain and mixed with the poor whites... And the last theory is that there is not any Indian blood in the Melungeons," Ben said, "but just a mixture of escaped slaves and trashy whites. And this is what the majority of people believe."[86]

Stoneking rejects the advice of his friends and, after the county clerk refuses to issue a marriage license, marries Deutsia in a ceremony conducted by a Melungeon preacher. Stoneking vows that he has become a Melungeon himself, that the Melungeons are "his people," but when Deutsia dies in childbirth, Stoneking abandons not only the Melungeons and Sanctuary Mountain, but his infant son as well. One can easily read into the novel's concluding of loss a sense of Stuart's own regret at not standing up to pressure from family and friends in his ill-fated romance with a Melungeon.

Katherine Vande Brake, author of *How They Shine: Melungeon Characters in the Fiction of Appalachia*, felt that Stuart's portrayal of the Melungeons left something to be desired. "I felt he was a little bit

---

[86] Stuart, *Daughter of the Legend*, 74–78.

condescending in his treatment of the Melungeon characters," she said. "I didn't feel like he had the kind of respect some of the [later] writers had. He had a kind of 'we—they' attitude."[87] Stoneking is appalled at the widespread superstitions prevalent among the Melungeons, and often displays an sense of superiority that was likely unintended, but unavoidable, by Stuart. Compared with what had been written about Melungeons before 1965, however, Stuart's portrayal was at least positive, and resulted in a new sense of pride for many Melungeons. This newfound pride led to the creation of the outdoor drama *Walk Toward The Sunset*, which resulted in nationwide interest in Melungeons.

Walk Toward the Sunset

Jesse Stuart's novel was just one factor in the transformation of Melungeon identity from "something bad" into "something good." Anthony Cavender noted that intermarriage and an improved socio-economic status had also helped change the negative image of Melungeons. "Very simply, the Whites who intermarried with the Melungeons were favorably impressed with their education and relatively high incomes. The Melungeons had proven they could achieve the goals of lower and middle class Whites."[88]

The stigma of being a Melungeon was disappearing—but so were the Melungeons themselves. In March of 1966, Rogersville attorney Henry Price spoke to the Spring Meeting of the American Studies Association of Kentucky and Tennessee in Cookeville, Tennessee. An amateur historian and Melungeon researcher, Price's topic was "Melungeons: The Vanishing Colony of Newman's Ridge." He concluded:

> The pure Melungeon (if there is or was such a thing) is rare today. Only among the older folk—deep in the ridge—does one see what must have been the original skin color characteristics, experience the wary, 'don't tread on me' atmosphere; hear the lament that young people are leaving the ridge in ever increasing numbers… The future for this remnant of the clan is not bright.

---

[87] K. Vande Brake, interview by Wayne Winkler, May 2001, Johnson City TN.

[88] Anthony P. Cavender, "The Melungeons of Upper East Tennessee: Persisting Social Identity," *Tennessee Anthropologist* 6/1 (Spring 1981): 32.

Unlike their origin, the destiny of the Melungeons of Newman's Ridge is certain. The day must surely come when the Melungeon is no more—a vanished people—gone without a trace except perhaps for the dark-eyed raven haired little girl or the olive skinned thin faced little boy who may appear among the posterity of East Tennessee."[89]

In the mid-1960s, an idea designed to bring tourism and economic opportunity to Hancock County engendered pride in the once-hated name "Melungeon." The University of Tennessee in Knoxville and Carson-Newman College in Jefferson City conducted studies on ways to bring economic development to Hancock County. Claude Collins participated, along with several other members of the Hancock County Human Resource and Leadership Development Association. Outdoor dramas were very popular throughout the South at that time, and Collins' panel discussed the possiblity of creating such an attraction in Hancock County. "My wife and I had been attending outdoor dramas—*Unto These Hills, Trail of The Lonesome Pine*... so we decided we would invite the area colleges to send in the heads [of their drama departments] to talk about outdoor dramas." The discussion soon led to the idea of staging a drama to attract tourists to Hancock County. It took an "outsider," someone not native to Hancock County, to suggest an idea that some locals might have seen as scandalous.

"The Methodist minister [R. B. Connor] spoke up and said, 'You've got a good story here if you'll just tell it,'" remembered Collins. "Somebody said, 'What's that?' He said, 'You need to tell the story of the Melungeons.' Oh, gosh! I scrinched down in my seat; I never opened my mouth, I just sat there and listened."[90] Collins, recalling the hard feelings that permeated Hancock County following Worden's *Saturday Evening Post* article, dreaded the reaction of the other Hancock Countians in the workshop. Connor, who had come to Sneedville from Morristown, was familiar with the story of the Melungeons, but apparently was not fully aware of the negative feelings that still clung to the very word "Melungeon." However, the idea caught on with others in the group. The local reaction to Jesse Stuart's novel had created an atmosphere in which Melungeon pride could finally take root.

---

[89] Price," Melungeons: The Vanishing Colony of Newman's Ridge."
[90] Collins interview, January 2002.

Carson-Newman College professors Gary Farley and Joe Mack High thought the idea had merit. They concluded that Hancock County had only two assets of interest to tourists: beautiful scenery and Melungeons. Poor roads prevented the exploitation of the scenery for the county's economic benefit, but the story of the Melungeons was seen as a possible subject for an outdoor drama. As a result, Dr. John Lee Welton of the Carson-Newman Drama Department entered into the discussions.[91]

The committee invited playwright Kermit Hunter to speak to the group. In an interview with Katherine Vande Brake, Hunter recalled receiving a letter from a woman in Sneedville, whose name he had forgotten, accompanied by some newspaper articles on the Melungeons. Claude Collins recalled that the letter was probably sent by Deborah Fannin, the drama teacher at Hancock County High School.[92]

Hunter, a native of Welch, West Virginia, was at that time the Dean of Arts at Southern Methodist University in Dallas. He had written more than forty scripts for outdoor dramas, including the successful *Unto These Hills*, performed on the Eastern Cherokee Reservation in the Smoky Mountains—a production with which many Hancock Countians were familiar. Hunter also authored a drama performed by the Cherokee nation at Talehquah, Oklahoma, entitled *The Trail of Tears*, and had helped to found the Institute for Outdoor Drama at the University of North Carolina in 1963.[93]

In January of 1968, Hunter attended a conference with community leaders and Dr. Welton in Sneedville. "Kermit Hunter was here from Southern Methodist University," Claude Collins remembers. "They had asked me to take him back to the airport, and going back to the airport, I was supposed to ask him if he would write us a play, and what he would charge." Hunter agreed to research and write the play for 10 percent of the first year's gate receipts.[94]

The *Knoxville News-Sentinal* reported:

---

[91] John Lee Welton, Wayne Winkler, in-person interview, March 2002, Jefferson City TN.

[92] Katherine Vande Brake, *How They Shine: Melungeon Characters in the Fiction of Appalachia* (Macon GA, Mercer University Press, 2000): 170; Collins interview, January 2002.

[93] Vande Brake, *How They Shine*, 169.

[94] Collins interview, January 2002.

> So serious has the project become that three top outdoor
> drama specialists are here for three days of conferences with
> backers and citizens of the county. The widely-known trio are
> Kermit Hunter ("Unto These Hills"), now dean of Southern
> Methodist University's School of the Arts in Dallas; Mark
> Sumner, an Asheville native who is director of the Institute of
> Outdoor Drama, University of North Carolina at Chapel Hill;
> and Earl Hobson Smith, professor of drama and playwright at
> Lincoln Memorial University, Harrogate…They are part of a six-
> member panel which today and tomorrow will discuss outdoor
> drama prospects with Hancock Countians. One theme under
> discussion is author Jesse Stuart's new book, "Daughter of the
> Legend."[95]

Hancock Countians Claude Collins and Corrine Bowlin were co-
chairs of the conference, which was also attended by Professors Farley,
High, and Welton from Carson-Newman College. The Reverend Connor
told a group meeting at the Methodist church that an outdoor drama
would help eliminate the stigma of the name "Melungeon;" in his words,
it would "lift their name from shame to the hall of fame." Connor
envisioned an economic revival for Hancock County, including "motels
and restaurants, bridle trails, and 18–hole golf course, quarters for drama
employees, a chairlift on Newman [sic] Ridge, heated swimming pool
and a landing strip for light planes. 'Might sound like much,' he said,
'but I know a fellow who's willing to put up $50,000 as a start.'"[96]

Anthony Cavender claimed in a 1981 article in the *Tennessee
Anthropologist* that, because the Melungeons had become a "hot topic,"
Sneedville's "elite" (merchants, educators, and prosperous farmers)
determined to exploit the widespread interest in the topic that had "put
the county on the map." "The elite," as Cavender wrote, "conceived of a
way to maximize the commercialization of the strong and growing
interest in Melungeons."[97]

Corrine Bowlin, the president of the newly-formed Hancock County
Drama Association, and Claude Collins, who served as secretary,

---

[95] Willard Yarbrough, "Maligned Mountain Folk May Be Topic of Drama,"
Knoxville News-Sentinel, 8 January 1968, 1.

[96] Yarbrough, "Maligned Mountain Folk," 1.

[97] Cavender, "The Melungeons of Upper East Tennessee," 33.

proudly acknowledged their Melungeon backgrounds. Most of the locals working on the project either had no Melungeon background or wouldn't acknowledge it. The Melungeons of the county were, for the most part, uncertain about the project. As Yarbrough wrote, "Key to an outdoor drama's success could well be the cooperation of the Melungeons themselves, who over the decades have come to mistrust those outsiders who distort their character and damage their image."[98]

"This was one of the problems that was faced by many of us in trying to do something for the county," recalls Dr. Welton, who agreed to direct the drama. "The Melungeon people simply did not want to admit that they were Melungeons—first of all because of the outlook of other people on the Melungeons and some the stories that had been started years ago, about how they were blood-drinking people and they've done witchcraft and all sorts of stories. I'm not really sure that some of those stories weren't started by the Melungeons themselves just to keep people away from them and make them leave 'em alone!"

To overcome local suspicions about the "outsiders" who were working on the drama, Welton asked cast and crew members to "go around to all the stores, to buy their supplies at each of the stores…We went to the churches…each Sunday to try to get acquainted with the community and let them get acquainted with us."

"We opened up the rehearsals; we never had a closed rehearsal. People could walk in, sit down, watch us work, and realize that we were not there to make fun of the Melungeons but rather to try and promote an interest in their heritage and a pride in their heritage."[99]

Obtaining the land for the amphitheater involved a bit of finesse on the part of Claude Collins. As a school administrator, Collins was familiar with grant applications and wrote a grant for a stage to be used as a teaching tool for his English classes. The grant was awarded, and Collins, on behalf of the Drama Association, negotiated to buy the land for the amphitheater. Setting his sights on a parcel of land next to the elementary school at the foot of Newman's Ridge, Collins recalls, "I went to talk to this man about it. I didn't tell him what we were going to do with the property. I just told him that we wanted the addition to the school, 'cause it was right back of where I was teaching. And I said 'It's

---

[98] Yarbrough, "Maligned Mountain Folk," 1.
[99] Welton interview, March 2002.

a possibility that I might carry on some classes down there in a theatre that we might build.'"

The property was bought and the amphitheater constructed. The former owner was not pleased with the Melungeon drama that was staged. "He certainly wasn't appreciative of what it turned out to be." Although Collins felt that the seller might have softened his attitude over the years, "I don't know that he ever came to see the play."[100]

Kyle Greene, president of the Hancock County Resource Development Association and co-chairman of the drama association's building committee, used eighteen workers from Operation Mainstream (a "War On Poverty" agency) to procure lumber by cutting trees from a road right-of-way. This lumber was used to build bleachers for the amphitheater and the log building which housed the theatre's box office and concession area.[101]

As the project drew closer to becoming a reality, the attitudes of many locals began to change. While many Hancock Countians had expressed skepticism about the drama and its topic, others grew enthusiastic. Welton noticed that several locals "who had never said that they were Melungeons [began] to come up and sort of nudge me on the shoulder and say, 'You know, I'm a Melungeon." We were quite proud that at least that change had come about."[102]

Walk Toward the Sunset opened as scheduled on 3 July 1969. The amphitheater was literally at the foot of Newman's Ridge, between the elementary school and the home of Elmer Turner and his wife, the former Hazel Winkler, who served as ticket manager and concessions manager, respectively. Scott Collins, who is today clerk and master of the Hancock County Court, was a high school senior who assumed the responsibilities of lighting director.

As visitors entered the amphitheater, they were treated to the dulcimer playing of Mollie Bowlin. Her husband Lonnie sat beside her and provided out-of-towners with a good look at a swarthy Melungeon. Theatregoers sat on smooth logs set into the hillside, and looked down on a stage which had Newman's Ridge as a backdrop. Local volunteers

---

[100] Claude Collins, *"Walk Toward The Sunset,"* presentation at Fourth Union, 22 June 2002, Kingsport TN.

[101] Juanita Glenn, "Hancock Countians Prepare For Drama About Melungeons," Knoxville *Journal*, Thursday, 1 May 1969, 5.

[102] Welton interview, March 2002.

filled out the cast, while the primary roles were acted by students from the drama department at Carson-Newman College.

Local acceptance of the play was not unanimous. Director Welton recalled a bomb threat on opening night. "As I understand, it was just 'word-of-mouth' coming around to us. Of course, we were a little uptight until the show was over that night and nothing popped." Claude Collins remembers, "We were really worried... We sat up the entire night [before opening] at the theatre, afraid somebody would bother it."[103]

The script of *Walk Toward the Sunset* was never formally published, but Katherine Vande Brake located a copy at Carson-Newman College, in a folder on a shelf in the drama department. The play is in two acts. The first act is set immediately after the American Revolution, while the second act takes place following the Civil War. Both acts take place in a time of change for the Melungeons, and both contain stories.[104]

In the first act, the Melungeons face the loss of their valley farms to whites because the Melungeons lack clear titles, and because they have dark skins. John Sevier and Daniel Boone argue over the issue. Boone supports the Melungeons, while Sevier, although sympathetic to the Melungeons, eventually gives in to pressure from white settlers who covet the Melungeons' land.

Pat Gibson and Alisee Collins are the romantic leads. Both characters provide information about the various legends surrounding the origin of the Melungeons. Attakullakulla is the Cherokee chief who offers to support the Melungeons if they wish to fight to hold their lands. Instead, Pat Gibson accepts an alternative Cherokee offer for land on what later became known as Newman's Ridge. The move is hastened by Gibson's accidental killing of a white scout in a fight. Act One ends with the Melungeons leaving the valley and the Cherokees setting the valley ablaze to cover the Melungeons' escape.

Act Two takes place in 1868. Civil War veteran and law student Vance Johnson falls in love with Cora Sylvester, a Melungeon girl.[105] This interracial relationship is controversial among both whites and

---

[103] Welton interview; Claude Collins, *"Walk Toward The Sunset.*

[104] Vande Brake, *How They Shine*, 172, 179.

[105] Vande Brake used a script for the 1976 production of *Walk Toward the Sunset* for her analysis. The program book for the 1971 season indicates that the lead female character in Act Two is named Alisee Gibson, and is the granddaughter of Pat Gibson and Alisee Collins from Act One.

Melungeons. Matters are complicated by the fact that Johnson is helping protect the Melungeons' interests in negotiations with a lumber company for timber rights on the Ridge. Discriminatory laws that had curtailed Melungeons' legal rights after 1834 had been repealed, and once again Tennessee politicians are at a loss as to how to deal with these non-black, non-white, non-Indian people.

A smallpox epidemic finally unites whites and Melungeons. As the whites are laid low by the disease, Melungeons—who are immune due to exposure to the disease in an earlier epidemic—come to Sneedville to nurse the sick and save the town. Cora's actions save the life of Vance's mother, ensuring her blessing for the coming marriage, and Cora's father becomes foreman of the logging crew, indicating the success of the negotiations with the logging company.

In her analysis of *Walk Toward the Sunset*, Katherine Vande Brake observes that the viewpoint taken by the author is reflective of the time—the mid-1960s—in which it was written.

> [S]omeone writing such a drama today might focus on the same issues—racial prejudice and local history—but in different ways. Racial equality was a 1960s crusade, and while still a problem in our society, the focus is different. The laws of the land now mandate equal opportunities for all; the problems are the more subtle ones of attitude. Certainly the Indians would be treated differently as well. In his play, Hunter buys into the stereotype of native Americans as violent warriors. The fact that the Cherokees invite the Melungeons to settle in their hunting ground seems unrealistic as well.[106]

In 1969, recognition of the basic equality of all humans was not as obvious as it is today. It was certainly not a given in Hancock County, where "George Wallace for President" bumper stickers still adorned many local cars years after Wallace's racially-charged 1968 campaign. Hunter's approach in *Walk Toward the Sunset*, so appropriate and even necessary in 1969, seems dated today. Had the drama continued to be performed, it seems likely that script revisions would have been made, as

---

[106] Vande Brake, *How They Shine*, 178.

they have been in many other long-running outdoor dramas, to reflect
modern attitudes.

Researcher Calvin Beale attended the second weekend's
performance of *Walk Toward the Sunset*. Beale had authored the 1957
article "American Triracial Isolates: Their Status and Pertinence to
Genetic Research," in *Eugenics Quarterly*. "I asked people downtown [in
Sneedville] who might be knowledgeable and could show me around
some, and they said 'Claude Collins.' It was summertime and he wasn't
teaching so he took me around for several hours that day."[107]

Collins and Beale traveled across Newman's Ridge into Snake
Holler and Vardy Valley and visited with a family named Bell. Collins
told Beale about the people who lived in the valley and on Newman's
Ridge, and about the Melungeons who left Hancock County for places
like Ellicott City, Maryland, or Kokomo, Indiana. In turn, Beale
informed Collins about other mixed-race communities in which names
associated with Melungeons were found.

At the amphitheater, Beale was given a special seat in the "dignitary
section." He described the play, particularly the second half, as
"skillfully done... In fact, there was hardly a dry eye in the place."
However, Beale noted that in the second half, playwright Kermit Hunter
"very distinctly and deliberately portrays the Melungeons as having gone
downhill socially and culturally in the previous hundred years... His
message to the Melungeons is that 'the world is passing them by' and
that despite the injustices of the past, they could not simply continue to
retreat to the mountain ridges."

Beale concluded that *Walk Toward The Sunset* "has been well
received by most of the Melungeon element of the population... The act
of sponsoring the play and thus confronting publicly the mystery of their
origin and their inferior status in the past seems to have been liberating in
itself."[108]

While some Hancock Countians were cynical and disparaging about
the drama, most of the residents were enthusiastic and enjoyed the out-
of-town visitors who streamed into Sneedville each weekend. The Rock
Hut restaurant advertised a "Melungeon Burger," and most of the

---

[107] Beale interview, June 2002.

[108] Calvin Beale, *A Taste of the Country: A Collection of Calvin Beale's Writings*,
Peter Morrison, editor (University Park PA: The Pennsylvania State University Press,
1990) 42–52.

residents were tolerant of outsiders who asked where Melungeons might be seen.

Not everyone in Hancock County was eager to exploit the Melungeon topic. As one county resident told Cavender, a Melungeon is someone who "has got nigger blood in 'em." Stories of unsolved murders, arson, and theft supposedly committed by Melungeons were still told to anyone who might ask. Some individuals were quite hostile about being labeled as "Melungeon," and denied the existence of any such people. Cavender related a conversation in the teachers' lounge of Sneedville's elementary school, when one teacher was singled out because of his Melungeon surname. "Everyone laughed... because no one considered him to be a 'real' Melungeon, and he certainly did not perceive himself to be one either. One teacher said, 'Well, Jim (pseudonym), I didn't know you had nigger blood in you!" Jim, who looks white in every respect, laughed and said, 'Yeah, I'm going to have to start charging money for you all to talk to me!'"[109]

Some Hancock Countians considered the tourists intruders who sought something that no longer existed. Cavender noted that the majority of whites he interviewed in Hancock County believed the Melungeons had disappeared. Some people with obvious Melungeon ancestry also sometimes denied the existence of Melungeons. A sixty-seven year old lifelong resident of Hancock County told Cavender he had never heard of the word "Melungeon."[110]

Other residents resented the tour buses that took tourists across Newman's Ridge into Blackwater in search of Melungeons. Claude Collins often accompanied these tours. "There were buses that came into Sneedville on Friday or Saturday nights, sometimes 10 or 12 buses in an afternoon. Well, I'd do a bus tour over into Vardy Valley, and show them the Presbyterian National Board of Missions, and this and that." Evidently, many residents were afraid Claude was pointing out individuals to the tourists instead of simply places of importance to the Melungeons. Melungeons didn't always care to be identified as such, particularly to tourists, and non-Melungeons *certainly* didn't want to be so identified. "Well, I was all but drug off that mountain," Collins recalled. "People in the valley didn't appreciate me doing it. So I soon had to quit doing that, because people resented it... I stopped over there

---

[109] Cavender, "Melungeons of Upper East Tennessee," 31.
[110] Ibid., 32–33.

in Vardy Valley once and there were some men who were going to drag me off there." Several complaints to the local magistrate put a stop to the tours.[111]

Collins found that not everyone approved of his emerging role as Melungeon spokesman. "It wasn't easy for Corinne or myself. But we had to do these things to keep the play going and to keep people coming in." He chuckled, and continued. "It was not easy."[112]

The first season closed with a total attendance of over 10,000. The second season of *Walk Toward the Sunset* opened on 2 July 1970, with improved lighting and seating. Corinne Bowlin's mother, Dora Bowlin, took over as president of the Drama Association. A few minor changes were made in the play itself, and word-of-mouth advertising attracted visitors from as far away as Pennsylvania, New York, Illinois, and elsewhere.[113]

In the spring of 1971, Collins, as secretary of the Drama Association, spoke with a reporter about some of the problems facing the production. "Our biggest problem is our lack of motels and restaurants. We can't keep people here when they come to see the play, and that keeps the drama from having as big an impact on the county's economy as it should have." Through ticket sales and donations, the Drama Association hoped to raise $30,000, which would wipe out the previous year's deficit of $2,600 and leave the production a profit besides. Collins hoped to see the production become profitable enough to pay the local actors and workers; only the production staff and principal actors were paid, and Hancock Countians were volunteers. "We have young people who are so interested in the play that they walk across Newman's [Ridge] each night to take part in it. It just doesn't seem right that we can't afford to pay them something." Collins saw the drama as a potential means of keeping young people in Hancock County, as well as a reason to develop motels, restaurants, and other tourist-oriented businesses in the county.[114]

The third season opened with Claude Collins taking over as president of the Drama Association. Despite a professional production

---

[111] Collins interview; Cavender, "Melungeons of Upper East Tennessee," 33.

[112] Collins interview, January 2002.

[113] Bible, *The Melungeons*, 116, Juanita Glenn, "Hancock Countians Aiding Dream With Drama," *Knoxville Journal*, Thursday, 11 March 1971.

[114] Glenn, "Hancock Countians Aiding Dream With Drama."

and an unprecedented community effort, the financial resources simply were not available to promote *Walk Toward the Sunset* well enough to attract large numbers of tourists to out-of-the-way Sneedville. Entertainer Tennessee Ernie Ford offered to help raise money and became chairman of the "Friends of the Melungeons." Contributors included the Dr. Pepper Bottling Company of Knoxville, Tennessee, the Rogersville Motor Company, and Alton Greene, a writer from Texas who contributed an article to the souvenir program entitled "The County That Time Forgot." Other individuals from nearby towns and cities contributed to the effort to keep *Walk Toward the Sunset* in production.[115]

Collins continued to serve as a spokesman for the Melungeons, but soon discovered that some reporters came to Sneedville with stereotypical ideas about mountain people, their stories already mentally composed before they asked the first question.

"This newspaper came in here from somewhere," Collins recalled years later. "They wanted to take my picture and interview me and so forth. I said, 'Fine, when do you want to interview me? So we decided on a time, and I said, "Well, now, you'll have to meet me at my house and let me dress up in my best suit and sit on my front porch. Because I don't want to be depicted in a little mountain cabin where I never lived. I never experienced that.' So they didn't interview me."[116]

In August of 1971, the New York *Times* published an article by Jon Nordheimer, entitled "Mysterious Hill Folk Vanishing." Nordheimer noted that many Melungeons had moved away from the poverty and limited opportunities of Hancock County. Citing many of the old theories and legends, Nordheimer touched on their uncertain ancestry. "For many years before the Civil War, Melungeons held an uncertain social status in Hancock County, somewhere between the whites and the 3,000 black slaves." Nordheimer never cited an authority for that number of slaves in the county, which didn't have 3,000 people in total at that time. "After the Civil War, however, intermarriage became acceptable, usually the son of a white family taking a hill girl for his bride, and there were reports of Melungeon males abducting white girls from distant farms to take into the hills with them." The notion that a white girl might voluntarily marry a Melungeon was apparently inconceivable.

---

[115] *Walk Toward the Sunset*, souvenir program, 1971.
[116] Collins interview, January 2002.

Nordheimer spoke with Taylor Collins and his wife, who were preparing to move to Ft. Wayne, Indiana, and with Monroe Collins, who said "All the ridge people have gone up from here and left, or else they're sleeping in their graves, and the ones that leave don't ever find their way back home no more." The article featured photographs that fit the common stereotype of mountaineers: shabbily-dressed people in a rickety cabin. Undeniably, these people existed in Appalachia, and still do. In objecting to having himself portrayed in this manner, Claude Collins had simply wanted to demonstrate that some Melungeons were well-educated and reasonably successful. The *New York Times*, America's newspaper of record, apparently chose not to cover that aspect of Melungeon life. Neither did it mention the outdoor drama, *Walk Toward the Sunset*, which could have benefitted greatly from the national exposure.[117]

On 19 April 1972, the *Kingsport Times* reported:

> "Walk Toward the Sunset," a story of the Melungeons of Hancock County, will be presented again this summer despite financial problems which almost closed the three-year-old drama after last season.
>
> The finances still aren't fully cleared with $3,000 of a $7,000 debt still to be paid, but supporters of the Kermit Hunter drama are planning to open again July 4 weekend and run through Labor Day.[118]

The 26 April 1972, issue of the *Knoxville News-Sentinel* carried an article which publicized the drama and the Melungeons in general.

> Spring air was nippy along Blackwater Creek in Vardy Valley.
>
> So chilly, in fact, that Howard Mullins lifted his hands with palms exposed to coal-fed flames of the open fire.
>
> Such delicate hands, calloused from field work and 110 winters spent in isolated hill country—where necessities of life

---

[117] Jon Nordheimer, "Mysterious Hill Folk Vanishing," *New York Times*, 10 August 1971, 33,38.

[118] "Melungeon Drama Goes On Despite Money Problems," *Kingsport Times*, Wednesday, 19 April 1972.

long since have become luxuries to a mysterious people to whom
Mullins belongs.

He is one of the last of the Melungeons, oldest of them all in
Hancock County. Which has been home to the Melungeons for
200 years.

Those left—in Snake Hollow, Blackwater, Vardy and
Mulberry—are few in number. Most have left the hills for jobs in
cities far and near. And time is catching up with those remaining.

In 1931 there were 40 Melungeon families living on
Newman's Ridge above their ancestral home. Today, only two
families remain on the steep ridges. Genealogist William P.
Grohse, Sr., who lives near Mullins, estimates there may be
under 200 families left in the county.

Melungeon youth, just as others, are leaving rural America
for jobs in towns and cities. Hancock's population of 12,000 in
1900 dropped to 6719 by 1970, according to the US Census....

The Melungeons... like many American traditions, are
passing, just as are some of their own traditions. Graveposts are
disappearing from their cemeteries...

The Melungeons aren't so reticent anymore, or so skeptical
of strangers, and this is largely because of Kermit Hunter's
outdoor drama that's shown here each summer, beginning July 4.
"The Melungeon Story: Walk Toward The Sunset" is staged at
the base of Newman's Ridge in Sneedville. It depicts their travail
and discrimination against them, from the time John Sevier
found them in 1784. It tells how racial bars were broken with the
marriage of a Sneedville white to a beautiful Melungeon lass.
These "people of free color" [sic] finally were permitted by the
Legislature to vote! And famed author Jesse Stuart tells in his
book "Daughter of a Legend" [sic] how he dated a Melungeon
when he was a student at LMU.[119]

Even today, however, Melungeons are lampooned. A recent
magazine article said the drama was concocted to bilk money
from tourists at a Melungeon trap that featured no Melungeons.
How sad! Melungeons built the outdoor theater, helped stage the
play, and performed in it. And Hancock Countians gave money

---

[119] Stuart's *Daughter of the Legend* is not autobiographical and does not mention
Stuart's own experiences.

and labor, signed notes for operating capital, and lost money in efforts to preserve the Melungeon culture and tradition.[120]

Despite the efforts of Tennessee Ernie Ford and the Friends of the Melungeons, production of *Walk Toward the Sunset* was cancelled for the summer of 1972 due to financial problems. Director John Lee Welton had left the production to pursue his doctoral degree; during the 1971 season, the play had been directed by members of the drama department at the University of Tennessee.[121]

In December 1972, Claude Collins and Elmer Turner attended the Eastern Indian Conference in Washington, DC. Sponsored by the Coalition of Eastern Native Americans, the conference was organized by Chief Curtis Custalow of the Mattaponi Reservation near West Point, Virginia. Collins and Turner registered as "Melungeon Indians," and one participant noted "First I ever heard of anyone *claiming* to be a Melungeon."[122] Thirty years later, Collins remembered little of the conference or why he and Turner attended, but he did remember that describing themselves as "Melungeon Indians" enabled them to get a grant to attend the conference. "I think maybe what we were doing [at the conference] was trying to find money," he speculated, recalling the financial difficulties faced by the Drama Association. "And, probably too, we were trying to figure out if we were connected with them."[123]

Dr. Welton returned to direct the drama in the summer of 1973, but the energy crisis caused the production to be cancelled again for the summer of 1974. Gas shortages were causing panic across the country, and Sneedville was a poor place to be stuck without fuel, considering that there were no motels and only one restaurant in the county.[124]

Walk Toward The Sunset closed permanently after the 1976 season. Ticket manager Elmer Turner had died in February 1974, and many other local participants had drifted away from the Drama Association. Cavender cites declining attendance and "bickering between members of

---

[120] Willard Yarbrough, "Melungeons Ways Are Passing," Knoxville *News-Sentinel*, 26 April 1972, 33.

[121] Bible, *The Melungeons*, 116; Welton interview, March 2002.

[122] Everett, "Melungeon History and Myth," 407.

[123] Collins interview, January 2002.

[124] Bible, *The Melungeons*, 116. The Town Motel downtown had only two rooms over the beauty shop and was not open on a regular bases.

the elite" as reasons for the closing of the drama. Claude Collins attaches more importance to the fact local people were not paid for their participation. "That's really why we had to quit. Carson-Newman students were getting paid to come over here. We were boarding them, and also they were getting some sort of a little salary. Our people [the locals] decided they wanted to be paid or they wouldn't be in it. Elmer Turner and I worked every night... we never got a penny." However, Collins also noted the drop in audience numbers. "What happened was, the attendance would drop a little every year, until we would have maybe, for the whole season, a thousand. And that was not enough people."

An observer could reasonably conclude that *Walk Toward the Sunset* never got a break. With just a little luck, the drama might have attracted enough tourists to become self-sustaining. A mention in the *New York Times* might have helped considerably, but the story of educated, self-motivated Melungeons putting on a play didn't fit the motif of despair sought by the author of the article, and so was not mentioned. And the gasoline shortages of 1974 again thwarted the best efforts of the Drama Association members. Some cynical Hancock Countians "knew all along" the play would be unsuccessful, but the show went on for six non-consecutive seasons, a tribute to the hard work and dedication of a few who wanted more opportunities for their children and neighbors. Jean Paterson Bible called *Walk Toward the Sunset* "a happy rendition of the Melungeon swan song. It is a fitting memorial to a vanishing race."[125]

After the *Sunset*: Status in Hancock County

Between 1978 and 1980, Anthony Cavender conducted interviews in Hancock County to determine, among other things, how county residents, both white and Melungeon, felt about the Melungeons. Cavender observed that Melungeon children were sometimes made to feel inferior due to their dark complexions. A 51–year old Melungeon woman, identified as "Elsie," said "I thought I was so ugly. I always thought that dark-skinned people were awful, you know... Well, you know how kids are when you are dark. Then, when I was home, I never

---

[125] Cavender, "The Melungeons of Upper East Tennessee," 34; Collins interview; January 2002; Bible, *The Melungeons*, 117.

realized how precious dark skin was till I left home. Everybody said 'Ahhh, I love your beautiful tan!' Everybody (here) was afraid they'd get brown, or at least us kids did."[126]

Cavender noted that the majority of "self-proclaimed Melungeons...do not look physically different from whites, and most of them occupy enviable positions in business and education."[127] While these "self-proclaimed" Melungeons, presumably including Corinne Bowlin, Claude Collins, Elmer Turner and others, did occupy leading positions in the county, nearly anyone with family ties in Hancock County knew Melungeons who were not, by any stretch of the imagination, part of any "elite." These Melungeons, however, were not as likely to acknowledge that heritage.

Cavender concluded that the majority of whites that he interviewed in Hancock County did not believe in the existence of the Melungeons. As late as 1981, those who did acknowledge the existence of Melungeons considered them people of low origin and even lower potential. A Sneedville merchant, commenting on the out-migration of Melungeons over the years, remarked that several had moved to the Back Valley area to be "closer to the welfare office" in Sneedville.[128]

According to Cavender's interviews, the definition of "Melungeon" in Hancock County depended largely on socio-economic status, and to a lesser extent, the willingness of the individual to proclaim a Melungeon heritage. "The definitional rules... are not uniformly applied to all individuals. Members of the middle and upper socio-economic levels who could be referred to as Melungeons, are not overtly referred to as such. Thus, it appears that the term Melungeon is used to both identify and stigmatize the poor. This observation is supported by the fact that some people use the term Melungeon in reference to any person who is on welfare, regardless of their kinship relations or ancestry."[129]

Daughter of the Legend and *Walk Toward the Sunset* gave many people a new and positive image of the Melungeons. A commonly-heard phrase in Hancock County after 1969 was "Once nobody would say the word 'Melungeon;' now everybody wants to be one." The term "Melungeon" had been transformed—for some, anyway—from an

---

[126] Cavender, "The Melungeons of Upper East Tennessee," 27, 29.

[127] Ibid., 32.

[128] Ibid., 28, 31.

[129] Ibid., 34.

epithet to a name worn proudly. However, many Hancock Countians, as evidenced by those who spoke to Cavender, maintained the same attitudes toward Melungeons as their grandfathers. Unfortunately, some of those who shared that opinion were swarthy-skinned people whose families bore the surnames Collins, Mullins, Gibson, Bowlin, etc. The shame of being called "Melungeon" would cause many to deny having any connection to "those people." Their children and grandchildren would have to learn of their heritage on their own.

6

INTO THE TWENTY-FIRST CENTURY

In 1969, just as the Hancock County Drama Association was about to retrieve the Melungeons' name "from shame to the hall of fame," in the words of the Reverend R. B. Connor, University of North Carolina anthropologists William Pollitzer and William Brown published the results of a genetic survey conducted in Hancock County. In 1965, Pollitzer and Brown made a health study of 72 individuals, identified as Melungeons by a local doctor. The following year, Pollitzer and Brown included 105 more Hancock Countians in their study.

In a later article, Pollitzer concluded that, based on comparisons of blood types, the Melungeons were "about ninety percent White, almost ten percent Indian, and relatively very little Negro in their origin. The analysis is not capable of differentiating between English versus Portuguese as the White component." Pollitzer did not specify what he meant by "relatively very little." By comparison, the Lumbees were determined to be "about forty percent White, forty-seven percent Negro, and thirteen percent Indian." Pollitzer concluded that the Melungeons were an ethnic group of the verge of dissolution through intermarriage with whites.[1]

In the late 1980s, James Guthrie re-analyzed the data collected by Pollitzer and Brown. Using techniques not available to the original study, Guthrie reached similar conclusions, but raised more questions relating to the age-old Melungeon controversy: the question of possible African ancestry. In the 1960s, Pollitzer and Brown were unable to tell whether the European component of the Melungeon makeup was English or Portuguese. Guthrie couldn't determine definitively either, but concluded

---

[1] William Pollitzer, "The Physical Anthropology and Genetics of Marginal People of the Southeastern United States," *American Anthropologist* 74/3 (1972) 723, 730.

that an African component was present in the genetic background of the Melungeons either way. "If it is assumed that the Melungeons are basically English," Guthrie wrote, "a considerable Black component is required" to account for the Melungeons' genetic makeup. That "Black component" would almost certainly have been added after the English arrived in North America. However, Guthrie stated that his findings were consistent with the Melungeons' tradition of Portuguese ancestry, and cited the "early incorporation of a Black component into Mediterranean populations." In other words, the mixture of African and European genes would have occurred much earlier, probably during the Moorish occupation of the Iberian peninsula.[2]

Guthrie offered a fascinating possibility for the origin of the term "Melungeon" from Rollin Gillespie's 1986 study of ancient Celtic Americans. Gillespie suggested that the Melungeons descended from Milesians, the founders of Milan, who left their homeland in Anatolia (present-day Turkey) after its invasion by Persia in 494 B.C. Most of the Milesians went to Ireland, but one group went to the island of Melun in the Seine. Gillespie "relates Caesar's difficulty in driving the 'Melungeons' from their island stronghold in 52 B.C., and suggests some escaped to America." Gillespie also presented evidence that the Melungeons absorbed members of the "Lost Colony" of Roanoke Island.[3]

Guthrie cited similarities in the Melungeons' genetic makeup to populations in Italy, Malta, Portugal, Cyprus, France, Spain, and the Canary Islands. He speculated that the Melungeons were primarily of Portuguese origin, with about five percent each of "Black and Cherokee." For the most part, Guthrie's finding's verified the claims of Portuguese ancestry that were a part of the Melungeon oral tradition—a tradition that had been labeled mythical six years earlier by David Henige.[4]

Henige and DeMarce Examine Legends

---

[2] James Guthrie, "Melungeons: Comparison of Gene Frequency Distributions to those of Worldwide Populations," *Tennessee Anthropologist* XV/I (Spring 1990): 13, 17.

[3] Rollin W. Gillespie, cited in Guthrie, "Melungeons," 13.

[4] Guthrie, "Melungeons," 17–18.

According to researcher David Henige, the Melungeons' claims of Portugese ancestry were a myth designed to deflect the belief of neighboring whites that the Melungeons had "black blood." Henige equated the Melungeons tradition of being "Portyghee" with the fanciful origin tales told by earlier writers, and those associated with (but not necessarily perpetuated by) the Guineas of West Virginia, the Lumbees of North Carolina, and the Jackson Whites of New Jersey. What they all had in common, Henige wrote, is that, like other American "racial isolates," they "have always defined themselves negatively; they have been willing to regard themselves as white and Indian but never as black..."[5]

Henige is the Africana Bibliographer at the University of Wisconsin—Madison. He has studied African oral traditions and became interested in the oral tradition of origin associated with the Lumbees, that of descent from the "Lost Colonists" or Roanoke Island. He expanded his study to include the Guineas, Melungeons, and Jackson Whites. "It occurred to me how extraordinarily similar these traditions were to the ones I had run across in Africa and Oceana and other places."[6]

Henige wrote in 1984 that "these groups perceived their distant past as being characterized by constant large-scale migrations." They came to their present location from somewhere far away: Portugal, for example. Henige cites Swan Burnett's recollection of Melungeons claiming Portuguese origin. He includes the "Celebrated Melungeon Case" in which Lewis Shepherd established, at least to the satisfaction of the Tennessee Supreme Court, an origin in ancient Carthage and a route to America through the Iberian peninsula. He also refers to Dromgoole's articles and her incorporation of "all the current notions of Melungeon origins into a single grand design," as well as more modern theories that popped up in twentieth century newspaper and magazine features. Henige dismisses all these theories in favor of census reports. The 1790 census showed numerous but unidentified "free persons of color" in areas where Melungeons lived. By 1830, Melungeon surnames were being listed as "free persons of color." However, Henige writes that "since the color line was inconsistently drawn from one locale to another, the Melungeons often managed to be classified as white during much of

---

[5] David Henige, "Origin Traditions of American Racial Isolates: A Case of Something Borrowed," *Appalachian Journal* (Spring 1984): 210.

[6] David Henige, interview by Wayne Winkler, telephone, September 1997.

this century. Even so, they must have regarded this good fortune as tenuous. In these circumstances, claims of Carthaginian, Portuguese, or merely English origins could help to reinforce and justify their endangered white status."[7]

Henige does not differentiate between what the Melungeons said of themselves and what was said about them. He makes that distinction in the case of the Lumbee in order to de-legitimize their particular origin theories. Henige does not point out that the Melungeons themselves only perpetuated two theories of origin: Portuguese, as documented by the *Littel's Living Age* article[8] at least as far back as the 1840s, and Indian, as related by Sneedville attorney Lewis Jarvis in 1903.[9] Other theories were the inventions of researchers and feature writers. By including them in such detail, Henige associates the Melungeons' own reasonable claims with the more fanciful claims made on their behalf, thereby dismissing their claims of origin along with those of the Guineas, Jackson Whites, and Lumbees.

Of course, the point of Henige's article is undeniable: there is a similarity in the oral traditions of origin among these groups, and much that is fanciful in those traditions—especially those traditions invented by feature writers. Henige believes that the tri-racials were the product of Colonial-era intermarriage between whites, blacks, and Indians. He acknowledges the social disadvantages inherent in such ancestry, and recognizes that individuals and groups would have a valid reason to create origin myths to explain their dark skins to a hostile white society. "I can't get into the minds of people who do this, of course," Henige said in 1997, "but if it were me and I had some choices, I'd make the choice that seemed to make me feel best about myself and made hope others would feel better about me than they did before." Discrimination against non-whites "was the principal motivation; it almost had to be, in terms of education, marriage, job opportunities, and so forth."[10]

Henige's assessment of why Melungeons in past generations might make up a story about being "Portyghee" is inarguable. His later application of that assessment to modern Melungeons touched on issues

---

[7] Henige, "Something Borrowed," 204.

[8] "The Melungeons," *Littel's Living Age.*

[9] Lewis M. Jarvis, *Hancock County Times,* 17 April 1903, cited in Elder, *Melungeons,* 74.

[10] Henige interview, September 1997.

that continue to divide Melungeons and researchers into the twenty-first century.

"The answer to the question, 'Where did the mysterious Melungeons come from?' is three words, and the three words are: Louisa County, Virginia, " says Virginia DeMarce, former president of the National Genealogical Society. "It's not that mysterious once you do the nitty-gritty research, one family at a time, the way one should.

"The great majority of the families that lived in Hawkins and then Hancock County, Tennessee, that is, the classic Melungeon area, can, using standard genealogical evidence, be traced back through a migration pattern that came either through central North Carolina and then western Orange County and Wilkes County and into that area, or through southwestern Virginia—Montgomery and Grayson County, and into [Hancock County]."[11]

In 1992 and 1993, DeMarce wrote two articles for the National Genealogical Society *Quarterly* concerning Melungeons and other tri-racial groups. In her second article, "Looking at Legends—Lumbee and Melungeon: Applied Genealogy and the Origins of Tri-racial Isolate Settlements," DeMarce recounts the tradition that British-American farmers found English-speaking Indian farmers when they moved into what is now Robeson County, North Carolina, then contrasts that tradition with records showing that no Indians were found in the area. "Mixed-bloods," however, were present. A North Carolina legislator complained that "The County of Robeson is cursed with a free-coloured population that migrated originally from the districts round about the Roanoke and Neuse Rivers."[12]

DeMarce traced the primary Lumbee families—Chavis, Goins, Cumbo, Sweat, Braboy (or Braveboy), Manuel (Emmanuel) and Locklear—from the Virginia Tidewater area to lower North Carolina and upper South Carolina. Finally, DeMarce declared that all evidence indicates the Lumbees had a tri-racial origin.[13]

In discussing the Melungeons, DeMarce states "Some writers today use the term generically, embracing the entire constellation of tri-racial groups. Technically, however, it belongs to the interrelated families

---

[11] Virginia Easley DeMarce, Wayne Winkler, telephone interview, August 1997.

[12] John Hope Franklin, *The Free Negro in North Carolina*, quoted by DeMarce, "Looking at Legends," 27.

[13] DeMarce, "Looking at Legends," 28–31.

along Newman's Ridge in Hawkins County, where they lived for forty years or so prior to 1844, when the area was cut away into the new county of Hancock." She suggests that many of the tri-racial families identified by Edward Price in the early 1950s as "Melungeons" have no connection with the "central group in Hawkins County."[14]

Using census and tax records, DeMarce traced those she defined as the primary Melungeon families—Collins, Gibson, Bowlin, Bunch, and Denham—back to central Virginia, primarily Louisa and surrounding counties. These families took two main migration paths to Newman's Ridge, and DeMarce maintains that they were a mixture of white, black, and Indian.

As for their claims of Portuguese ancestry, DeMarce saw much the same motivation as that noted by Henige. "Part of it, I think, was deliberate obfuscation—people who didn't want outsiders involved with their communities, fobbing them off with all sorts of stories." The truth of the Melungeons ancestry, she says, has been available to anyone who wanted to check. "People have tended to rely on oral tradition and folklore rather than the long, tedious process of sitting down with county records. I'm not the only person who's tracing it. Jack Goins over in Rogersville, Tennessee has traced his own family lines and has come up with almost precisely the same conclusions I have... Journalists have tended to track through other journalists, and go back to those imaginative feature articles Will Allen Dromgoole wrote in the late nineteenth century. They simply haven't done their homework."[15]

DeMarce concedes that there might have been a Portuguese connection through one family, but notes that claims of "Portuguese " ancestry were associated with many tri-racial groups, likely in response to "the perpetual wish for non-African ancestry. "A claim to Mediterranean ancestry offered a logical and viable alternative" to being considered black, with the resulting loss of social status.[16]

As writer Chris Everett points out, "throughout much of the nineteenth century and well into the early twentieth, 'Portuguese' was regularly nothing other than a euphemism for mixed African-American heritage."[17] DeMarce related a tale of her early genealogical research into

---

[14] Ibid

[15] Demarce interview, August 1997.

[16] DeMarce, "Looking at Legends," 36–37.

[17] Everett, "Melungeon History and Myth," 369.

her own family, when her grandfather warned her that she might find some "Carolina Portuguese" in the family. When she asked what a "Carolina Portuguese" was, her grandfather replied, "A mulatto who's got too much money for anyone to call him that to his face."[18]

Still, DeMarce recognizes another possibility—"that there might be a kernel of truth in the tradition" of Portuguese ancestry among the Melungeons, "even though literary attempts to prove it are faulty." She concludes, however, that although "[m]any isolate groups still resist the idea of African-American ancestry," if they wish to learn the truth about their origins they "must be willing to consider the possibility" of European, Native American, and African components in their backgrounds.[19]

Brent Kennedy and the "Melungeon Movement"

In the mid-1980s, Atlanta resident Brent Kennedy realized that something was very wrong with his health. Bouts of exhaustion turned into painful swelling in his arms and legs. He had spells of fever, difficulty in breathing, and blurred vision, and doctors were unable to determine what was wrong.

Kennedy was a senior vice-president and Chief Operating Officer for Jerold Panas Linzy and Partners, a development consulting firm specializing in campaign planning and direction for non-profit institutions. He had come a long way from his roots in Wise, Virginia, where he earned an undergraduate degree at Clinch Valley College. He went on to the University of Tennessee, eventually earning a doctoral degree in communications. Brent Kennedy had built a successful life which now seemed in danger of ending because of a disease no one could identify.

Finally, in 1988, Kennedy learned that he had sarcoidosis, a disease most prevalent in those of Mediterranean and Middle Eastern descent.[20] Kennedy, however, believed he was of Scots-Irish descent, as were most of his neighbors Wise County. As Kennedy began researching his family

---

[18] Virginia Easley DeMarce, Wayne Winkler, in-person interview, September 1998.

[19] DeMarce, "Looking at Legends," 36–37.

[20] Kennedy was later diagnosed with Familial Mediterranean Fever, which is even more rare among people of northern European background.

history, he was astonished to learn that many of his ancestors were Melungeons. A lot of mysteries were cleared up by this knowledge.

"I had known that [my family] had a different heritage," said Kennedy in 1997. "The purely physical characteristics of my family told me that. My mother, my brother, my aunts and uncles all had a Mediterranean or Middle Eastern look, but it didn't make sense because the family said 'No, we're English and Scots-Irish.'And frankly, the genealogy said that. The census records said that."[21]

Kennedy tried to interest scholars and scientists in examining the ethnic background of the Melungeons, but to no avail. In 1992 he organized a group of researchers into the Melungeon Research Committee. This group included researchers from various institutions, including historian Eloy Gallegos, Arlee Gowen of the Gowen Research Foundation, Robert Elston of Louisiana State University, Khalid Awan of the University of Virginia, Jeffrey Chapman, Charles Faulkner, Benita Howell, Richard Jantz, and Jack Williams, all from the University of Tennessee, and Chester DePratter from the University of South Carolina. Some of these researchers have since left the Committee and some disagree to varying degrees with the conclusions Kennedy eventually put in a book, entitled *The Melungeons: The Resurrection of a Proud People; An Untold Story of Ethnic Cleansing in America.*[22]

"You have to go back to the 1500s, I think, to get to the primary origin of the Melungeons," says Kennedy.[23] He wrote:

> I contend that the remnants of Joao ("Juan") Pardo's forts, joined by Portuguese refugees from Santa Elena, and possibly a few stray Dominicans and Jesuits, exiled Moorish French Huguenots, and escaped Acadians, along with [Sir Francis] Drake's and perhaps other freed Turkish, Moorish, and Iberian captives, survived on these shores, combined forces over the ensuing years, moved to the hinterlands, intermarried with various Carolina and Virginia Native Americans, and eventually became the reclusive Melungeons.[24]

---

[21] Brent Kennedy, Wayne Winkler, in-person interview, July 1997, Wise VA.

[22] C. S. Everett, "Melungeon History and Myth," 360, 391.

[23] Kennedy interview, July 1997.

[24] Kennedy, *The Melungeons*, 137.

In his preface, Kennedy acknowledges that he is expressing his own opinions rather than the findings of the Melungeon Research Committee. He describes his book as a "manifesto," rather than an academic treatise.

> I strongly emphasize that I am not an historian, an anthropologist, or a professional writer. I continue to need—and energetically seek—the assistance of others. If there are errors in my work, or if any readers have information or insight that could further refine or illuminate the sometimes hesitant conclusions in these pages, please share that information with me and I will see that it is incorporated into our research.[25]

Kennedy hypothesizes that the term *Melungeon* "has its base in the Arabic *melun jinn* which means 'cursed soul' or 'one who has been abandoned by God.' It's also found in Turkish [*melun can*[26]], where it's pronounced 'melun-JUHN, and it's found in Portuguese, where it's pronounced 'melun-JHAHN. But all three have their base in Arabic and all three are Muslim terms used by Muslim people to describe themselves when their luck had run out."[27]

Most researchers in the past had observed that the Melungeons resented the term and did not use it to identify themselves, leading to the natural assumption that the name had been imposed on the Melungeons by their Anglo neighbors. Kennedy contends that the name had been turned into an epithet over time, but had originated with the Melungeons themselves. Referring to the ethnic mixture that made up the early Melungeons, Kennedy argues that "the Turkish/Moorish element was at least in the beginning the predominant one, explaining why the probable Turkish self-descriptive term 'Melungeon' came to be associated with the various populations regardless of their location."[28]

Kennedy's claim of a Turkish origin for the Melungeons interested the Turkish government, and in April of 1995, Kennedy visited Turkey as a guest of the Turkic World Research Foundation, a group of scholars who explore the dispersal of Turkic peoples around the world. The Foundation had already been studying the possible connections between

---

[25] Ibid., viii.

[26] In Turkish, the letter "c" is pronounced as the English "j."

[27] Kennedy interview, July 1997.

[28] Kennedy, *The Melungeons*, 137.

Turks and American Indians. Recognizing that many Turkish and Moorish sailors became galley slaves on Portuguese ships, some of which went to the "New World," Turkish researchers were intrigued by the possibility that a population of Turkish descendants existed in southern Appalachia.[29]

Kennedy met Nuri Ertan, the mayor of Çesme, a fishing village on the Aegean coast. The region around Çesme provided many of the Ottoman seamen who were captured by the Spanish and Portuguese and who never returned home. Kennedy and Ertan developed a warm friendship, and Wise, Virginia, and Çesme became sister cities. Turkish officials later named a mountain outside Çesme "Melungeon Mountain" and maintained it as a memorial to Turkish sailors who were "taken away to America by Portuguese people in 16th century."[30]

In an appendix entitled "Common Melungeon Related Surnames," Kennedy does not restrict the list of Melungeon name to the commonly-cited names of the Newman's Ridge Melungeons—Gibson, Collins, Mullins, Bunch, Denham, and Goins—or even the expanded list compiled by Edward Price, which included families such as Nichols, Sexton, Perkins, and others from Melungeon communities in Kentucky and Virginia. Kennedy listed 137 family names as "Melungeon-Related."

The immediate effect of Kennedy's book was not just a renewal of interest in the Melungeons, but an expansion of that interest. The story has always attracted readers, as evidenced by generations of feature writers. Kennedy's book suggested to a lot of people that they might be Melungeons themselves. With 137 possible names, the odds of finding one of those names in one's individual family tree were pretty good—especially if one lived in or had ancestors from southern Appalachia.

Kennedy left his job in Atlanta and took the position of vice-chancellor at his *alma mater*, Clinch Valley College in Wise, Virginia. He hit the lecture and media circuit in the upper South, and word of his book began to spread. Audiences were fascinated by the idea of Turkish sailors adapting to a new life among North American Indians, and enthralled by the possibility that they were descended from such "exotic" forebears. Reporters were intrigued by Kennedy's speculation that

---

[29] Ibid., 130–31.
[30] Sign on Melungeon Mountain, Çesme, Turkey.

Abraham Lincoln and Elvis Presley were descended from Melungeons.[31] Helping to spread the word about this historical phenomenon was the rapidly growing modern phenomenon of the Internet.

A relative told Mary Goodyear about Kennedy's book, and she began researching the Melungeons in the belief that she would find a connection to her own family. "I wanted to know who [the Melungeons] were," says the Shauk, Ohio, native. "People weren't talking about it. I asked many people and nobody had an answer who they were, or if they really existed or if they were a figment of somebody's imagination. I searched the Internet, encyclopedias, dictionaries, everything—you couldn't even find the word." Believing that others shared her interest in the subject, Goodyear began coordinating a Melungeon e-mail list in the fall of 1996.[32]

On weekends, Mary Goodyear's mail list had as many as 650 messages from people seeking genealogical data or general information about the Melungeons. The *Wall Street Journal* printed an article about the renewed interest in the Melungeons and the role played by the Internet in feeding that interest. With so many people talking to each other, Goodyear felt that they were almost like family, and proposed a get-together in Wise, Virginia, home of Clinch Valley College where Brent Kennedy worked. Someone suggested this would be like a family reunion, but Goodyear pointed out they'd never gotten together before, therefore it couldn't be a *re*-union. Thus the name "First Union" was given to the gathering; organizers expected about 50 people to show up.[33]

Instead, more than 600 people showed up in tiny Wise, Virginia on Satruday, 26 July 1997. From the steps of the Wise County Courthouse, the mayor of Çesme, Turkey, Nuri Ertan, welcomed the citizens of Çesme's sister city. Brent Kennedy spoke briefly, inviting everyone to the Clinch Valley College campus where presentations would be made. Then Connie Clark, a high school teacher from nearby Big Stone Gap, Virginia, took the microphone.

---

[31] Kennedy, *The Melungeons*, 28–31, 140.

[32] Mary Goodyear, Wayne Winkler, in-person interview, July 1997, Wise, VA.

[33] Goodyear interview, July 1997; Fred. R. Bleakley, "Appalachian Clan Mines Web Sites for Ancestral Clues," *Wall Street Journal* (14 April 1997): B-1, B-5.

"Fifty years ago, cousins" she intoned, "we couldn't have stood right here on these courthouse steps. We could not have been here; we probably wouldn't have been *allowed* to be here!"[34]

At the gathering on the CVC campus, Bill Fields of Seymour, Tennessee, talked about hearing Brent Kennedy speak for the first time. "I went in [to the lecture] absolutely sure that my family was white...I came out, and I was absolutely sure that they weren't." His newsletter *Under One Sky*, is sent to Melungeon researchers across the country.

> What people want to know is whether or not their ancestors were Melungeon—and that's a really difficult question. There's no paper trail. A lot of people come at this research from family history research, and traditional genealogy will teach you that you have to have paper documentation, you have to have evidence to say that this person is the son of this person is the son of this person. There's no paper to say, "This person is a Melungeon, this person is a Lumbee..." In the case of the Melungeons, often people were trying to hide that identity. The last thing they were going to do was get it written down on a piece of paper.[35]

Kennedy's Critics

Not everyone shared the enthusiasm of the First Union participants for Brent Kennedy's work. "Of course, the amount of publicity that is being generated for the unverified theories," Virginia DeMarce commented, "in my view, leads to people believing things roughly equivalent to the people who believe that aliens landed in Roswell, New Mexico, but there's really nothing one can do about that."[36]

DeMarce wrote a very critical review of Kennedy's book in the June 1996 issue of the National Genealogical Society's *Quarterly*.

> Kennedy does not use the term Melungeon in its anthropological sense—that is, the interlocking families who moved into, existed in, and dispersed from Hawkins and

---

[34] Connie Clark, Wayne Winkler, audio recording, July 1997, Wise, VA.

[35] Bill Fields, Wayne Winkler, in-person interview, July 1997, Wise, VA.

[36] DeMarce interview, August 1997.

Hancock Counties, Tennessee. Rather, he coins a very loose definition, expanding it to cover essentially all colonial-era Virginians and Carolinians who (in whatever records he consulted) are not clearly stated to be European American or African American. *Melungeon* thus becomes a catchall description for dark-skinned individuals whose ancestry does not seem to be sub-Saharan Africa—as well as their lighter-skinned relatives and descendants, whom he presents as subjects of racial prejudice.[37]

DeMarce questions Kennedy's claim that the Melungeons faced discrimination, persecution, and even "ethnic cleansing." In the introduction to his book, Kennedy describes the Melungeons as a people "ravaged, and nearly destroyed, by the senseless excesses of racial prejudice and ethnic cleansing."[38] DeMarce writes that this assertion "begs for supporting evidence—as does his contention that Melungeon families were originally large landowners, deprived and marginalized by Scotch-Irish and other northern-European settlers... The author's theme of ancestral persecution by other community settlers is difficult to uphold... Kennedy's own accounts of twentieth-century oppressions and slights reveal that members of these families who had risen in social rank were among those who discriminated against those of lesser social rank. The question arises whether the issue of prejudice was one of ethnicity or socioeconomics."[39]

A major part of Kennedy's book is devoted to tracing his own genealogy. DeMarce takes issue with his findings."I identified many inaccuracies in the family lines that he published in the book. I did a great deal of background research. Basically, I said the evidence in all of the documents such as the census does not substantiate Dr. Kennedy's claim that his family lines were Melungeon. There is no evidence anywhere in the documentary record that they were other than white."[40]

Kennedy depicts the 1790 census as "grounds for stripping Melungeons of their properties and their rights." Because the

---

[37] Virginia DeMarce, "The Melungeons" (review essay), *National Genealogical Quarterly* (June 1996): 135.

[38] Kennedy, *The Melungeons*, xiii.

[39] DeMarce, "The Melungeons," 137, 149.

[40] DeMarce interview, August 1997.

Melungeons did not fit the convenient legal categories of "White," "Negro," "Indian," or "Mulatto," the Melungeons were classified as "free persons of color," or "fpc." The result, according to Kennedy, was a loss of rights, and often of property.[41]

"In checking Kennedy's family lines," DeMarce writes, "this reviewer consistently found the opposite—not a single instance in which his named ancestors, from 1790 through 1900, appear in public documents as anything but white. The legal acceptance of these lines as white by local officials contrasts curiously with the author's repeated statements that they were routinely labeled *fpc*." She also pointed out several mistakes in Kennedy's analysis of his genealogy.[42]

DeMarce concludes, "If the motto of Romantic literature was "any time but now, and any place but here," then Kennedy's motto appears to be, "any ancestry is preferable to northern European... he has—through his redefinition of the word *Melungeon*—essentially invented a 'new race,' a new and historically non-existent oppressed minority that belies his own ancestry."[43]

Kennedy wrote a reply to DeMarce's review which was not published in the *Quarterly*. As he explained in a later interview:

> Virginia [DeMarce] relies totally on the written record. The written record is only as good as the people who wrote that record. With the Melungeons, several things are at play. First of all, the genealogical records pertaining to race and ethnicity are woefully inadequate and inaccurate. You know, people who were chosen to be census takers in the 1700s were not anthropologists and physicians; these [jobs] were political payoffs, and if the person could read and write, that was a real plus. These were the people who were designating race. That worked both ways. Sometimes if a person was "too dark," he became "mulatto" or "black" or "Melungeon" or whatever. And sometimes that same person might, if they happened to have a friendship with the census taker, might be white in the next census and then hang onto that classification. So we have to recognize that that sort of thing happened.

---

[41] Kennedy, *The Melungeons*, 12–13.
[42] Demarce, "The Melungeons," 137.
[43] Ibid., 149.

The other thing, which is to me the real crux of the issue here, is that so much of the admixture of these Melungeons—and by Melungeons, I mean this broad-based Mediterranean/ Middle Eastern population, and they were people from everywhere, not just a few isolated families on hilltops—but the broad base of these people had already admixed before the first census was taken. So there's no way to go back prior to that period and be able to point out with any certainty that these people either were or were not Melungeons. What you do is you go back as far as you can genealogically, and then make certain assumptions. The written record does not, at least in this country, reflect the reality of who we are and where we came from.[44]

In a reply published on a now-defunct Melungeon website, Kennedy writes:

I continue to be amazed that DeMarce is seemingly genuinely convinced that a few isolated Melungeon families in the 1600s remain but a few isolated Melungeon families in the 1990s. Did these people not reproduce?... She is wrong. Her mistake falls into the same vein as her other mistakes: she assumes the written record is the only reality and that it is always accurate. DeMarce identifies a few early Melungeon families, assumes that those are the only ones, and the excludes all other populations and individuals from kinship.

The reality is that those she identified were merely the "tips of icebergs," metaphorically speaking.[45]

David Henige also criticizes Kennedy's work. "I don't think that it has a right to be called a scholarly book and I'm astonished that it was published by a scholarly press. To me, it falls well short of the accepted principals for tying evidence and argument together. It's just bad history."

---

[44] Brent Kennedy, Wayne Winkler, in-person interview, April 1998, Johnson City, TN.

[45] Brent Kennedy, "Kennedy Response to DeMarce," 15 September 1997, *A Melungeon Homepage*, Darlene Wilson webmaster, http://www.clinch.edu/appalachia/ melungeon, page now defunct.

Referring to the various theories that have been expounded about the Melungeons over the years, Henige says, "Kennedy has kind of taken them all and made sort of a mega-theory out of it where everything fits in somehow—some more than others. The Turkish thing is, I think, the one he pushes the hardest. This is definitely a case of taking what's out there, building on it, and using it as a form of corporate self-esteem.

"I don't begrudge groups who feel they need to feel better about themselves to find whatever way they want to make that happen. That's fine; we all do that. But then you fall back on what we generally call scholarship... I feel that you have to make a better case than [Kennedy] has made. I'm a bit, I suppose, befuddled that people don't seem to care that he can't make his case. Or else they just assume he does."[46]

Henige's review of *The Melungeons* in the *Appalachian Journal* was even more scathing that DeMarce's. In his review, entitled "The Melungeons Become a Race," Henige quotes Ian Hacking, who wrote "Do I want to live in a scholarly community where so many bad arguments are taken seriously?" He then proceeds to savage Kennedy's book, criticizing even the cover art.

It must be said out the outset that *The Melungeons* is a remarkably egocentric work. N. Brent Kennedy is not only its author but its centerpiece from whom all description and argumentation radiate. This is never in doubt. Already in the frontispiece he and five relatives gaze back at the reader... Two chapters, more than 40 percent of the text, are devoted to detailing the authors maternal and paternal ancestors, not without, as noted below, numerous misattributions, and for good measure he traces his own ancestry back to Pocahontas.[47]

Henige repeatedly uses Kennedy's rejection of the traditional "tri-racial isolate theory" to argue that Kennedy rejects the notion of an African component in the Melungeons' background. Commenting on Kennedy's claim that some ancestors of the Melungeons might be of mixed Berber, Jewish, and Basque heritage, Henige writes that they

---

[46] Henige interview, September 1997.

[47] David Henige, "The Melungeons Become a Race," *Appalachian Journal* 25.3 (Spring 1998): 270–271.

would "therefore [be] one of the very tri-racial groups that he otherwise finds offensive!"[48]

Henige is not the only observer to see in Kennedy's work—or more precisely, in its acceptance by so many "white" people of possible Melungeon ancestry—yet another Melungeon denial of African ancestry. Kennedy acknowledged that some people were quick to accept his hypothesis of a Mediterranean/Middle Eastern origin as an explanation for the Melungeon complexion that rejects the possibility of black forebears. However, Kennedy includes an African component in his suggested Melungeon gene pool,[49] and consistently argues that the Melungeons were of partial African ancestry. "My contention is this: We Melungeons are absolutely tri-racial—or quad-racial, or however many races there are. We are that. There is no doubt in my mind... Anyone who says that we are not related to all people is totally wrong."[50]

Henige, like DeMarce, repeatedly criticizes Kennedy for sloppy scholarship. "Several examples have already illustrated that *The Melungeons* is a fabric of assertions that are almost never supported by documentation and never by original sources, thus depriving Kennedy's argument of the credibility that comes from being able to be tested.... From all this a question naturally arises. Is there a point in demonstrating the many defects of N. Brent Kennedy's scholarship? It must be conceded immediately that it is unlikely that doing this will dissuade believers who will see such criticism as nothing more than hegemonic behavior quite in line with that which, as Kennedy and others argue, has come before."[51]

The *Appalachian Journal* published a reply to Henige's article in the same issue. Darlene Wilson, then a Ph.D. candidate at the University of Kentucky, attended high school with Brent Kennedy, and has done considerable Melungeon research. She points out in the first paragraph of her reply that "Kennedy clearly states that he is not a historian. To hold a non-academic writer to a standards of scholarship that he didn't aim to

---

[48] Henige, "The Melungeons Become a Race," 274.
[49] Kennedy, *The Melungeons*, 143.
[50] Kennedy interview, April 1998.
[51] Henige, "The Melungeons Become a Race," 278, 282.

meet provides the academic reviewer an unwarranted platform from which to lecture."[52]

Wilson continues, "Both DeMarce and Henige have a legitimate grievance and that is with Mercer University Press or with whoever gave them the idea in the first place that Kennedy's work should be considered a scholarly work of history... Kennedy would have been better served had his editor eliminated all attempts at notes and merely included a bibliography of suggested reading."

The Melungeons had, by November of 1997, sold over 10,000 copies, "roughly three-to-four times the average initial sales of an academic work by any university press, especially a minor one," writes Wilson. "Kennedy's book is indeed considered a single family's history by the readers I have heard from; only a fraction of that audience are academics. Thus we need to consider *The Melungeons'* impact among a predominantly Appalachian-oriented lay-readership."[53]

Scholars like Henige, Wilson argues, have discouraged scholarly studies of the Melungeons' history "by treating the topic with derision and contempt," and she points to Henige's 1984 article as an example. Kennedy's book, she maintains, rang "loudly and convincingly with many Appalachian people who have begun to re-examine their own de-racialized histories and genealogical myths... Simply stated, Kennedy opened the closet door on Appalachia's ugly history of racism, caste- and class-differentiation, and showed that it isn't ancient history but something quite current."[54]

Kennedy's work, Wilson argued, inspired non-academics to explore their own family histories in a way that an academic like Henige never could. Furthermore, "present-day Melungeons aren't going to go back into the historical closet simply because Henige chides Kennedy in print for scholarly sins."[55]

In still the same issue of *Appalachian Journal*, Henige has the last word in what was becoming a tiresome debate. "Wilson absolves Kennedy on the grounds that he does not pretend to be a historian. True enough, but he very much pretends to be writing history."

---

[52] Darlene Wilson, "A Response to Henige," *Appalachian Journal* 25/3, Spring 1998, 287.

[53] Wilson, "Resonse," 287.

[54] Ibid., 288.

[55] Ibid., 294.

Acknowledging the sales figures of *The Melungeons*, Henige declares that "it should not be granted the amnesty that Wilson would confer on it. After all, taking a sledgehammer to a gnat is a compliment to the gnat."[56]

Turkey and Melungeons

As noted earlier, Brent Kennedy's hypothesis that Melungeons had a genetic connection to Turks—or more precisely, to ethnic groups commonly found in the former Ottoman Empire—did not go unnoticed in Turkish academic circles. The Turkic World Research Foundation is devoted to the study of Turkic peoples around the world. Much of their research involved possible connections between Turkic peoples and American Indians.

In the revised 1997 edition of his book, Kennedy recounts his first trip to Turkey in 1995, and points out several linguistic similarities between Turkish words and phrases that have always been assumed to have originated with Native Americans. For example, "Kentucky," thought to have originated with a phrase from an unspecified Indian language, *kan tok*, meaning "dark and bloody ground. The Turkish phrase *kan tok* means "full of blood." "Alabama" is very similar to *Allah bamya*, meaning "God's graveyard," while "Tennessee" is close to the Turkish *tenasüh*, meaning "a place where souls move about."[57]

Although Kennedy and other researchers compiled a long list of "Indian" words which have parallels in the Turkish language, linguistic similarities can be drawn between many languages, and are usually merely coincidental. The Turkic World Research Foundation, founded in 1980 and directed by Professor Turan Yasgan, sponsored further research, and hosted various delegations of Melungeons in Turkey. A Melungeon delegation visited in 1998 and met with Turkey's president, Suleymann Demeril, along with other cabinet officials, members of the Turkish Parliament, and of course, Turkish journalists. The media coverage of the visiting Melungeons was so extensive that the proprietor of a remote gasoline station in the Taurus Mountains recognized several members of the delegation from television.

---

[56] David Henige, "Henige Answers Wilson," *Appalachian Journal* 25/3 (Spring 1998): 297–98.

[57] Kennedy, *The Melungeons*, 132–33.

The Turkish Minister of Culture, Istemehan Talay, explained why Melungeons were so interesting to the Turkish people. "We see the Melungeons as our relatives in the United States, and we are also proud and happy that, after so many years, they still continue their relationship with Turks, with Turkey, and are conscious of their roots and of their cultural heritage. In the last two years, in the media and in the press, many publications and many speeches about the Melungeons took place. So public opinion is very much aware of the presence of Melungeons in the United States and their interests [in] Turkey."[58]

Turkish interest in the Melungeons has a geo-political aspect. An under-appreciated ally of the US, Turkey has long supported American interests, including support for Israel, often to the displeasure of its more hard-line Muslim neighbors. However, Turkish interests—particularly those which place Turkey in conflict with Greece—have routinely been ignored or thwarted by the US government. Turkish politicians realized that the discovery of a sizable population of Turkic people in the United States might help counter the influential "Greek lobby" in America.

President Suleymann Demeril recognized that the research connecting Melungeons and Turks was still at an early stage, and was far from conclusive. "But if [the theories of Turkish origin can be proved], we will make a big information campaign in Turkey, showing that we have some brothers and sisters in the United States... It will be a bridge."[59]

The work of the Turkic World Research Foundation was hampered by economic downturns in Turkey caused by the devastating 1999 earthquake and the resulting political turmoil. In the meantime, Brent Kennedy, in his capacity as vice-chancellor at Clinch Valley College (renamed the University of Virginia's College at Wise), had established student and faculty exchanges with Istanbul University and Dumlupinar University.

Examining the Iberian Connection

---

[58] Istemehan Talay, Wayne Winkler, in-person interview, June 1998, Ancara, Turkey.

[59] Suleymann Demeril, Wayne Winkler, in-person interview, June 1998, Ankara, Turkey.

Following the publication of Kennedy's book, other researchers took on the Melungeon legend. Eloy Gallegos and Manuel Mira published books in the 1990s arguing that the European component of Melungeon ancestry originated on the Iberian peninsula. Gallegos, in his 1997 book *The Melungeons: The Pioneers of the Interior United States, 1526–1997*, argues that the Melungeons descended from Spanish families, many of whom occupied Juan Pardo's series of forts in what became the southeastern United States. Mira's 1998 book *The Forgotten Portuguese: The Melungeons and Other Groups; The Portuguese Making of America* contends that the Melungeons are of Portuguese descent.[60]

The Spanish and Portuguese men who entered the southern Appalachian mountains with Juan Pardo in the sixteenth century meant to stay, according to Gallegos. "They did not come as explorers, they weren't *conquistadores*. They came to conquer no one and they conquered no one." When the Spanish abandoned Santa Elena in 1587 about 125 men were left at forts scattered across the interior. Records indicate that they and their families still occupied these interior forts twenty years later, after some of the men had married women of the Cherokee, Creek, and Catawba tribes. Gallegos speculates that as the half-Indian children of these Spanish and Portuguese began to multiply, they formed a separate culture, one more European than Indian. "Many of them would have had, by necessity, to have married Indian women. But I feel, based on some of the evidence we have, that probably after the first generation they married within their own community... [They] were a community apart from the total Indian community."[61]

"By the later part of the 1700s," Gallegos writes, "the descendants of Pardo's 'The Few' were no longer Spanish or Portuguese. They numbered in the tens of thousands and had spread out all over the Southeastern United States... They had become a *melange*, a mixture, by the beginning of the 1800s."[62] These descendants of Iberian settlers then formed the core of not only the Melungeons, according to Gallegos, but the Brass Ankles, Redbones, and Lumbees as well.

---

[60] Gallegos, *The Melungeons*; Manuel Mira, *The Forgotten Portuguese: The Melungeons and Other Groups* (Franklin NC: Portuguese-American Historical Research Foundation, Inc., 1998).

[61] Gallegos, *The Melungeons*, 60, Eloy Gallegos, Wayne Winkler, in-person interview, September 1998, Knoxville, TN.

[62] Gallegos, *The Melungeons*, 153.

Gallegos, an original member of Brent Kennedy's Melungeon Research Committee, does not completely reject Kennedy's theory of a Turkish component in the ancestry of the Melungeons. However, he "very emphatically disagrees that the Turkish input was provided as early as the sixteenth century, i.e. by way of the Drake/Roanoke episode. The Turkish input probably was not provided until late in the seventeenth century; by that time the Melungeons, descendants of the Pardo people, had already been in the interior of the Southeastern United States for more than one hundred years."[63]

One of the most persistent legends associated with the Melungeons is that they claimed Portuguese, or "Portyghee" ancestry. However, in the earliest documents relating to Melungeons, that claim is never attributed to a specific Melungeon. The earliest written claim of a Melungeon/Portuguese connection was in *Littel's Living Age* in 1849.

> The legend of their history, which they carefully preserve, is this. A great many years ago, these mountains were settled by a society of Portuguese Adventurers, men and women—who came from the long-shore parts of Virginia, that they might be freed from the restraints and drawbacks imposed on them by any form of government. These people made themselves friendly with the Indians and freed, as they were from every kind of social government, they uprooted all conventional forms of society and lived in a delightful Utopia of their own creation, trampling on the marriage relation, despising all forms of religion, and subsisting upon corn (the only possible product of the soil) and wild game of the woods. These intermixed with the Indians, and subsequently their descendants (after the advances of the whites into this part of the state) with the negros and the whites, thus forming the present race of Melungens.[64]

Hale and Merritt also made an unattributed claim of Portuguese ancestry on behalf of unnamed Melungeons in their *History of Tennessee*

---

[63] Ibid., 26.

[64] "The Melungeons" *Littel's Living Age*, March 1849.

in 1913. "They call themselves Portuguese... As a body, they were as concrete as the Jews, and their descendants are still to be found."[65]

The claim of Portuguese ancestry is repeated, this time with attribution (albeit indirect), in Bonnie Ball's *The Melungeons*. She relates an interview conducted by G. M French with a Scott County, Virginia resident named "Uncle Washington" Osborne. "Osborne" is a surname often associated with Melungeons, but Osborne never claims any connection with the Melungeons other than knowing several. He stated that an "Uncle Poke Gibson" claimed to be a "Portuguese Indian," which was presumably a cross between Portuguese and Indian, and referred to the Melungeons as *melongo*, which Osborne described as "pure Portuguese."[66] Ball herself concluded that "Portuguese ancestry is likely; all the older Melungeons have claimed it."[67]

Manuel Mira also contends that the Melungeons descended from the Portuguese. In his 1998 book *The Forgotten Portuguese* (revised in 2001 as *The Portuguese Making of America*), Mira theorizes that the first European ancestors of the Melungeons arrived from Portugal in the sixteenth century. He further states that in order for the Melungeons to survive for such a long period of time while maintaining their group identity, women as well as men made up the initial group of European ancestors.[68]

Portugal was an important seafaring nation in the century leading up to the European colonization of America. As Mira points out, while most of the Portuguese exploration of the American continent "was done under the Spanish flag and paid for by the Spanish crown, it was their [the Portuguese'] individual work and pioneering spirit that contributed to the making of this nation...The first Spanish discovery was made when the grandchildren of the first Portuguese navigators were already adults."[69]

Recognizing the diverse ethnic groups that occupied Portugal, Mira accepts that the ancestors of the Melungeons may have originally been

---

[65] Will T. Hale, and D. L. Merritt, *A History of Tennessee and Tennesseans* (Chicago Lewis Publishing Company, 1913) 180.

[66] Bonnie Ball, *Melungeons: Their Origin and Kin* (1992, Johnson City TN: Overmountain Press, 1969), 76-77.

[67] Ball, *Melungeons*, 95.

[68] Manuel Mira, *The Portuguese Making of America* (Franklin, NC: Portuguese-American Historical Research Foundation, Inc., 2001) 283–84.

[69] Mira, *The Portuguese Making of America*, xviii.

Berbers, Moors, Turks, or Sephardic Jews; they may have come from India, Africa, or anywhere else the Portuguese were influential. "Although some of the Melungeons may have originated outside Portugal proper," he writes, "they were Portuguese by nationality. The Melungeons may have come from continental Portugal, the Azores, Madeira, or other Atlantic islands, Africa, Brazil or the Far East. All of these places, or parts of them, were Portuguese territories and under the Portuguese flag."[70]

Mira argues that the origin of the word Melungeon is Portuguese, that older Melungeons claimed Portuguese ancestry, and that the Portuguese regularly sailed to America and almost certainly left people on American soil. Therefore, Mira claims the most plausible explanation for the origin of the Melungeons is that they came from Portugal.[71]

Melungeon Heritage Association

First Union, the Melungeon gathering in Wise, Virginia in July 1997, was successful enough to inspire another gathering in 1998. Second Union was a much more elaborate event than its predecessor. Part academic conference and part family reunion, Second Union attracted approximately 2,000 people to the campus of The University of Virginia's College at Wise. While Second Union was in the planning stages, the organizers were simultaneously forming a non-profit organization to promote knowledge and understanding of the Melungeons. The Melungeon Heritage Association received a charter from Commonwealth of Virginia in the summer of 1998. Audie Kennedy, a Wise, Virginia, police officer, became the first president of MHA.

The mission statement posted on the MHA website outlines the purpose of the organization:

> The Melungeon Heritage Association is a non-profit organization.
>
> Our purpose is to document and preserve the heritage and cultural legacy of mixed-ancestry peoples in or associated with the southern Appalachians. While our focus will be on those of

---

[70] Ibid., 292.
[71] Ibid., 291–92.

Melungeon heritage, we will not restrict ourselves to honoring only this group. We firmly believe in the dignity of all such mixed ancestry groups of southern Appalachia and commit to preserving this rich heritage of racial harmony and diversity that years of legalized racism almost annihilated from our history and memory....

Our goals include:

1. To set up a "clearinghouse" of Melungeon related information and an archives of Melungeon related materials

2. To facilitate future Melungeon gatherings and events.

3. To make research and information about the Melungeons and other similar groups available to the general public.

4. To become a central exchange registry for mixed-ancestry groups in the southern Appalachians whereby we can exchange relevant information and documents.[72]

Although Second Union was a success, drawing nearly 2,000 participants, the high overhead of the event left MHA in debt, and the effort involved had depleted the energies of the all-volunteer organization. The MHA Board of Directors decided to sponsor large gatherings, or "Unions," every other year, with smaller events to be held during the "off" years.

Members of MHA attended a January 1999 hearing held by the Tennessee Bureau of Indian Affairs. Assistant director Eddie Nickens proposed that the state recognize Melungeons as an Indian population. Attending this meeting were descendants of non-recognized tribes, descendants who could not prove descent from recognized tribes, and numerous ostensibly "white" people dressed in feathers and other Indian regalia who bemoaned the fact that none of the established tribes would accept them because they lacked any documentation of their Indian ancestry. Since there is no established method of determining who is and who is not a Melungeon, this proposal, if enacted. would effectively grant "Indian" recognition to any individual who claimed to be Melungeon.

MHA did not follow up on this proposal for state recognition even though the organization proudly acknowledges the Indian component of

---

[72] Melungeon Heritage Association website, www.melungeon.org.

Melungeon ancestry. Though some of the early Melungeon families traveled with the Saponi Indians, and other tribes almost certainly contributed to the Melungeon gene pool, those early Melungeons did not maintain ties with those tribes and did not live as Indians after settling on Newman's Ridge and elsewhere. MHA acknowledges a variety of ancestries for the Melungeons and the members in attendance at the meeting felt that it would be inappropriate to claim that the Melungeons were primarily an Indian people.[73]

MHA sponsored a one-day Melungeon genealogy workshop in Berea, Kentucky in June 1999. This event featured workshops where genealogical research methods were discussed, and "family chats" where those researching particular family lines could meet and exchange information. Following the gathering, the MHA Board elected Connie Clark president, and assigned committee positions for the planning of Third Union. Most rewarding was the report from treasurer S.J. Arthur that MHA was able to completely pay off its remaining debt.

Third Union, again held in Wise, Virginia in May 2000, had a slightly smaller turnout than Second Union, but left the organization with a modest profit. At Third Union, Brent Kennedy began collecting hair samples from Melungeons for use in a DNA study. MHA's next project was to fulfill a long-held desire on the part of many to hold an event in Hancock County. MHA began working with the Vardy Community Historical Society to present a one-day event at the site of the old Vardy Presbyterian Church.

Vardy Community Historical Society

The genesis of the Vardy Community Historical Society was a suggestion made to Claude Collins about the possibility of a school reunion for former Vardy students. "I got all the school registers from the [county school] superintendent's office," Collins said, "and we had a little committee, and went through all those registers from 1910 to 1973. We picked out all the people that we knew who were still living, and we had about 350. We notified those people; we set out to find all those people and we found them. We wrote them letters and told them we wanted to have a school reunion. Well, that first year, we had about about 300 people."

---

[73] Observations of author, who attended the meeting.

The first Vardy School reunion, held in 1996, was plagued by bad weather. "Oh, it was raining, it was terrible," Collins recalled. "We didn't know what we were going to do; we had no place to meet, because the church was falling down. [By this time, the Vardy School building was beyond repair.] So, the evening before [the reunion], we asked Elm Springs Church to let us meet in their Fellowship Hall."

The reunion was a success, and Collins felt that the students needed to commemorate their school. "When we got ready to close that afternoon, I told them, 'We need to put up a marker down at Vardy in memory of our teachers.' They took up $600 dollars and gave it to me." Meanwhile, another former student and descendant of original property owner Batey Collins, DruAnna Overbay, along with her husband, bought the church and the house where faculty members had lived. At the next Vardy School reunion, discussion on where to put the commemorative marker evolved into a decision to buy and restore the church on behalf of the former students. To accomplish this, the Vardy Community Historical Society was chartered in 1998.[74]

The online mission statement of VCHS reads:

> The mission of the Vardy Community Historical Society, Inc. is to record and report on the lives, times, and culture of the people living in the Vardy Valley along Blackwater Creek in East Tennessee; to document the Presbyterians' contributions to the health, education and religious needs of the resident families from 1862 to 1974; to restore and maintain certain properties of historical interest built during the late 19th and early 20th centuries; and to participate with individuals, groups, and educational institutions with like interest in the origins, migration, and lives of people living in Vardy and elsewhere known as Melungeons.[75]

"We bought the church for $5,000... all the people [at the reunion] were interested in restoring the church [to] the way it was," according to Collins. VCHS restored the church as a museum commemorating the Presbyterian mission, and the state of Tennessee designated Vardy

---

[74] Collins interview, January 2002.

[75] VCHS Mission Statement, http://hometown.aol.com/vardyvalley/vchsmission.html.

Church a state historical site. The next project for VCHS was the restoration of Mahala Mullins' cabin.

Mahala Mullins, well-known from the many stories of her size and her moonshining activities, was a matriarch of the Melungeon community, with many descendants still living in Hancock County. Her cabin was in disrepair, and VCHS decided to move it from its remote location on Newman's Ridge to a spot across Vardy Road from the old church. The group moved the cabin in early 2000 and began restoration.

The Vardy Gathering, co-sponsored by VCHS and MHA, took place on Saturday, 23 June 2001. More than 400 people attended from as far away as Texas and Vermont. The Mahala Mullins cabin had a steady stream of visitors. R. C. Mullins, who lived in the cabin as a child and again following his marriage, talked on the front porch about the early history of the structure, while inside the cabin, graduate student Katie Doman related information gathered in her oral history project about the Vardy community. Claude Collins conducted walking tours of the grounds, and DruAnna Overbay presented the history of the Vardy School and mission.

Claude Collins, treasurer of VCHS, hoped to expand the membership of the organization and re-furnish the Mullins cabin. The group also planned to purchase the building where the Vardy School faculty lived and establish a "bed-and-breakfast."[76]

DNA study

DNA (deoxyribonucleic acid) constitutes the genetic material of all cellular organisms and the DNA viruses; DNA replicates and controls through messenger RNA the inheritable characteristics of all organisms. A molecule of DNA is made up of two parallel twisted chains of alternating units of phosphoric acid and deoxyribose, linked by crosspieces of the purine bases and the pyrimidine bases, resulting in a right-handed helical structure, that carries genetic information encoded in the sequence of the bases.[77]

---

[76] Collins interview, January 2002.

[77] http://www.academicpress.com/insight/04221999/DNA1.htm

In the spring of 2000, Brent Kennedy was the vice-chancellor at the University of Virginia's College at Wise. Thanks to Kennedy's contacts with Turkish academics, UVA-Wise has a large number of Turkish students and hosts a celebration on Turkish Independence Day. "I was there as a supportive European," English-born Kevin Jones recalls, "and he was there as a supportive Melungeon. We got to talking, and as he told me about the Melungeon phenomenon, there were a number of things that, as a biologist, intrigued me."[78]

Jones was born in a suburb of London, and received both his undergraduate and Ph.D. degrees from the University of Reading. He did post-doctoral research at Louisiana State University, and in 2000 was a professor of biology at UVA-Wise, teaching courses including cell biology and genetics.

"Brent Kennedy... explained the controversy that surrounded the origins of the Melungeons [and] realized that I had the DNA expertise to look at that," Jones related. "The subjects were largely chosen by Brent Kennedy on the basis of pursuing as many of the known Melungeon lineages that existed in the area and taking advantage of his genealogical expertise. People were then asked to donate samples to the study, and in the majority of cases they kindly did so." Such a study would utilize technology not available to Brown and Pollitzer or to Guthrie, who studied blood samples taken from Hancock County Melungeons in the 1960s.[79]

Deciding who is and who is not a Melungeon has always been a tricky proposition. Prior to about 1965, no one used the term "Melungeon" to describe themselves. "Melungeon" was a term used to describe, in a derogatory way, people of swarthy complexions, and the definition was strictly subjective. An individual was a Melungeon if his or her neighbors called that individual a Melungeon, and there was no scientific or objective way of defining this population. After Kennedy's 1994 book generated considerable interest in Melungeons, many people suspected some sort of Melungeon ancestry, could not prove it, but identified themselves as Melungeons anyway.

"The first problem we run into, or I run into, is that Melungeons, as far as I can tell, are a self-defining population," Jones told an audience at

---

[78] Kevin Jones, "DNA Study Results," presentation at Fourth Union, 20 June 2002.

[79] Kevin Jones, Wayne Winkler, in-person interview, February 2002; Minneapolis, Minnesota.

Fourth Union, the Melungeon gathering in Kingsport, Tennessee in June 2002.

> You could claim to be Melungeon because you read a book once and you live in Big Stone Gap [Virginia]. You may have had an oral tradition a hundred years ago of being Melungeon, and managed to escape it. And, having once escaped it, in view of the serious and very detrimental effects that being labeled 'Melungeon' used to have, gave you a perfectly valid reason to deny it forevermore. And when you got to the point where you were no longer even suspected of it, why, turn black the clock.
>
> And so in sampling a population of female lines, we're firstly dealing with the problem that we have lines which are Melungeon often because they say they are. This is where I needed help, because if I walk through the streets of Wise, or indeed through the streets of Vardy, chances are at that point I wouldn't have known a Melungeon if he jumped up and bit me... I had to rely on Brent and some others to decide who was valid for inclusion as a true Melungeon line on the maternal side.[80]

Brent Kennedy chose samples from people who had "known" Melungeon ancestry. These people were primarily those who knew of their biological kinship with families that had been labeled "Melungeon" in the past. Since the term "Melungeon" was used primarily in Hancock County, Tennessee, and Lee, Scott, and Wise Counties in Virginia, the subjects chosen for the DNA study were descended from families in that geographic area. Hair samples for mitochondrial DNA were gathered at Third Union in Wise, Virginia, in 2000 and from a Melungeon gathering in Vardy in 2001.

Mitochondrial DNA is particularly suited for tracing female lines. "That DNA has two huge advantages," said Jones.

> Firstly, you only get it from your mother, so it's not like other genes that you have where your mother and father contribute something and mix them up. The [mitochondrial]

---

[80] Jones, "DNA Study Results."

DNA you get from your mother is the same DNA that she got from her mother, and so on.

Its second big advantage is that there's areas of that DNA which change over time. They mutate, in effect, without hurting you...But that fast mutation rate means that, in the history of people in the world, as populations have started and moved and migrated, their DNA has changed. And increasingly, we can tie particular DNA to a particular group of people or a particular area of the world...What we get from those [hair samples] is a DNA sequence which we can think of as being about an 800–long letter code, and we can take that string of 800 letters and compare those to what now is literally thousands of samples from around the world. We're interested both in the number of different sequences that we get from the population and also how they appear to relate to other samples worldwide.[81]

Jones compared these samples to the thousands available through GenBank and the Mitochondrial DNA Concordance, databases containing DNA sequence information. Looking at the maternal lines of the Melungeons who were tested, Jones found considerable variation in ethnicity among the samples. "It's comparatively straightforward to link particular sequences to particular ethnic groups and different areas of the world," he noted, "and the majority of those Melungeon-derived sequences were European in origin. Within those European samples, though, there is an awful lot of diversity, and some seem to reflect areas outside the traditional northern European sphere."

The ability to tie a sequence to a particular area is dependent upon the historical occurrence of any given sequence somewhere, and the places that are easy to track are where we've had populations existing for a long time, and not being affected by a lot of different people coming in. So some, perhaps more isolated, areas of Europe are easier to track than more cosmopolitan [areas]. For example, it would be almost impossible to say "This is a German or a French sequence." It's often easier if you've got an area, as is true of some of eastern

---

[81] Jones, "DNA Study Results."

Europe, and indeed the Iberian peninsula, where populations are traditionally more insular.[82]

According to Jones, it is relatively simple to put these sequences into one of three broad ethnic categories: African (including African-American), native American (which is similar to some Asian sequences), and what Jones called "Eurasian." "That is a far wider area than what you may think of as Europe," said Jones. "It's not just northern Europe, it's areas of the Middle East, heading on a little into India, coming across the Mediterranean." In short, just about anything not covered by Africa, the Americas, or eastern Asia falls into this category.

Since we can fairly readily put sequences into one of those three categories, we can ask what is my first question: on the female side, is this a tri-racial group of people? Are the Melungeons truly tri-racial?...Is there any evidence that this Melungeon community has married somewhere, on the female lines, with Native Americans and African-Americans? And the answer to that is, yes they have.

The numbers are relatively small, and I don't want people to get tied up with numbers because numbers are only important when you deal with thousands of people. But nevertheless about five percent of people who claim to be Melungeon reflect a Native American ancestor on their female side, and about five percent reflect an African-American [ancestor]. All three of these broad categories have contributed, genetically at least, to the people who define themselves as "Melungeon."

That leaves an awful lot of people who fall under the "Eurasian" category. That perhaps is no real surprise. Dealing with Eurasian sequences is one of the hardest things that scientists have to do, because populations have moved around Europe so much that there are some sequences that you find anywhere in Europe. They don't tell us anything about likely origins. When we look at the Eurasian Melungeon samples, an awful lot of them fall within that category. They are generic-type sequences. They could be from England, they could be from

---

[82] Jones interview, February 2002.

Ireland, they could be from France, they could be from Spain, they could be from Turkey—anywhere within that Eurasian category. Some sequences have become incredibly widely distributed, and indeed Melungeons show a high percentage of those.

All that really tells us is that the Melungeon population, if we look at it overall, is not genetically narrow. There's been all sorts of input, even on the European side. And this population, genetically on the female side, in essence is as diverse, just about, as anywhere you're likely to find. So if anyone has ever said "You inbred Melungeon," they are lying.[83]

Some of these "Eurasian" sequences closely match sequences found among the Siddi population of northern India. During medieval times, European slave traders took East Africans to India as slaves. Many of these slaves took advantage of the complicated kingdom boundaries and dense forests of northern India to set themselves free. Those that converted to local religions, including Islam, Hinduism, and Roman Catholicism, and adopted local ways became known as Siddis. Many became sailors and established kingdoms along the western coast of India and eventually spread throughout India. The Siddis are ancestors of the modern-day Romany, or Gypsy, people.[84]

Though the number of sequences consistent with Turkish or northern Indian ancestry were few, their distribution indicates to Jones the strong possibility that some of the Melungeons' ancestry came from those regions. "I think one of the problems here is that we tend to think of 'Turkish' in terms of the dimensions of modern Turkey, not of the original scale of people of Turkish origin who, in essence, were spread throughout the European world. Perhaps the best I can say is that some of those sequences are a little more 'exotic' than Anglo-Irish sequences, and some of those could reflect, perhaps, populations that were associated with or moved through Turkey."[85]

---

[83] Jones, "DNA Study Results."

[84] "Siddis and Habshis," http://www.colorq.org/MeltingPot/Asia/Habshi.htm. The Siddis are not to be confused with *siddhis*, described by yogis and supernaturalists as a magical or spiritual power for the control of self, others and the forces of nature.

[85] Jones interview, February 2002.

One hundred twenty hair samples were studied for mitochondrial DNA. Thirty samples of cheek cells were taken to study the Y-chromosome, or male, DNA.

> The use of the Y-chromosome on a large world-wide scale has been a relatively recent phenomenon. Indeed, if one went back three years, there were really no worldwide data available. Y data is also not sequenced data like the female is, and I at UVA-Wise do not have the capability to analyze patterns of Y chromosomes. But there are a number of groups in the world who most certainly do; indeed, we're fortunate enough that one of them, Benny Greenspan, who works with Michael Hammer, is one of the people who can look at Ys very effectively. I actually relied [at first] on Dr. Mark Thomas at the University College of London, and he too is a world-wide Y expert.[86]

Jones isolated the DNA from cheek swabs representing 30 male lines from the major Melungeon male linages.

> With only 30 samples in there, it would be wrong for me to draw any obvious conclusions, because when you deal with populations—and all of this genetic work is a population study—you need to generate a certain finite speed and mass before you can start to make sense of the patterns that you see. Arguably we would want about twice as many Y samples as we've got to start to do that. But what I can do today is to point out some things that I find interesting.
>
> Mark [Thomas] has performed some very stringent analysis on 20 of the 30 samples. Those 20 samples reveal a range of different types of Y chromosomes. In fact the diversity of different Y-chromosomes within those 20 samples is greater than has been reported for the moment for the whole of England on the basis of several hundred Y-chromosomes.
>
> So, again, on the male side as well, this is a genetically diverse population. And you become genetically diverse either

---

[86] Jones, "DNA Study Results."

by having unusual people come in from the beginning or by marrying unusual people who live around you...

Y chromosomes can be grouped into a number of major types, and within the 20 samples that have been looked at, we have some types who, on a worldwide basis, show up in one percent of people from northern Europe and show up in 22 percent of people from Syria, or 12 percent of people from Turkey. That doesn't mean that they are definitively Middle-Eastern, but we have to pay attention to those numbers and say "What's the most logical explanation for this?" And the most logical explanation at this point is that these reflect people who came in from those areas of the world or somewhere around.

Because often with this data if you've got 22 percent here and one percent here, you see a progression of decrease to get from 22 to one. So even if you're not from the 22 percent area of the world, chances are you're going to be from somewhere fairly close if you're turning up with a certain frequency.

Mark has also compared some of those Y chromosomes to a database of 5,000 other Y chromosomes from thirty populations across the world. What do we see from that? Just as on the female side, within the male side... there are African lineages. So that tri-racial aspect of the Melungeon culture appears to extend to both the male and the female side.[87]

Many of the male haplotypes studied are quite common in Europe, and could have originated in a variety of places. But some of those haplotypes only match an Anatolian Turk; another type was definitely Arabic. Jones stressed that the Melungeons were not at all identical in their genetic makeups, and that the genetic mixture was different in each subject.

Such testing is not perfect, of course, and does not tell researchers everything about an individual's inheritance. One drawback to this DNA testing is that the tests show only one ancestor. Theoretically, and individual could have ancestors who came from Finland, Africa, Iran, China, and Samoa, and have a DNA test result reflecting only the Finnish ancestor. Therefore, DNA studies cannot tell researchers everything

---

[87] Ibid.

about an individual's ancestry. These tests can only show that a particular ancestry is present in an individual's genetic makeup. However, the study was not concerned with individual results. "We're looking for patterns that exist in the population as a whole," according to Jones. "Now, obviously, each individual sample contributes to that, but I think that for an individual you can say relatively little. Looking at the patterns that occur throughout the population becomes important. And that means the number of samples that are looked at is also significant, and we've tried to do as many as is reasonably possible."[88]

> If you are hoping for a DNA sequence, a Y chromosome type, that says "You are a Melungeon"—forget it. It doesn't exist. This is a very heavily mixed genetic population that appears to extend, certainly on the female side, and from the look of it on the male side, and amongst that mixture are some people outside of northern Europe…
>
> It's a cultural identity which is real and important but it does not reflect any genetic basis. I hope that with that variability that exists, apparently, within this population, that's something to be proud of, because that culture and identity has been maintained in the face of input from all sorts of people. You are the product of a truly multi-national, tri-racial mix of genetic types, but you have that commonality of being Melungeon and knowing what that means.[89]

Jones believes the results of his research match up quite well with those obtained by Pollitzer and Brown, and by James Guthrie. "I think, actually, that all of those studies approximately reached the same kind of conclusions. I don't think that any of those discounted a basic tri-racial mixture… It's very hard with all this data, indeed including theirs as well as mine, to reach definitive conclusions. One is taking one's snapshot of a population and seeing how one interprets that. That doesn't mean that it's the definitive answer; it's always going to be open to refinement, certainly."

The long-held belief that the Melungeons originated in Portugal is neither borne out nor negated by Jones' research. "To date we've found

---

[88] Jones interview, February 2002.

[89] Jones, "DNA Study Results."

no sequences that can be definitively traced back to uniquely Portuguese sequences. That doesn't mean that they don't exist. A large number of the European sequences are now widely spread throughout Europe, and if one of those generic sequences happened to come from Portugal we would not detect that. We can't dismiss that theory at the moment, but we can't provide additional support for it."[90]

The DNA test results show that, as a group, the Melungeons are definitely tri-racial. While nearly all Melungeons have been willing to accept the idea of Indian descent, the notion of African ancestry has been anathema to many, particularly in the years when African-Americans faced state-sanctioned segregation and discrimination. "I can hear my grandma spinning in her grave right now," said one Melungeon descendant upon hearing the results of the DNA test. He said it with a smile, however, indicating that the present generation of Melungeon descendants is much more willing to accept an African ancestry than their forebears.

In short, the DNA study indicates today's Melungeons are primarily of European descent, with some Native American and African-American ancestry. Some Melungeons have genetic sequences matching the Siddis of northern India, others reflect a Turkish or Syrian ancestry. Some of those who consider themselves "Melungeon" possess all of those "exotic" genes; others have some of them—and others reflect only the "generic" European genes. The Melungeons are by no means uniform in their genetic backgrounds; they are a mixed-ethnic population with varying degrees of mixture within that population.

The DNA study seems to confirm most of the theories proposed by Kennedy. In doing so, the study did not negate most of the other popular and/or scientific theories about the Melungeons. Family lines originating in northern India or in Turkey could have been in Portugal for several generations before coming to America, where they would have considered themselves descendants of Portuguese or "Portyghee," having lost all knowledge of the family's true geographic origins. The only researchers whose theories have been refuted by the DNA study are those who claim that the Melungeons were strictly a mix of Native American, African-American, and northern European.

---

[90] Jones interview, February 2002.

The surprising revelation in Jones' study is that some of these Turkish- and northern Indian- like sequences have been passed through the Melungeons' maternal lines, indicating that their overseas ancestors included not only male sailors and explorers, but females as well. What Darlene Wilson called the "offshore male other" in the genetic makeup of the Melungeons was, in reality, often a female. While the legends of shipwrecked sailors and pirates marrying Indian women may still have some validity, we know that some women made the voyage to America.

These are the people who have been largely left out of America's English-oriented history books. How they arrived in America, how they banded together in family groups and eventually migrated to the mountains of southern Appalachia, is a question for future historians and genealogists. The European/Middle Eastern ancestors of the Melungeons arrived in America with the intention of establishing their families in a new land. Through intermarriage with Indians and African-Americans, they managed to do so; their descendants are at the forefront of the effort to find out who they were and how they eventually became the people known as Melungeons.

7

CONCLUSIONS AND SPECULATIONS

The historical record tells us relatively little about the Melungeons, who became a fixture in Appalachian folklore over 200 years ago. Thanks to the efforts of genealogists like Virginia DeMarce and Jack Goins, we know of the travels and land ownership of some of the "core" Melungeon families on and near Newman's Ridge in the early nineteenth century. Geographers, demographers, and researchers like Edward Price, Calvin Beale, Donald Ball and John Kessler provide insights on where members of those families migrated from there. Anthropologists and geneticists like William Brown and William Pollitzer, James Guthrie, and Kevin Jones offer tantalizing glimpses of the Melungeons' mysterious ancestors. But the primary questions which have fascinated scientists and storytellers alike remain unanswered.

Where did the Melungeons originate? Did bonds of kinship or culture maintain them as a cohesive people, or were they united merely by their uncertain ethnic status in a white-dominated society? What does the word "Melungeon" mean? And is there a kinship between Melungeons and other tri-racial groups, such as the Lumbees, the Brass Ankles, the Redbones, etc.?

The Melungeons themselves, according to several accounts, claimed to be Portuguese. The first mentioned of Portuguese ancestry among the Melungeons was in the 1849 *Littel's Living Age* article. We do not know which individuals and families made that claim, but since Vardemon Collins is the only Melungeon identified in the article by his real name, we might reasonably assume he made the first recorded claim. Even if we accept that Vardemon Collins had Portuguese ancestry, other Melungeons might not have shared that genetic heritage. Later generations of Melungeons may have believed themselves of Portuguese ancestry simply based on "Ol' Vardy's" statement—or they may have simply preferred people to think that their swarthy completions were the result of Portuguese—rather than African or Indian—ancestry.

However, the blood studies done by Pollitzer and Brown and reviewed by Guthrie bolstered the idea that Melungeons shared a genetic heritage—or at least several genetic traits—with people who once lived in or had extensive contact with Portugal and Spain. Kevin Jones' DNA study indicated that some Melungeon haplotypes matched populations in Turkey, the Middle East, Africa, and the Siddi regions of northern India—all areas which were at one time under Portuguese domination or visited heavily by Portuguese merchant ships.

Both the Spanish and Portuguese populations share a wide range of ethnic backgrounds as a result of centuries of Muslim occupation and assimilation. Nearly all the populations found in Jones' Melungeon study (with the exception of Native American) could be found in a typical group of Portuguese. After a few generations in Portugal, families from a variety of locations would naturally come to consider themselves "Portuguese."

The presence of genetic markers from Turkey, Africa, and India among present-day Melungeons could plausibly be explained by the just a few individuals from those respective areas arriving in America in the seventeenth or even eighteenth centuries. However, Portuguese individuals and families were known to be in America along with the very first European colonists; they brought a wide variety of ethnic and genetic heritages to the American shores, including those indicated in DNA tests of Melungeons. Beyond that, the very fact that the Melungeons claimed Portuguese ancestry adds considerable weight to the argument that the Melungeons were, indeed, what they claimed to be: Portuguese. In the case of the Melungeons, the term "Portuguese" would represent individuals and families from a wide range of ethnic and genetic backgrounds whose forebears either lived in Portugal or in a Portuguese-dominated area. In calling themselves that, however, the early Melungeons were leaving out a considerable portion of their story.

Some have looked to Juan Pardo's series of forts protecting the road from Santa Elena to the Gulf of Mexico as a possible source for the Portuguese component in the Melungeons' heritage. Several of the soldiers and families that occupied these forts, including Pardo himself, were of Portuguese ancestry, and the forts they occupied were not far from the territory where Melungeons were first documented in the early

1800s. The Spanish abandoned these forts when they evacuated Santa Elena, and the occupants either assimilated with local Indians or died out. It *is* possible that a Portuguese-Indian people survived and eventually moved to the Clinch River region of northeast Tennessee and southwest Virginia,

Weighing against this theory is the fact that the Melungeon families traced by genealogists are first identified in areas considerably to the north and east of the area containing Pardo's forts. The names of some of early Melungeon settlers, and those of their probable ancestors, are found in the tax and census records of North Carolina and Virginia. The Orange County tax list of 1755 includes several names associated with Melungeon families, and Melungeon names are also found in the 1782 tax lists for Montgomery and Grayson Counties in Virginia, and Wilkes County, North Carolina. Vardemon Collins, one of the original Melungeon settlers on Newman's Ridge, is found on the Wilkes County list for 1787. If any of these families were part of the Pardo expeditions, they would have taken the unlikely migration pattern of north and east out of the mountains of North Carolina and Tennessee, into the piedmont of Virginia (where they first appeared on tax rolls), then back to the south and west toward the area they had originally left.

If we accept the Melungeons' claims of Portuguese ancestry, we must recognize that their Portuguese forebears, for some reason, did not assimilate into the larger European-American population, not did they coalesce into a Portuguese-American community, such as those established in New England. Instead, as indicated by the tax lists cited above, these "Portuguese" stayed on the edges of the frontier, continually moving into newly-opened areas of settlement. Such a pattern suggests that these individuals and families were somehow separate from the predominant white society, whether by choice or by the antipathy of that larger community. A community or extended family group representing a dark-skinned fusion of Portuguese and remnant Indian tribes would almost certainly exist on the fringes of colonial white society.

The Melungeons who came to Fort Blackmore in southwest Virginia and later settled on Newman's Ridge in Tennessee most certainly had ties—either genetic, social, or both—with various groups of Indians. Researchers have identified early Melungeon family heads as living with Indians and being officially classified as such in tax and census records. Sneedville attorney Lewis Jarvis asserted, 100 years after the event, that "The white emigrants and friendly Indians erected a fort on the bank of the river and called it "Fort Blackmore'...From here they came on to Newman's Ridge...They all came here simultaneously with the whites from the State of Virginia between the years 1795 and 1812..."

The Melungeons may have lived and traveled with the Indians, but they did not maintain an Indian identity. The "friendly Indians" with whom the Melungeons traveled were almost certainly remnant members of the Powhatan or Monacan tribes, tribes which were in an advanced stage of dissolution by the end of the eighteenth century. We have no record of what became of the "friendly Indians" after their arrival at Fort Blackmore. We can assume that their tribal structure was so decayed by that time that there was no cohesive Indian society for the Melungeons to join, and the individual tribal members eventually went their own way and assimilated to some degree into the surrounding white society. The family groups of the Melungeons who settled in southwest Virginia and northeast Tennessee may not have been merely affiliated with these tribal groups, but instead were all that remained of those groups.

The African element of the Melungeons' ancestry may have been present among the Portuguese prior to their arrival in America, or it might be the result of later intermarriage with members of the sizable free black population of the southern colonies. Either scenario or both would have intensified hostility among white colonists about these dark-skinned people who didn't fit into convenient categories of white, black, or Indian.

The Melungeons, like nearly all the other tri-racial groups, usually denied having any African ancestry. Their white neighbors generally believed that some, if not all, Melungeons *did* have African ancestry. The question of "Negro blood" affected the social and legal status of all tri-racial groups until very recently. White-dominated American society stigmatized those with African ancestry, and in many ways the stigma was even worse for those of tri-racial ancestry. Tri-racials inhabited an ethnic no-man's land. They usually shunned association with nearby African-American communities (which often, in turn, shunned the tri-racials). They were rejected by white society. They had no surviving connection or identity with any stable Indian communities. As Melungeon families moved westward through Virginia and North Carolina in the late eighteenth century, they were escaping an increasingly rigid racial hierarchy that had no convenient or consistent status for families of mixed ethnic background.

In 1813, the word "Melungin" appeared in the minutes for Stony Creek Baptist Church. No explanation for the term is given, and we can only guess at its origins. The simplest and most logical explanation for the name "Melungeon" is that the word derived from the old English term "malengin," meaning "mischievous intent." It was a word used in the works of John Gower, Sir Thomas Malory, and Edmund Spenser, works almost as well known in colonial America as those of Shakespeare. Many researchers have opined that "Melungeon" derived from the French term *melange*, meaning "mixture." While the Melungeons were certainly of mixed-ethnic background, it seems likely that if the white settlers wanted to use a name to describe a mixed-race people, they would have used a simpler English term such as "half-breed" or "mulatto." English-speaking people on the frontier were much more likely to have used an English term to describe these swarthy newcomers than to have used a derivation of the French *melange*. "Malengin" suggests the feeling whites had about these dark-skinned people: they were different-looking, they traveled with Indians, and therefore were not to be trusted.

There is certainly no documentation which supports this—or any other—theory behind the origin of the word "Melungeon." Good arguments exist for other theories as well. One participant on a Melungeon e-mail list reported a conversation with a Portuguese woman who said that in Portugal, "Melungeon" describes the type of person who would move without paying back rent. Many researchers still believe "Melungeon" came from the French *melange*. And the theory that the word originated with the Arabic *melun-jinn* and the Turkish *melun-can* resonates strongly with those who accompanied Brent Kennedy on one of his visits to Turkey; they acknowledge that the Turkish people seemed familiar with the word "Melungeon" (which they pronounced *MELON-juhn*). Admittedly, the Turks were familiar with the word largely through publicity surrounding Kennedy's work with the Turkic World Research Foundation, but they spoke the word with such affection that one observer wished his Hancock County grandmother could have heard the word spoken the way the Turks said it.

Any speculation on the origin of the name "Melungeon" is based on the flimsiest of evidence. We do not know whether the Melungeons of

Stony Creek used that word for themselves or if it was a name imposed on them by their neighbors. If the term originated with the Melungeons, it is unlikely they would describe themselves with a word meaning "evil machination; guile; deceit." Unless further documentation relating to the name is uncovered, the origin of the word "Melungeon" will probably remain shrouded in mystery.

Whatever the source for the word "Melungeon," by the time it was written in the Stony Creek Church minutes in 1813, Melungeon families had already settled on and near Newman's Ridge in the new state of Tennessee. Tennessee had been formed in 1786 without the restrictive racial laws that were in effect in Virginia and North Carolina, making it a haven for free African-Americans and mixed race families and individuals. This fact probably accounted for the migration of the Melungeons into Tennessee, and the environs of Newman's Ridge became the central location of this particular mixed-race population. When Tennessee re-wrote its constitution in 1834, racial restrictions were put into place, and some families and individuals moved on. Some moved into Kentucky, others moved into southeastern Tennessee, and there are suggestions that at least a few Melungeons moved into territories west of the Mississippi River.

The "core" group of Melungeons stayed in the remote isolation of the Newman's Ridge area, avoiding contact with whites as best they could—except for those whites captivated by the Melungeons' exotic good looks. Since their arrival in southwest Virginia and northeast Tennessee, Melungeons tended to either marry within their own group or to marry whites. As a group, they became "whiter"—but never white enough to completely avoid the hostility and suspicion of their Caucasian neighbors or the damning epithet "Melungeon." The only way to avoid that name and the reputation that went with it was to move far away, to a place where no one had ever heard that mysterious word. By the 1950s, Melungeons were a part of the large scale migration of Appalachian people to the Midwest and other regions, which offered more economic opportunities—and a chance to leave behind epithets like "Melungeon."

Melungeon Identity in the 21st Century

In less than half a century, the Melungeons went from being an ethnic curiosity, a folktale, one of America's dirty little racial secrets, to being an Internet phenomenon, an ethnic identity with which thousands of ostensibly "white" Americans sought to establish a connection. The Melungeons of just a couple of generations ago, most of whom never used the term "Melungeon" to describe themselves, would have been astounded at the number of people today who eagerly embrace that once-hated name.

When Dr. Kevin Jones said, "You could claim to be Melungeon because you read a book once and you live in Big Stone Gap," he was only half-joking. The outdoor drama *Walk Toward the Sunset* engendered a sense of pride in many of the Melungeons living in and near Hancock County, Tennessee. However, it was the work of Brent Kennedy that spread interest in the Melungeons beyond a small circle of researchers and folklorists. Kennedy suggested that the Melungeons, along with other tri-racial groups, represented just the tip of an American multi-racial iceberg, and that thousands of ostensibly "white" Americans shared a multi-racial heritage. The publicity generated by Kennedy's 1994 book and subsequent gatherings sponsored by the Melungeon Heritage Association led many people to claim a Melungeon connection, a claim often based on very flimsy evidence.

As many Hancock Countians said during the run of the outdoor drama *Walk Toward the Sunset*, "It used to be no one ever said the word 'Melungeon.' Now everyone wants to be one." That statement is even more true today than was in the 1970s. Hundreds of people share the experience of Bill Fields, publisher of the Melungeon newsletter *Under One Sky*, who attended a Brent Kennedy lecture in the mid-1990s. "I went in [to the lecture] absolutely sure that my family was white... I came out, and I was absolutely sure that they weren't." Kennedy adhered to a very broad definition of "Melungeon," and people who had grown to middle age believing themselves to be "white" began to proudly proclaim—often with scant evidence—a Melungeon identity.

Virginia DeMarce, a former president of the National Genealogical Society, decried the number of people assuming they had Melungeon ancestry without adequate documentation. She felt that most of the people who believed they had Melungeon ancestry after reading Kennedy's book were "roughly equivalent to the people who believe that aliens landed in Roswell, New Mexico." DeMarce believed that the name "Melungeon" applies to only a small group of people: "...the interrelated families along Newman's Ridge in Hawkins County, where they lived for forty years or so prior to 1844, when the area was cut away into the new county of Hancock."

A few members of a Melungeon e-mail list echoed DeMarce's "narrow" definition of Melungeon. One individual, who traces his ancestry back to the original Collins and Gibson families who settled on Newman's Ridge, said to this author at a Melungeon gathering, "If you can't trace your family back to Hancock County, you ain't a Melungeon. Period."

This narrow definition of "Melungeon," which restricts the term only to those who lived on or near Newman's Ridge, ignores a great deal of documentation of Melungeon families who lived far from Hancock County. For example:

• The 1830 census, which showed 331 "free persons of color" in Hawkins County, also noted the presence of four separate units of the Goins family in Hamilton County, in southeastern Tennessee. Though this family group appears to have originated in the neighborhood of Newman's Ridge, they migrated to the southwest within a short time. So, even before the *Littel's Living Age* article of 1849, Melungeons were documented some 200 miles away from the Hancock County area. The available records do not indicate whether these families and individuals were known by the name "Melungeon," but by 1872 that name would be demonstrated as having been in use in southeastern Tennessee.

• While the evidence of "Lungeons" in Arkansas in 1811 does not offer any solid connection with the Melungeons in northeast Tennessee and southwest Virginia, it offers a tantalizing—if uncorroborated—suggestion that the term, or variants thereof, were in use far from Newman's Ridge even prior to the first documented use of the word in 1813.

• The "Celebrated Melungeon Case" of 1872 is another instance of Melungeons documented outside the area defined by DeMarce. In his memoirs, published in 1915, Judge Lewis Shepard recounts how, as a young attorney, he defended a Melungeon girl in an inheritance case. During the trial, Shepard presented some theories about the origin of the Melungeons which seem somewhat fanciful, but the point is there *were* Melungeons in this area who were known by that term.

• Some time after about 1880, Melungeons from Hamilton County, Tennessee moved into the community of Graysville in neighboring Rhea County to the north. The first Melungeon in Graysville was George Goins, who was born in Hamilton County in 1865 and married to a woman who claimed to be Cherokee. Surnames in the Graysville community include Goins, Bolin, Collins, and Bell. Other surnames associated through intermarriage with Melungeons include Hambrick, Henderson, Leffew, and Patton.

• In 1897, author John Fox Jr. used a Melungeon character in his short story "Through The Gap," published in his book *"Hell Fer Sartain" and Other Stories.* Fox was familiar with Melungeons in southwest Virginia and southeastern Kentucky; not only had he grown up near Melungeons in that region, he later had business dealings with them.

• The Federal Writer's Project *Guide To The States* for Tennessee contains O. N. Walraven's brief entry in a section about Oakdale, near Harriman, about thirty miles west of Knoxville: "In the village is a small colony of Melungeons, a dark-skinned people found only in the mountainous regions of East Tennessee and western North Carolina." While Walraven also tries to define a narrow geographic habitat for the Melungeons, it is a completely different region than that defined by DeMarce.

• Geographer Edward Price acknowledged that Hancock County was the center of the Melungeon population, but he also noted populations in Bristol and Kingsport, Tennessee, Dungannon (Scott County), Virginia, and Wise County, Virginia. In addition, a group of Melungeons was cited in the eastern Kentucky counties of Letcher and Knott; while not identified locally as Melungeons, many of this group of a few hundred had the names Collins, Gibson, and Sexton. Price also mentioned Melungeons in Graysville, Bazeltown (near Harriman, Tennessee) and groups of Melungeons near Nashville and in Bell's Bend on the Cumberland River. Price traced the migration of Melungeon families from the boundary region of Virginia and North Carolina to northeastern Tennessee, spreading as far as Magoffin County, Kentucky, and Highland County, Ohio.

While it is true that the Hancock County Melungeons were the best known group, the definition of "Melungeon" espoused by DeMarce is obviously too narrow for accuracy. The people identified in the examples presented above certainly shared a genetic heritage with the Melungeons of Newman's Ridge and were in many cases known by that name. Others shared the heritage but not necessarily the name. Many of the Melungeon families in southwest Virginia were known as "Ramps," but their family ties to the Hancock County Melungeons have been long established. Donald Ball and John Kessler were among the first to call the "Carmel Indians" of Ohio by the term "Melungeon," but the genealogies of the Carmel group tie them to families in southeastern Kentucky who were also known as Melungeons to their neighbors. A family identified by the surrounding community as "Melungeon" is, by definition, Melungeon; however, lack of such community identification does *not* necessarily mean that a family is not Melungeon—at least, depending on one's definition of the word.

One major difficulty in deciding who is a Melungeon in the 21st century is the fact that there has never been a precise definition of either the word "Melungeon" or the people whom it describes. There is not, and never has been, the equivalent of a tribal association or government agency to say who was and who wasn't a Melungeon. There is also no equivalent to the "blood quantum" test sometimes used to determine whether a person is an Indian. Those who would look to documentation to identify the earliest Melungeon families find that documentation is both scarce and flawed. As noted earlier, no census or tax records used the term "Melungeon,' and whether a dark-skinned family or individual was listed as "white" or "black" was at best a subjective matter. An examination of known written accounts of the Melungeons in the nineteenth century provide little assistance in identifying Melungeon individuals or families.

   • The 1813 Stony Creek Church minutes do not identify the "melungins" by name.

   • The 1840 *Jonesboro Whig* article did not identify the "impudent Malungeon" by name.

   • In 1846, eight Melungeons were charged with illegally voting in an election held that previous August. The defendants were Melungeon patriarch Vardemon "Vardy" Collins, Solomon Collins, Ezekial Collins, Levi Collins, Andrew Collins, Wiatt Collins, and brothers Zachariah and Lewis Minor. Existing court records do not, however, refer to these individuals as Melungeons; they were charged with voting illegally "by reason of color."

   • The 1849 *Little's Living Age* article uses obvious pseudonyms (Jord Bilson, Syd Varmin) for most of the characters portrayed. The one exception was "Ol' Vardy," who was surely Vardemon Collins.

   • Swan Burnett's 1889 article did not mention any Melungeons by name.

   • One of Will Allen Dromgoole's 1890 *Nashville American* articles stated; "There are but three names among them—real Malungeon names—Collins, Mullins, Gorvens. Lately the name of Gibbins has found a way among them, but the first three are their real names." Dromgoole also mentioned Calloway Collins and his wife and children by name.

   • Dromgoole's first 1891 *Arena* article asserted, "They are limited somewhat as to names: their principal families being the Mullins, Gorvens, Collins, and Gibbins." Her second article specifically named Vardy Collins and Buck Gibson, as well as other Melungeons, and included the Denhan and Goins surnames.

Prior to Dromgoole's articles, "Ol' Vardy" Collins was the only individual ever identified in print as a Melungeon, and Dromgoole's informal census of Melungeon family names occurred nearly a century after the first Melungeons moved to the area. Since no official documents ever identified anyone as a Melungeon, those looking for solid documentation of that ancestry are likely to be disappointed in their search, unless an ancestor happened to be one of the very few Melungeons named in a newspaper or magazine article. Usually, the genealogist can only make an educated assumption based on knowledge of Melungeon families and migration patterns.

Another problem in identifying Melungeon ancestors is the fact that the name was not commonly used by those to whom it referred. Edward Price noted in 1951, "There is no group of people who call themselves Melungeons or who would recognize themselves as thus separated from the rest of the country population." Melungeons were defined by their neighbors; they did not define themselves. Furthermore, "Melungeon" has traditionally implied more than just the genetic and ethnic makeup of an individual or family—which, until very recently, were largely a matter of speculation. The word also reflected the community's attitude about those to whom it was applied. "Melungeon" indicated someone of a lower social class, someone on welfare, someone who was considered inferior to neighboring whites. Melungeon researcher Darlene Wilson argues that the socio-economic implications of the term were far more significant than the ethnic implications. Thus a family could—at least in theory—lose the designation "Melungeon" by improving its socio-economic position and moving to an area where neighbors did not know of their earlier status.

Those who seek to define "Melungeon" are faced with the question of whether to define the term in a genetic sense or in a socio-economic sense. Using the former definition, anyone with a genetic connection to the families identified at some time and place, as "Melungeon" is also a Melungeon. Under the latter definition, only those who were known in their communities as "Melungeon," only those who suffered the stigma and discrimination associated with that name, can rightfully claim to be

Melungeon. Of course, most of those who fit that second definition of "Melungeon" are elderly now, and, because they well remember the stigma, are the least likely people in the world to embrace that name.

To illustrate the difficulty in defining who is and who is not a Melungeon, one can look at the many descendants of Mahala Mullins, the legendary Melungeon matriarch and moonshiner. Those of Mahala's descendants who stayed in Hancock County and the surrounding area are certainly Melungeons and have always been considered as such by the community. Other descendants moved away, and their children never heard the term "Melungeon." One of Mahala's great great grandsons, "John," grew up in the Midwest, graduated from college, and has had a successful career. While his cousins in Hancock County lived with the knowledge and stigma of their Melungeon status, "John" did not know of his Melungeon ancestry until he was middle-aged. Genetically, "John" is as much a Melungeon as his cousins. One might argue that his cousins are "more Melungeon" in a cultural sense, having grown up with the word and all it implied. Before making that argument, however, one must also take into account that "John" proudly proclaims his Melungeon ancestry while some (but certainly not all) of Mahala's other descendants refuse to acknowledge themselves or their families as Melungeon.

The stigma associated with the name "Melungeon" began to disappear when the Hancock County Drama Association staged the outdoor drama *Walk Toward the Sunset*. The play generated a sense of pride in having a Melungeon heritage, and eliminated much of the negative connotation associated with the name. Furthermore, many Melungeons had broken the cycle of poverty and achieved success—some in Hancock County, and some elsewhere. Thus, the socio-economic definition of "Melungeon" is no longer valid. No one uses the word in the way it was used a couple of generations ago. "Melungeon" was originally an epithet, which implied more than just a mixed-ethnic heritage; it meant one who was sneaky, disreputable, poor, ignorant, and untrustworthy—at least in the eyes of the people who used the term. If "Melungeon" meant all those things today, very few people would desire such identification However, if one argues that the word means the same thing it did in 1900, one must also argue that Melungeons no longer exist, since the social conditions attached to the word in 1900 also, for the most part, no longer exist.

Thousands of Americans have a genealogical and genetic connection with the Melungeons and that fact insures that "Melungeon" is a word that continues to have a meaning, albeit a different meaning than it held a century ago. Many people today use the term "Melungeon descendant" to describe themselves, recognizing that they do not live under the same conditions that made "Melungeon" such an epithet to their ancestors. This description both celebrates the user's unique ethnic heritage and recognizes that the user can never truly know what once meant to be called "Melungeon."

Melungeons do not exist today in the way they existed a century ago, as objects of suspicion and discrimination, defined by the community through legend and folklore. To be a Melungeon descendant today is to recognize one's multi-ethnic heritage, and the fact that one's ancestors faced some degree of discrimination for being non-white in a racist society. That recognition will probably lead to a fuller understanding of America's tumultuous history of race relations and the absurdity of the concept of race in general. And in recognizing the difficulties faced by our ancestors, we can also celebrate their perseverance, their determination, and their drive for a better future that allows us to celebrate a heritage that they could not even acknowledge. Simply having Melungeon heritage does not make one a better person, but understanding the ramifications of that heritage may well do so.

Melungeons and Other Tri-Racials

Some of those who are trying to find evidence of their Melungeon ancestry today have discovered a tri-racial or multi-ethnic background, but have not connected these ancestors to any known Melungeon family or location. Some of these tri-racial ancestors may not have been Melungeon, but were known by another name—Croatan, Brass Ankle, Redbone, or one of the other group names. Some of these groups may have been related to one another. Genetic testing of members of these groups could possibly show common ancestry with the Melungeons, and might possibly provide further clues to the origins of some or all of these groups.

Unfortunately, there has been little apparent desire among these groups to date for identification with the Melungeons or for identification of themselves as tri-racial groups. Invitations to several of these groups for participation in a Melungeon gathering in June 2002 were almost all ignored—with the notable exception of a delegation of Redbones from Louisiana. Many of the group identified by Gilbert and others as "tri-racial" are working instead toward recognition as Indians. The Lumbees, once known as Croatans, are the only one of these tri-racial groups so far to have received federal recognition as an Indian tribe, and that recognition is limited, providing no Federal benefits such as a reservation or educational grants. The Commonwealth of Virginia has extended state recognition to several groups once denied such recognition by the policies of Walter Plecker, including the Monacans, the Chickahominy, the Mattaponi, and the Pamunkey. As of this writing, the Virginia tribes were still struggling for federal recognition—something also attempted by recently-created tribal organizations that represent the people once known as Brass Ankles in South Carolina, and the Ramapough Mountain People ("Jackson Whites") in New Jersey and New York.

These tribal organizations have a valid reason to avoid association with self-acknowledged tri-racials like the Melungeons. A serious obstacle to federal recognition of these groups as Indians seems to be their tri-racial backgrounds. In an echo of the odious "one-drop rule," the varying degrees of African ancestry—the "taint" of Negro blood, as Plecker might have put it —among these groups has been cited, albeit subtly, as justification for denial of federal recognition. Adding to the difficulty facing these groups is the reluctance of those tribes, which already have federal recognition to share scarce federal resources with "questionable" newcomers.

Further research, including DNA testing, may well reveal genetic and genealogical links between the Melungeons and other tri-racial groups. If so, genealogists and historians may someday uncover information which will shed further light on the origins of the Melungeons and of other tri-racial people. As noted earlier, the Goins family might well be the key to unlocking these mysteries, as nearly every tri-racial group in America contains individuals and families with this surname. Until such time, the Melungeons are likely to retain a large measure of the mystery that has branded them "sons and daughters of the legend."

The Sunset Approaches

In 1975, author Jean Patterson Bible predicted the disappearance of the Melungeons as a distinct people. That disappearance is, sadly, inevitable.

The Melungeons, as a people, are surely walking toward the sunset. Most of the Melungeons whose features branded them African-American long ago assimilated into that population. Those with primarily Indian or Caucasian features have intermarried with whites for so many generations that most have lost any distinguishing characteristics. This disappearance could not have been prevented even if the Melungeons had set out to preserve themselves as a distinct ethnic group. There were never enough Melungeons for that to be possible without considerable inbreeding among the families. As Bible prophesied, "They'll be gone in a generation or two, except for an occasional dark-complected [*sic*] child as a reminder of the past."

The Melungeons will not disappear without notice, however. The Reverend Chester Leonard, Miss Mary Rankin, and the faculty and staff at the Vardy Community School created a community of confident, educated Melungeons who would reject the stereotypes imposed on them by generations of folklore. Claude Collins, Corrine Bowlin, Dora Bowlin, Elmer and Hazel Turner, and the other members of the Hancock County Drama Association began the process of reversing the prevailing negative attitudes toward Melungeons, attitudes shared by whites and Melungeons alike. Authors Jean Patterson Bible, Brent Kennedy, and others have continued that process, and organizations like the Melungeon Heritage Association and the Vardy Community Historical Society are helping to firmly establish the Melungeons' place in history. Families with Melungeon ancestry will hopefully celebrate that heritage for generations to come.

One can only hope that other tri-racial groups will embrace their own multi-ethnic heritages with similar pride. Some of these groups, such as the Lumbee and the Virginia Indian tribes vilified by Walter Plecker and the Racial Integrity Act, can acknowledge their tri-racial heritage while retaining a primarily Indian identity. Other groups, such as the Red Bones, Brass Ankles, Wesorts, and others, can emulate the Melungeons and embrace their own unique ancestries, celebrating their ethnic diversity. Our ancestors created the people we are today, and we should acknowledge *all* the components of our respective heritages.

American history has largely ignored the part played by the non-white and non-European people who helped create this nation. In many cases, whites who did not follow the genocidal example of their fellow Europeans joined these non-white people. People from widely different backgrounds and ethnicities merged their fates and created families that, because of their efforts in the face of harsh discrimination, survive to this day. These individuals and families had lives that should be acknowledged and celebrated. It is up to the present generation of tri-racial descendants to give them their due.

APPENDIX A

Will Allen Dromgoole's Articles for the *Nashville Sunday American*
31 August and 14 September, 1890

Land Of The Malungeons

Written for the *Sunday American*

Away up in an extreme corner of Tennessee I found them—them or it, for what I found is a remnant of a lost or forgotten race, huddled together in a sterile and isolated strip of land in one of the most inaccessible quarters of Tennessee. When I started out upon my hunt for the Malungeons various opinions and vague whispers were afloat concerning my sanity. My friends were too kind to do more than shake their heads and declare they never heard of such a people. But the less intimate of my acquaintances cooly informed me that I was "going on a wild-goose chase" and were quite willing to "bet their ears" I would never get nearer a Malungeon than at that moment. One dear old lady with more faith in the existence of the Malungeons than in my ability to cope with them begged me to insure my life before starting and to carry a loaded pistol. Another, not so dear and not so precautious *[sic]*, informed me that she "didn't believe in women gadding about the country alone, nohow." Still, I went, I saw and I shall conquer.

How I chanced to go and how I first heard of the Malungeons was through a New York newspaper. Some three years since I noticed a short paragraph stating that such a people exist somewhere in Tennessee. It stated that they were rather wild, entirely unlettered and largely given to illicit distilling. It spoke of their dialect as something unheard of, but failed to locate the human curiosities. I had but one cue by which to trail them—voz: they were illicit distillers. After repeated inquiry, and no end of laughter at my expense, I went to Capt. Carter B. Harrison, who was once United States marshall and did a good deal of work in this district.

"The Malungeons?" said Capt. Harrison. "O yes; you will find them in ———county [I will give the county later], and Senator J———, of the state senate, can tell you all about them."

I trailed Senator J——— for six months, and with this result:

"Go to ———," said he, "and take a horse forty miles across the country to ———, Tenn. There strike for ——— ridge, the stronghold of the Malungeons."

I have followed directions faithfully, and just here let me say if any one supposes I made the trip for the fun it might afford, he is mistaken. If any one supposes it was prompted by a spirit of adventure, or a love for the wild and untried, he is grievously in error. I have never experienced more difficulty in traveling, suffered more inconvenience, discomfort, bodily fatigue, and real dread of danger. It required almost superhuman effort to carry me on, and more than once, or a dozen times, was I tempted to give it up.

The Malungeons are a most peculiar people. The occupy an isolated and, except for horse or foot passengers, inaccessible territory, separated and alone, not mixing or caring to mix with the rest of the world. There are, however, a few, a very few, exceptions. I went one day to preaching on Big Sycamore, where the people are more mixed than on their native mountains. I found here all colors—white women with white children and white husbands, Malungeon women with brown babies and white babies, and one, a young copper-colored woman with black eyes and straight Indian locks, had three black babies, negroes, at her heels and a third [sic] at her breast. She was not a negro. Her skin was red, a kind of reddish-yellow, as easily distinguishable from a mulatto as the white man from the negro. I saw an old colored man, black as the oft-quoted ace of spades, whose wife is a white woman. I am told, however, the law did take his case in hand, but the old negro pleaded his "Portyghee" blood and was not convicted.

Many Malungeons claim to be Cherokee and Portuguese. Where they could have gotten their Portuguese blood is a mystery. The Cherokee is easily enough accounted for, as they claim to have come from North Carolina and to be a remnant of the tribe that refused to go when the Indians were ordered to the reservation. They are certainly very Indian-like in appearance. The men are tall, straight, clean-shaven, with small, sharp eyes, hooked noses and high cheek bones. They wear their hair long, a great many of them, and evidently enjoy their resemblance to the red man. This is doubtless due to the fact that a great many are disposed to believe them mulattos, and they are strongly opposed to being so classed. The women are small, graceful, dark and ugly. They go barefooted, but their feet are small and well shaped. So, too, are their hands, and they have the merriest, most musical laugh I have ever heard. They are exceedingly inquisitive, and will ask you a dozen questions before you can answer two.

The first question that greets you at every door is—even if you only stop for water—"Whatcher name?" the next is, "How old yer?" and then comes the all-important—"Did yer hear an'thin' o' ther railroad cumin' up ther ridge?"

They look for it constantly and always, as if they expect to see, some glad day, the brunt of the iron track, the glorious herald of prosperity and knowledge, come creeping up the mountains, horseback or afoot, bringing joy to the cabin even of the outcast and ostracised Malungeon; ostracised indeed. Only the negroes, who have themselves felt the lash of ostracism, open their doors to the Malungeons. They are very dishonest, so much so that only a few, not more than half a dozen, of the best are admitted into the house of the well-to-do native.

During the war they were a terror to the women of the valley, going in droves to their homes and helping themselves to food and clothing, even rifling the beds and closets while the defenseless wives of the absent soldiers stood by and witnessed the wholesale plundering, afraid to so much as offer a protest. After the war the women invaded their territory and recovered a great deal of their stolen property. They are exceedingly lazy. They live from hand to mouth and in hovels too filthy for any human being. They do not cultivate the soil at all. A tobacco patch and an orchard is the end and aim of their aspirations. I never saw such orchards, apples and apples and apples, peaches and peaches and peaches, and soon it will be brandy and brandy and brandy. They all drink, men, women and children, and they are all distillers; that is, the work of distilling is not confined to the men. Indeed, the women are the burden-bearers in every sense. They cook, wash, dig, hoe, cut wood, gather the fruit, strip the tobacco and help with the stills. There is not so much distilling now among them as there was a few years back. Uncle Sam set his hounds upon their trail, and now they are more careful of the requirement of the federal law at all events, as their miserable little doggeries, dotted here and there, go to prove.

They wondered very much concerning my appearance among them. Yes, I am right in the midst of them, and such an experience is almost beyond my power to picture. My board rates 15 cents per day. (Let the Maxwell blush.)[1] Thank fortune, my purse and my destiny have at last "met upon a level." No, do not say I am swindling my poor hosts. (I go from place to place.) Wait until I tell you. After I really struck their settlement, I entered upon a diet of cornbread and honey. Coffee? Oh yes, we have "lots" of coffee. It sets (or stands according to its age) in a tin pot in the shed (or under it), between the two rooms. There are never more than two rooms. Any one who is thirsty helps himself to coffee. Cold? Aye, cold as this world's charity and as comfortless. But it saves a walk to the spring and so we drink it. I had some trouble in getting board, because I asked "for board." And let me say, I have never drawn a good easy breath since I landed and found a dozen pairs of little black Indian eyes turned upon me. Always they are at the cracks, the chimney corner, "window hole," the door, peeping through the chinquapin and wahoo bushes, until I feel as if forty thousand spies were watching my movements. I had not dared to take out a pencil for three days, except last Monday night after I went to bed. I tried to write a letter in the dark, by a streak of light which fell through a chink in the door. But the next morning, when my hostess—a little snap-eyed, red-brown squaw—flung open my door (the room had but one, and she had removed the fastening, a wooden button, the night before) and sung out:

---

[1] A reference to Nashville's famous hotel, the Maxwell House.

"You Joe!—time you's up out'n ther," and a little, limp, sleepy-looking Indian crawled out from a pallet of rags in the corner. I felt pretty sure the boy had been put there to watch me, and so didn't try that kind of writing again. They are exceedingly suspicious and are as curious about me as can be. They received an idea that I am traveling for my health, as quite a number come from the valley to drink the mineral water with which this magnificent country abouts. Still, they suspect me, and they come in droves to see me. Seven little brown women, with bare feet and corncob pipes, sat on the doorstep yesterday to see me go out. I stopped a moment to speak to them; told them my name (which is the greatest puzzle to them, not one daring to try it), my age, and was informed that if I wasn't married "it wair time." And then one grizzle face old squaw kindly offered me a "pull at her pipe."

I visited one house of two rooms—Mrs. Gorvins'. She was out in the orchard gathering apples to dry, and out to the orchard I went. The prettiest girl I ever saw came to meet me with her lap full of apples. She pointed to a seat on a rude bench and poured the apples into my lap, at the same time calling, "Mai! Mai! Come er-here!" (Please call that word Mai as it is called in hair or after.) Mai came, and the saints and hobgoblins! The witch of Endor calling dead Saul from sepulchral darkness would have calked her ears and fled forever at the sight of this living, breathing Malungeon witch. Shakespeare would have shrieked in agony and chucked his own weird sisters where neither "thunder, lightning nor rain" would ever have found them more. Even poor tipsy, turvy Tam O'Shanter would have drawn up his gray mare and forgotten to fly before this, mightier than Meg Merrilles herself. She was small, scant, raw-boned, sharp-ankled, barefoot, short frock literally hanging from the knee in rags. A dark jacket with great yellow patches on either breast, sleeves torn away above the elbow, black hair burnt to an unfashionable auburn long ago, and a corncob pipe wedged between the toothless gums. A flock of children came in her wake, and full one dozen more (indeed I am telling the unvarnished truth) came from bush and brake. I never saw as many, seventeen by actual count, and two missing "count o' bein' dead."

Mrs. Gorvins was silent until I spoke to one of the children, and then, let me tell you something, I never saw an uglier human creature, or one more gross-looking and unattractive, and I never saw a gentler, sweeter, truer mother. She called up her children—little brown fellows, bearing the unmistakable mark of the Indian, all but one, a little white-headed boy with blue eyes and dimpled chin, who seemed as much out of place among them as a lily in a dungeon. One was Maggieleny (Magdeline), and one was Ichabady (Ichabod), and one was Archivale (Archibald). Another was Kat (Kathleen), another Hanny (Hannah), and the baby-names giving out, as the mother told me, she "had jes' been plumb erbliged ter name one over twict," and so the baby was called Katty (Kathleen).

They lived on corn bread and honey, coffee without cream or sugar, and found life full and glad and satisfactory.

I could run on forever telling you of these queer, queer people, who are a part of us, have a voice in our politics and a right to our consideration. They are a blot upon our state. They are ignorant of the very letters of the alphabet, and defiant (or worse, ignorant) of the very first principles of morality and cleanliness. It is no sensational picture I have drawn; it is hard truth, hard to believe and hard to understand. They are within five miles of one of the prettiest county seats in Tennessee. In politics they are republican to a man, but sell their votes for 50 cents and consider themselves well paid. They are great "charmers" and "herb doctors." I have a string of "blood beads" I bought of an old squaw, who assured me they would heal all "ailmint o' the blood." They are totally unlike the native Tennessee mountaineer, unlike him in every way. The mountaineer is liberal, trustful and open. The Malungeon wants pay (not much, but something) for the slightest favor. He is curious and suspicious and given to lying and stealing, things unknown among the native mountaineers.

I must tell you of a sermon I heard down in Black Water swamp. I do not know what the text was, but the preacher, a half-breed, was telling of the danger of riches. He told them of Mr. Vanderbilt, "the riches' man et ever trod on God a-mighty's yearth," he said. And then he told how, when he came to die he called his wife and asked her to sing, "Come, Ye Sinners." He drew his point: the rich man wanted the beggar's song sung over him. And he lamented that it was "tu late, tu late" for Mr. Vanderbilt. He died and went to torment, "an wher uz all his money?" I took it upon myself to tell him where a good slice of it was. I could not call myself a Tennesseean and sit by and hear Mr. Vanderbilt slandered, and right here in Tennessee, too, preached right into hell by the people his wealth was given to bless. So when the service was over I went to the preacher and I said: "Brother, you are doing the memory of Mr. Vanderbilt a great wrong. He was a good man, if a rich one, and Tennessee is indebted to him for the grandest school she has."

He looked at me a minute, and then he said:

"He uz a Christian?"

"Yes," I said, "and had a Christian wife."

His face brightened. "Waal," he said, "I air glad to know that; I'll tell 'em so nex' time I preach."

I hope he did.

Will Allen[2]

A STRANGE PEOPLE

———

Habits, Customs and Characteristics of Malungeons.

———

Little Given to Social Intercourse With the Neighbors.

———

A School Teacher Who Can Neither Read Nor Write—Dancing the Favorite Pastime

———

(Written for The American)

---

[2] Will Allen Dromgoole, "Land of the Malungeons," Nashville *Sunday American*, 31 August 1890, 10.

I have made a careful study and inquiry as to the name Malungeon, but have been unable as yet to place it. It has an Indian sound, but the Malungeons themselves have no idea as to its origin or meaning.

These people, of whom so little is known, inhabit an isolated corner of the earth, known as Newman's ridge, in Hancock county. They are within five miles of one of the prettiest county seats in Tennessee. They mix very little with the natives of the county, and seem to care very little about the world beyond their isolated habitation. Their homes are miserable hovels, set in the very heart of the wilderness. There is not, I am told, a family on the ridge other than the Malungeons.

At one house where I stopped I was put in a closet to sleep. The room had no windows and the door opened into my landlady's room. The latch was removed before I retired. My bed was made of straw and I was not its sole inhabitant, not by an overwhelming majority. My food consisted of corn bread, honey and bitter coffee. At another place, I climbed a ladder to the roof-room, which had neither windows nor floor. I did not meet a man or woman on the ridge who could read.

At the foot of the ridge in what is known as Black Water swamp, the country is simply magnificent. I boarded there for several days and found the people exceedingly kind. The ridge proper is the home of the Malungeons.

I visited one house where the floors were of trees, the bark still on them, and the beds of leaves. The owner was a full-blooded Indian, with keen, black eyes, straight black hair, high cheeks, and a hook nose. He played upon his violin with his fingers instead of a bow, and entertained us with a history of his grandfather, who was a Cherokee chief, and by singing some of the songs of his tribe. He also described the Malungeon custom of amusements. The dance is a favorite pastime consisting of a two, four or six-handed reel. Whiskey is a very popular guest at their entertainments, and fights are not an uncommon result. In a fight each man's friends are expected to take sides and help, and the fight continues until one side at least is whipped.

———————

At another house I visited (if I may call it a house) I found the family, nine in number, housed in one room of a stable. There were three rooms to the establishment. The stock (belonging to some one else) was fed in one department and the family lived in the next. The living room was about 12 feet square and had neither chinking or daubing. There were two beds, and one of them stood alongside the partition where there were cracks large enough for a child of 5 years to step through the hay rick on the other side. The space unoccupied by the beds was about 1 feet [*sic*], and there being no chairs, and old quilt was spread upon the floor, and three poor old women were scattered upon it arranging their Indian locks. The third room was the cooking department, although several dirty-looking beds occupied space here and there. I forgot to mention a heap of white ashes in the living room, which the women utilized for spitting upon. The Malungeons are great lovers of the weed and all chew and smoke—men, women and children.

———————

I also visited the cabin of a charmer, for you must know these people have many superstitions. This charmer can remove warts, moles, birth-marks, and all ugly protuberances by a kind of magic known only to herself. She offered to remove the mole from my face for 10 cents, and became quite angry when I declined to part with my lifetime companion.

"Tairsn't purty, nohers," she said; "an 't air ner sarvice, nurther."

I cannot spell their dialect as they speak it. It is not the dialect of the mountaineers, and the last syllable of almost every word is omitted. The "R" is missing entirely from their vocabulary. There is also a witch among them who heals sores, rheumatism, "conjures," etc. They come from ten miles afoot to consult her

———————

They possess many Indian traits, that of vengeance being strongly characteristic of them.

They, likewise, resemble the negro in many things. They are sticklers for religion, and believe largely in water and the "mourner's bench." They call themselves Baptists, although their form of worship is really that of the Dunkard. They are exceedingly illiterate, but are beginning to take some interest in educational matters. I visited one of their schools, taught by a native Malungeon. He could not read, and his pronunciation of the words given to the spelling class was exceedingly peculiar, as well as ridiculous. Mr. Thomas Sharpe, of Nashville, made an excellent sketch of this teacher while he was busy with his class and unconcious that he was "being tuk fur a pictur."

_____

There are but three names among them—real Malungeon names—Collins, Mullins, Gorvens. Lately the name of Gibbins has found a way among them, but the first three are their real names. They distinguish each other in a most novel manner. For instance, Calloway Collins' wife is Ann Calloway, his daughter is Dorous Calloway, and his son is Jim Calloway.

_____

How they live is a mystery. Their food is the hardest kind, and their homes unfit shelter for man or beast. In many cases they are extremely immoral and seem utterly unconscious of either law or cleanliness. Their voices are exceedingly sweet, and their laugh the merriest, most musical ripple imaginable, more like the tinkle of a happy little brook among beds of pebbles than the laugh of a half civilized Malungeon. Even the men speak low and their voices are not unpleasant. The women are quick, sharp, bright. The men are slow, lazy, shiftless and shirking, and seem entirely unacquainted with work, God's medicine for the miserable.

_____

Their dress is ordinary calico, or cotton, short blouse, without buttons or other fastenings than brass pins conspicuously arranged, or narrow white strings tacked on either side the waist and tied in a bow knot.

_____

These strange people have caught, however, the fever raging throughout the south, and especially through Eastern Tennessee, the iron fever. They believe their sterile ridges to be crammed full with the

precious ore. If it is, the rocks give no sign, for there are no outcroppings
to be found as yet.

At one place I staid to dinner. No one ate with me except my own
guide, and the food and shelter were given grudgingly, without that
hearty willingness which characterizes the old Tennessee mountaineer,
who bids you "light and hitch, feed your critter and be ter home." I was
invited to eat, to be sure, but the family stood by and eyed me until my
portion of bread and honey almost choked me. Corn bread, thick, black,
crusted pones, steaming hot, and honey sweet enough and clean—aye,
clean, for the wild bees made it from the wild flowers springing straight
from God's planting. I paid 15 cents for my dinner. A mountaineer
would have knocked you down had you offered money for dinner under
such circumstances. Bah! The Malungeon is no more a mountaineer than
am I, born in the heart of the old Volunteer state.

Will Allen[3]

---

[3] Will Allen Dromgoole, "A Strange People," Nashville *Sunday American*, 14
September 1890, 10.

APPENDIX B

Will Allen Dromgoole's *Arena* Articles

The Malungeons

by Will Allen Dromgoole

Were you ever when a child half playfully told "The Malungeons will get you?" If not, you were never a Tennessee child, as some of our fathers were; they tell all who may be told of that strange, almost forgotten race, concerning whom history is strangely silent. Only upon the records of the state of Tennessee does the name appear. The records show that by act of the Constitutional Convention of 1834, when the "Race Question" played such a conspicuous part in the deliberations of that body, the Malungeons, as a *"free person of color,"* was denied the right of suffrage. Right there he dropped from the public mind and interest. Of no value as a slave, with no voice as a citizen, what use could the public make of the Malungeon? When John Sevier attempted to organize the State of Franklin, there was living in the mountains of Eastern Tenessee a colony of dark-skinned, reddish-brown complexioned people, supposed to be of Moorish descent, who affiliated with neither whites nor blacks, and who called themselves Malungeons, and claimed to be of Poruguese descent. They lived to themselves exclusively, and were looked on as neither negroes nor Indians.

All the negroes ever brought to America came as slaves; the Malungeons were never slaves, and until 1834 enjoyed all the rights of citizenship. Even in the Convention which disfranchised them, they were referred to as *"free persons of color"* or "Malungeons."

Their condition from the organization of the State of Tennessee to the close of the civil war is most accurately described by John A.

McKinley, of Hawkins County, who was chairman of the committee to which was referred all matters affecting these *"free persons of color."*

Said he, speaking of free persons of color, "It means Malungeons if it means anything. Although 'fleecy locks and black complexion' do not forfeit Nature's claims, still it is true that those locks and that complexion mark every one of the African race, so long as he remains among the white race, as a person doomed to live in the suburbs of society.

"Unenviable as is the condition of the slave, unlovely as slavery is in all its aspects, bitter as is the draught the slave is doomed to drink, nevertheless, his condition is better than that of the *'free man of color'* in the midst of a community of white men with whom he has no interest, no fellow-feeling and no equality." So the Constitutional convention left these the most pitiable of all outcasts; denied their oath in court, and deprived of the testimony of their own color, left utterly helpless in all legal contests, they naturally, when the State set the brand of the outcast upon them, took to the hills, the isolated peaks of the uninhabited mountains, the corners of the earth, as it were, where, huddled together, they became as law unto themselves, a race indeed separate and distinct from the several races inhabiting the State of Tennessee.

So much, or so *little*, we glean from the records. From history we get nothing; not so much as the name—Malungeons.

In the farther valleys they were soon forgotten: only now and then and old slave-mammy would frighten her rebellious charge into subjection with the threat,—"The Malungeons will get you in you ain't pretty." But to the people of the foot hills and nearer valleys, they became a living terror; sweeping down upon them, stealing their cattle, their provisions, their very clothing, and household furniture.

They became shiftless, idle, thieving, and defiant of all law, distillers of brandy, almost to a man. The barren height upon which they located, offered hope of no other crop so much as fruit, and they were forced, it would appear, to utilize their one opportunity.

After the breaking out of the war, some few enlisted in the army, but the greater number remained with their stills, to pillage and plunder among the helpless women and children.

Their mountains became a terror to travelers; and not until within the last half decade has it been regarded as safe to cross Malungeon territory.

Such they *were*; or so do they come to us through tradition and the State's records. As to what they *are* any who feel disposed may go and see. Opinion is divided concerning them, and they have their own ideas as to their descent. A great many declare them mulattoes, and base their belief upon the ground that at the close of the civil war negroes and Malungeons stood upon precisely the same social footing, "*free men of color*" all, and that the fast vanishing handful opened their doors to the darker brother, also groaning under the brand of social ostracism. This might, at first glance, seem probable, indeed, reasonable.

Yet if we will consider a moment, we shall see that a race of mulattoes cannot exist as these Malungeons have existed. The race goes from mulattoes to quadroons, from quadroons to octoroons, and there it stops. The octoroon women bear no children, but in every cabin of the Malungeons may be found mothers and grandmothers, and very often great-grandmothers.

"Who are they, then?" you ask. I can only give you their own theory—If I may call it such—and to do this I must tell you how I found them, and something of my stay among them.

First. I saw in an old newspaper some slight mention of them. With this tiny clue I followed their trail for three years. The paper merely stated that "somewhere in the mountains of Tennessee there existed a remanant of people called Malungeons, having a distinct color, characteristics,and dialect." It seemed a very hopeless search, so utterly were the Malungeons forgotten, and I was laughed at no little for my "new crank." I was even called "a Malungeon" more than once, and was about to abandon my "crank" when a member of the Tennessee State Senate, of which I happened at that time to be engrossing clerk, spoke of a brother senator as being "tricky as a Malungeon."

I pounced on him the moment his speech was completed. "Senator," I said, "what is a Malungeon?"

"A dirty Indian sneak," said he. "Go over yonder and ask Senator ———; they live in his district."

I went at once.

"Senator, what is a Malungeon?" I asked again.

"A Portuguese nigger," was the reply. "Representative T____ can tell you all about them, they live in his county."

From "district" to "county" was quick travelling. And into the House of Representatives I went, fast upon the lost trail of the forgotten Malungeons.

"Mr. ____," said I, "please tell me what is a Malungeon?"

"A Malungeon," said he, "isn't a nigger, and he isn't an Indian, and he isn't a white man. God only knows *what* he is. *I* should call him a *Democrat*, only he always votes the Reublican ticket." I merely mention all this to show how the Malungeons to-day are regarded, and to show I tracked them to Newman's Ridge in Hancock County, where within four miles of one of the prettiest county towns in Tennessee, may be found all that remains of that outcast race whose descent is a riddle the historian has never solved. In appearance they bear a striking resemblance to the Cherokees, and they are believed by the people round about to be a kind of half-breed Indian.

Thier complexion is a reddish brown, totally unlike the mulatto. The men are very tall and straight, with small, sharp eyes, high cheek bones, and straight black hair, worn rather long. The women are small, below the average height, coal black hair and eyes, high cheek bones, and the same red-brown complexion. The hands of the Malungeon women are quite shapely and pretty. Also their feet, despite the fact that they trravel the sharp mountain trails barefoot, are short and shapely. Their features are wholly unlike those of the negro, except in cases where the two races have cohabited, as is sometimes the fact. These instances can be readily detected, as can those of cohabitation with the mountaineer; for the pure Malungeons present a characteristic and individual appearance. On the Ridge proper, one finds only pure Malungeons; it is in the unsavory limits of Black Water Swamp and on Big Sycamore Creek, lying at the foot of the Ridge between it and Powell's Mountain, that the mixed races dwell.

In Western and Middle Tennessee the Malungeons are forgotten long ago. And indeed, so nearly complete has been the extinction of the race that in but few counties of Eastern Tennessee is it known. In Hancock you may hear them, and see them, almost the instant you cross into the county line. There they are distinguished as "Ridgemanites," or pure "Malungeons." Those among them whom the white or negro blood has entered are called the *"Black-Waters."* The Ridge is admirable adapted to the purpose of wild-cat distilling, being crossed by but one road and crowned with jungles of chinquapin, cedar, and wahoo.

Of very recent years the dogs of the law have proved too sharp-eyed and bold even for the lawless Malungeons, so that such of the furnace fires as have not been extinguished are built underground.

They are a great nuisance to the people of the county seat, where, on any public day, and especially on election days, they may be seen squatted about the streets, great strapping men, or little brown women baking themselves in the sun like mud figures set to dry.

The people of the town do not allow them to enter their dwellings, and even refuse to employ them as servants, owing to their filthy habit of chewing tobacco and spitting upon the floors, together with their ignorance or defiance of the difference between *meum* and *tuum*.

They are exceedingly shiftless, and in most cases filthy. They care for nothing except their pipe, their liquor, and a tramp "ter towin." They will walk to Sneedville and back sometimes twice in twelve hours, up a steep trail though an almost unbroken wilderness, and never seem to suffer the least fatigue.

They are not at all like the Tennessee mountaineer either in appearance or characteristics. The mountaineer, however poor, is clean—cleanliness itself. He is honest (I speak of him as a class) he is generous, trustful, until once betrayed; truthful, brave, and possessing many of the noblest and keenest sensibilities. The Malungeons are filthy, their home is filthy. They are rogues, natural, "born rogues," close, suspicious, inhospitable, untruthful, cowardly, and to use their own word, "sneaky." They are exceedingly inquisitive too, and will trail a visitor to the Ridge for miles, through seemingly impenetrable jungles, to discover, if may be, the object of his visit. They expect remuneration for the slightest service. The mountaineer's door stands open, or at most the string of the latch dangles upon the "outside." He takes you for what you *seem* until you shall prove yourself otherwise.

In many things they resemble the negro. They are exceedingly immoral, yet are great shouters and advocates of religion. They call themselves Baptists, although their mode of baptism is that of the Dunkard.

There are no churches on the Ridge, but the one I visited in Black Water Swamp was beyond question and inauguration of the colored element. At this church I saw white women with negro babies at their breasts—Malungeon women with white or with black husbands, and some, indeed, having the three separate races represented in their children; showing thereby the gross immorality that is practised among them. I saw an old negro whose wife was a white woman, and who had been several times arrested, and released on his plea of "Portygee" blood, which he declared had colored his skin, not African.

The dialect of the Malungeons is a cross between that of the mountaineer and the negro—a corruption, perhaps, of both. The letter R occupies but a small place in their speech, and they have a peculiar habit of omitting the last letter, sometimes the last syllable of their words. For instance "good night"—is "goo' night." "Give" is "gi'" etc. They do not drawl like the mountaineers but, on the contrary, speak rapidly and talk a great deal. The laugh of the Malungeon women is the most exquisitely musicle jingle, a perfect ripple of sweet sound. Their dialect is exceedingly difficult to write, owing to their habit of curtailing their words.

The pure Malungeons, that is the old men and women, have no toleration for the negro, and nothing insults them so much as the suggestion of negro blood. Many pathetic stories are told of their battle against the black race, which they regard as the cause of their downfall, the annihilation, indeed, of the Malungeons, for when the races began to mix and to intermarry, and the expression, "A Malungeon nigger" came into use, the last barrier vanished, and all were regarded as somewhat upon a social level.

They are very like the Indians in many respect, their fleetness of foot, cupidity, cruelty (as practised during the days of their illicit distilling), their love for the forest, their custom of living without doors, one might almost say,—for truly the little hovels could not be called homes,—and their taste for liquor and tobacco.

They believe in witchcraft, "yarbs," and more than one "charmer" may be found among them. They will "rub away" a wart or mole for ten cents, and one old squaw assured me she had some "blood beads" the "wair bounter heal all manner o' blood ailimints."

They are limited somewhat as to names: their principal families being the Mullins, Gorvens, Collins, and Gibbins.

They resort to a very peculiar method of distinguishing themselves. Jack Collins' wife for instance will be Mary Jack. His son will be Ben Jack. His daughters' names will be similar: Nancy Jack or Jane Jack, as the case may be, but always having the father's Christian name attached.

Their homes are miserable hovels, set here and there in the very heart of the wilderness. Very few of their cabins have windows, and some have only an opening cut through the wall for a door. In winter an old quilt is hung before it to shut out the cold. They do not welcome strangers among them, so that I went to the Ridge somewhat doubtful as to my reception. I went, however, determined to be one of them, so I wore a suit as nearly like their own as I could get it. I had some trouble securing boards, but did succeed at last in doing so by paying the enormous sum of fifteen cents. I was put to sleep in a little closet opening off the family room. My room had no windows, and but the one door. The latch was carefully removed before I went in, so that I had no means of egress, except through the family room, and no means by which to shut myself in. My bed was of straw, not the sweet-smelling straw we read of. The Malungeons go a long way for their straw, and they evidently make it go a long way when they do get it. I was called to breakfast the next morning while the gray mists still held the mountain in its arms. I asked for water to bathe my face and was sent to "ther branch," a beautiful little mountain stream crossing the trail some few hundred yeards from the cabin.

Breakfast consisted of corn bread, wild honey, and bitter coffee. It was prepared and eaten in the garret, or roof room, above the family room. A few chickens, the only fowl I saw on the Ridge, also occupied the roof room. Coffee is quite common among the Malungeons; they drink it without sweetening, and drink it cold at all hours of the day or nights. They have no windows and no candles, consequently, they retire with the going of the daylight. Many of their cabins have no floors other than that which Nature gave, but one that I remember had a floor made of trees slit in half, the bark still on, placed with the flat side to the ground. The people of h te house slept on leaves with an old gray blanket for covering. Yet the master of the house, who claims to be an Indian, and who, without doubt, possesses Indian blood, draws a pension of twenty-nine dollars per month. He can neither read nor write, is a lazy fellow, fond of apple brandy and bitter coffee, has a rollicking good time with an old fiddle which he plays with his thumb, and boasts largely of his Cherokee grandfather and his government pension. In one part of his cabin (there are two rooms and a connecting shed) the very stumps of the trees still remain. I had my artist sketch him sitting upon the stump of a monster oak which stood in the very center of the shed or hallway.

This family did their cooking at a rude fireplace built near the spring, as a matter of convenience.

Another family occupied one room, or apartment, of a stable. The stock fed in another (the stock belonged, let me say, to someone else) and the "cracks" between the logs of the separating partition were of such depth a small child could have rolled from the bed in one apartment into the trough in the other. How they exist among such squalor is a mystery.

Their dress consists, among the women, of a short loose calico skirt and a blouse that boasts of neither hook nor button. Some of these blouses were fastened with brass pins conspicuously bright. Others were tied together by means of strings tacked on either side. They wear neither shoes nor stockings in the summer, and many of them go barefoot all winter. The men wear jeans, and may be seen almost any day tramping barefoot across the mountain.

They are exceedingly illiterate, none of them being able to read. I found one school among them, taught by an old Malungeon, whose literary accomplishments amounted to a meagre knowledge of the alphabet and the spelling of words. Yet, he was very earnest, and called lustily to the "chillering" to "spry up," and to "learn the book."

This school was located in the loveliest spot my eyes ever rested upon. An eminence overlooking the beautiful valley of the Clinch and the purple peaks beyond/billows and billows of mountains, so blue, so exquisitely wrapped in their delicate mist-veil, one almost doubts if they be hills or heaven.While through the slumbrous vale the silvery Clinch, the fairest of Tennessee's fair streams, creeps slowly, like a drowsy dream river, among the purple distances.

The eminence itself is entirely barren save for one tall old cedar, and the schoolmaster's little log building. It presents a very weird, wild, yet majestic scene, to the traveller as he climbs up from the valley.

Near the schoolhouse is a Malungeon grave-yard. The Malungeons are very careful for their dead. They build a kind of floorless house above each separate grave, many of the homes of the dead being far better than the dwellings of the living. The grave-yard presents the appearance of a diminutive town, or settlement, and is kept with great nicety and care. They mourn their dead for years, and every friend and acquaintence is expected to join in the funeral arrangements. They follow the body to the grave, sometimes for miles, afoot, in single file. Their burial ceremonies are exceedingly interesting and peculiar.

They are an unforgiving people, although, unlike the sensitive mountaineer, they are slow to detect an insult, and expect to be spit upon. But injury to life or property they never forgive. Several odd and pathetic instances of Malungeon hate came under my observation while among them, but they would cover too much space in telling.

Within the last two years the railroad has struck within some thiry miles of them, and its effects are becoming very apparent. Now and then a band of surveyors, or a lone mineralogist will cross Powell's mountain, and pass through Mulberry Gap just beyond Newman's Ridge. So near, yet never nearer. The hills around are all said to be crammed with coal or iron, but Newman's Ridge can offer nothing to the capitalist. It would seem that the Malungeons had chosen the one spot, of all that magnificent creation, *not* to be desired.

Yet, they have heard of the railroad, the great bearer of commerce, and expect it, in a half-regretful, half-pathetic way.

They have four questions, always, for the stranger: -

"Whatcher name?"

"Wher'd yer come fum?"

"How old er yer?"

"Did yer hear en'thin' er ther railwa' comin' up ther Ridge?"

As if it might step into their midst any day.

The Malungeons believe themselves to be of Cherokee and Portuguese extraction. They cannot account for the Portuguese blood, but are very bold in declaring themselves a remnant of those tribes, or that tribe, still inhabiting the mountains of North Carolina, which refused to follow the tribes to the Reservation set aside for them.

There is a theory that the Portuguese pirates, known to have visited these waters, came ashore and located in the mountains of North Carolina. The Portuguese "streak," however, is scouted by those who claim for the Malungeons a drop of African blood, as, quite early in the settlement of Tennessee, runaway negroes settled among the Cherokees, or else were captured and adopted by them.

However, with all the light possible to be thrown upon them, the Malungeons are, and will remain, a mystery. A more pathetic case than theirs cannot be imagined. They are going, the little space of hills 'twixt earth and heaven alloted them, will soon be free of the dusky tribe, whose very name is a puzzle. The most that can be said of one of them is, "He is a Malungeon," a synonym for all that is doubtful and mysterious—and unclean.[1]

The Malungeon Tree And It's Four Branches

By Will Allen Dromgoole

Somewhere in the eighteenth century, before the year 1797, there appeared in the eastern portion of Tennessee, at that time the Territory of North Carolina, two strange-looking men calling themselves "Collins" and "Gibson". They had a reddish brown complexion, long, straight, black hair, keen, black eyes, and sharp, clear-cut features. They spoke in broken English, a dialect distinct from anything ever heard in that section of the country.

They claimed to have come from Virginia and many years after emigrating, themselves told the story of their past.

These two, Vardy Collins and Buck Gibson, were the head and source of the Malungeons in Tennessee. With the cunning of their Cherokee ancestors, they planned and executed a scheme by which they were enabled to "set up for themselves" in the almost unbroken Territory of North Carolina.

Old Buck, as he was called, was disguised by a wash of some dark description, and taken to Virginia by Vardy where he was sold as a slave. He was a magnificent specimen of physical strength, and brought a fine price, a wagon and mules, a lot of goods, and three hundred dollars in money being paid to old Vardy for his "likely nigger." Once out of Richmond, Vardy turned his mule's shoes and struck out for the wilderness of North Carolina, as previously planned. Buck lost little time ridding himself of his negro disguise, swore he was not the man bought of Collins, and followed in the wake of his fellow thief to the Territory. The proceeds of the sale were divided and each chose his habitation; old Vardy choosing Newman's Ridge, where he was soon joined by others of his race, and so the Malungeons became a part of the inhabitants of

---

[1] Dromgoole, "The Malungeons," 470–79.

Tennessee. This story I know is true. There are reliable parties still living who received it from old Vardy himself, who came here as young men and lived, as the Malungeons generally did to a ripe old age.

The names "Collins" and "Gibson" were also stolen from the white settlers in Virginia where the men had lived previous to emigrating to North Carolina.

There is, perhaps, no more satisfactory method of illustrating this peculiar race, its origin and blood, than by the familiar tree.

Old Vardy Collins, then, must be regarded as the body, or main stem, in this state, at all events.

It is only of very late years the Melungeons have been classed as "families". Originally they were "tribes", afterward "clans" and at last "Families". From Old Vardy the first tribe took it's first name "COLLINSES". Others who followed Vardy took the Collins name also. Old Benjamin Collins, one of the pioneers, was older than Vardy, but came to Tennessee a trifle later. He had quite a large family of children, among them Edmond, Mileyton (supposed to have meant Milton), Marler, Harry, Andrew, Zeke, Jordon. From Jordan Collins descended Calloway Collins who is still living today and from whom I obtained some valuable information.

But to.go back a step. Benjamin Collins was known as old Ben, and became the head of the Ben tribe. Old Solomon Collins was the head of the *Sols*. The race was increasing so rapidly, by emigration and otherwise, that it became necessary to adopt other names than Collins. They fell, curiously enough, upon the first or christian name of the head of a large family connection or tribe. Emigrants arriving attached themselves as they chose to the several tribes. After a while, with an eye to brevity, doubtless, the word "tribe" was dropped from ordinary, everyday use. The *"Bens"* the *"Sols"* meant the Ben and Sol Tribes. It appeared that no tribe was ever called for Old Vardy, although as long as he lived he was reconized as head and leader of the entire people.

This is doubtless due to the fact that in his day the settlement was new, and the people, and the one name *Collins* covered the entire population. The original Collins people were Indian, there is no doubt about that, and they lived as the Indians lived until sometime after the first white man appeared among them. All would huddle together in one room (?), sleep in one common bed of leaves, make themselves such neccessary clothing as nature demanded, smoke, and dream away the good long days that were so dreamily delightful nowhere as they were on Newman's Ridge.

The Collins tribe multiplied more and more; it became necessary to have names, and a most peculiar method was hit upon for obtaining them.

Ben Collins children were distinguished from the children of Sol and Vardy by prefixing the Christian name either of the father or mother to the Christian name of the child. For instance; Edmund Ben, Singleton Ben; Andrew Ben; Zeke Ben, meant that Edmund, Singleton, Andrew, and Zeke were the sons of Ben Collins. Singleton Mitch; Levi Mitch, and Morris Mitch, meant that these men were the sons of Mitchel Collins. In the next generation there was a Jordan Ben (a son of old Benjamin Collins) who married Abbie Sol, had a son, who is called (he is still living, as before stated) Calloway Abby for his mother. The wife before marriage takes her father's Christian name; after marriage that of her husband. Calloway's wife, for instance, is Ann Calloway. It is not known, and cannot by any possibility be ascertained at what precise period other races appeared among the "Collinses." For many years they occupied the Ridge without distrurbance. The country was new, wild, and few straggling settlements were glad of almost any new neighbors. Moreover, these strange people, who were then called the "Ridgemanites", the "Indians", and the "Black Waterites" (because of a stream called Black Water, which flows through their territory, the bed of which was, and is, covered with a peculiar dark slate rock which gives the black appearance to the stream), had chosen the rocky and inaccessible Ridge, while the fertile and beautiful valley of the Clinch lay open and inviting to the white settler. The Ridgemanites were not striving for wealth evidently, and as land was plentiful and neighbors few, they held their bit in the creation without molestation or interruption for many years. They were all Collinses, as I said; those who followed the first-comers accepting the name already provided them. There was no mixture of blood: they claimed to be Indians and no man disputed it. They were called the "Collins Tribe" until having multiplied to the extent it was necessary to divide, when the descendants of the several pioneers were separated, or divided into *clans*. Then came the Ben clan, the Sol clan, the Mitch clan, and indeed every prominent head of a large relationship was recognized as the leader of his clan, which always bore his name. There was, to be sure, no set form or time at which this division was made. It was only one of those natural splits, gradual and necessary, which is the sure result of increasing strength.

They were still, however, we must observe, all Collinses, The main *tree* had not been disturbed by foreign grafting, and while all were not blood descendants of old Vardy they, at all events, had all fallen under his banner and appropriated his name.

The tree at last began to put forth branches, or rather three foreign shoots were grafted into the body of it; the English (or white), Portuguese, and African.

The English branch began with the *Mullins* tribe, a very powerful tribe, next indeed for a long time to the Collins tribe, and at present the strongest of all the several branches, as well as the most daring and obstinate.

Old Jim Mullins, the father of the branch, was an Englishman, a trader, it is supposed, with Indians. He was of a roving, daring disposition, and rather fond of the free abandon which characterized the Indian. He was much given to sports, and was always "cheek by jowl" with the Cherokees and other Indian tribes among which he mingled. What brought him to Newman's Ridge must have been, as it is said, his love for freedom and sport, and that careless existence known only to the Indians. He stumbled upon the Ridge settlement, fell in with the Ridgemanites, and never left them. He took for a wife one of their women, a descendant of old Sol Collins, and reared a family known as the "*Mullins* tribe." This is said to be the first white blood that mingled with the blood of the dusky Ridgemanites.

By marriage I mean to say (in their own language) they "took up together" having no set form of marriage service. So old Jim Mullins took up with a Malungeon woman, a Collins, by whom he had a large family of children. Sometime after he exchanged wives with one Wyatt Collins, and proceeded to cultivate a second family. Wyatt Collins also had a large family by his first wife, and equally fortunate with the one whom he traded her for.

After the forming of Hancock County (Tennessee) old Mullins and Collins were forced to marry their wives according to the law of the land, but all had children and grandchildren before they were lawfully married.

The Mullins tribe became exceedingly strong, and remains today the head of the Ridge people.

The African branch was introduced by one Goins (I spell it as they do) who emigrated from North Carolina after the formation of the state of Tennessee. Goins was a negro, and did not settle upon the Ridge, but lower down the Big Sycamore Creek in Powell's Valley. He took a Malungeon woman for his wife (took up with her), and reared a family or tribe. The Goins family may be easily reconized by their kinky hair, flat nose and foot, thick lips, and a complexion totally unlike the Collins and Mullins tribes. They possess many negro traits, too, which are wanting to the other tribes.

The Malungeons repudiate the idea of negro blood, yet some of the shiftless stragglers among them have married among the Goins people. They evade slights, snubs, censure, *and the law*, by claiming to have married Portuguese, there really being a Portuguese branch among the tribes.

The Goins tribe, however, was always looked upon with touch of contempt, and was held in a kind of subjection, socially and politically, by the others.

The Mullins and Collins tribes will fight for their Indian blood. The Melungeons are not brave; indeed, they are great cowards and easily brow-beaten, accustomed to receiving all manners of insults which it never occurs to them to resent. Only in this matter of blood will they "show fight"

The Portuguese branch was for a long time a riddle, the existence of it being stoutly denied. It has at last, however, been traced to one "Denhan," a Portuguese who married a Collins woman.

It seems that every runaway or straggler of any kind whatever, passing through the country took up with abode temporarily or permanently, with the Malungeons, or as they were then called the Ridgemanites. They were harmless, social, and good-natured when well acquainted with one—although at first suspicious, distant, and morose. While they have never encouraged emigration to the Ridge they have sometimes been unable to prevent it.

Denhan, it is supposed, came from one of the Spanish settlements lying further to the south. He settled on Mulberry Creek, and married a sister of Old Sol Collins.

There is another story, however, about Denham. It is said that the first Denham came as did the first Collins from North Carolina, and that he (or his ancestors) had been left upon the Carolina coast by some

Portuguese pirate vessel plying along the shore. When the English wrested the island of Jamacia from Spain in 1655, some fifteen hundred Spanish slaves fled to the mountains. Their number grew and their strength multiplied. For more than a hundred years they kept up a kind of guerilla warfare, for they were both savage and warlike. They were called "mountain negroes," or "maroons". The West Indian waters swarmed with piratical vessels at that time, the Portugese being the most terrible and daring. The crews of these vessels were composed for the most part of these "mountain negroes." When they became insubordinate, or in any way useless, they were put ashore and left to take care of themselves. It is said the Denhans were put ashore on the Carolina coast. Their instincts carried them to the mountains, from which one emigrated to Newman's Ridge, then a part of North Carolina territory.

So we have the four races, or representatives, among, as they then began to be called, the Malungeons; namely, the Indians, the English, the Portuguese, and the African. Each is clearly distinct and easily recognized even to the present day.

The Portuguese blood has been a misfortune to the first Malungeons inasmuch as it has been a shield to the Goins clan under which they have sought to shelter themselves and repudiate the African streak.

There is a very marked difference between the two, however. There is an old blacksmith, a Portuguese, on Black Water Creek, as dark as a genuine African. Yet, there is a peculiar tinge to his complexion that is totally foreign to the negro. He has a white wife, a Mullins woman, a descendant of English and Indian. If Malungeon does indeed mean mixture, the children of this couple are certainly Malungeons. The blacksmith himself is a Denhan, grandson of the old Portugese emigrant and a Collins woman.

This, then, is the account of the Malungeons from their first appearance in that part of the country where they are still found, Tennessee.

It will be a matter of some interest to follow them down to the present day. Unlike the rest of the world they have progressed slowly.

Their huts are still huts, their characteristics and instincts are still Indian, and their customs have lost but little of the old primitive exclusive and seclusive abandon characteristic of the sons of the forest.[2]

---

[2] Will Allen Dromgoole, "The Malungeon Tree and Its Four Branches," *The Arena*, Vol. 3, June 1891, 745–51.

APPENDIX C

Sons Of The Legend

By William L. Worden

Surrounded by mystery and fantastic legends, the Malungeons live on Newman's Ridge, deep in the Tennessee Mountains. The story of a colony whose background is lost in antiquity.

About the people of Newman's Ridge and Blackwater Swamp just one fact is indisputable: There are such strange people. Beyond that, fact gives way to legendary mystery, and written history is supplanted by garbled stories told a long time ago and half forgotten.

Today, even the legend is in the process of being forgotten, the strange stories are seldom remembered and the people are slipping away to cities and to better farms, there to tell anyone who asks them, all they can about where they came from, but never to tell who they are. Because they do not know.

Newman's Ridge lies beyond Blackwater Swamp, and Blackwater lies beyond Sneedville. Sneedville, war-swollen to a population of about 400 persons, is the county seat of Hancock County, Tennessee, just below Virginia, in the mountains through which no principal highway runs, no railroad has tracks, and only a single, insecure telephone line with five or six connections straggles. To get to Sneedville, an outsider can drive up the wandering bank of the Clinch River from Tazewell though Xenophon, which can be missed if the traveler is not looking carefully; or he can go over the switchbacks of Clinch Mountain from Rogersville to Kyle's Ford and down the river from the east. Either pinestudded route is beautiful. Neither has ever been used by very many people who did not live in Sneedville.

Nothing much ever happened in Sneedville. There is no industry, no mining now. Only once did the town ever get its name into newspapers farther away than Knoxville, when once some years before the war, Charlie Johns, a lank mountaineer, married Eunice Winstead, who was certainly not more than thirteen years old and was variously reported as being only nine. Their pictures and story made most of the United States newspapers in a dull news period.

Charlie and Eunice still live near Sneedville, but nothing has been written about them for a long time. They do not want anything more written.

From Sneedville, a few small roads lead northward toward the swamp and the ridge. One is passable, when the weather permits, through Kyle's Ford all the way to Vardy, where Presbyterians maintain a mission school. But weather does not permit with any regularity. There are in Rogersville a few tall, olive-skinned people with dark eyes and high cheekbones, small hands and feet and straight black hair, the men gaunt, the young women often remarkably beautiful.

In Sneedville on a "public day" when a lawing of some interest is under way in the county courthouse, many country people come to town from the rich farms along the Clinch River bottoms. Walking among them along the one muddy main street or leaning against the stone wall around the courthouse square will be other dark people—old women withered or excessively fat, inclined to talk very fast in musical voices, old men spare and taciturn, thinlipped, rather like Indians, but not quite like them. Either they have some Latin characteristics or the effect of the legend is to make the stranger think they have. Some few of them—the daughters of these people are very often lovely, soft and feminine, in striking contrast to the bony appearance of most mountain women—live in the town. Of them, their neighbors will say, "Well, they don't talk about it, but I happen to know her pappy used to make whiskey up on the ridge;" or "He might not tell you, but he never came to town from Vardy until he was growed."

But for all that some of them live there, these are strangers in Rogersville, strangers in Kyle's Ford and Sneedville. They are not fully at home where the telephones are or the highways go. The small roads lead up out of Sneedville across the swamp and end at the base of Newman's Ridge, nearly twenty miles long, a mile or so across at its most narrow point, virgin except for small clearings which dot its high slopes—clearings with log houses in them, corn patches growing beside the doors. That is, those houses that have doors. Many have no floors and some have no doors; only burlap hanging across the openings in cold weather.

Here, beyond where the roads end, in the clearings on the ridge, the dark people are at home. This is the Malungeon country. This is the country where no one ever uses the word "Malungeon." As a matter of fact, nobody is entirely sure what the word is. Perhaps "Malungeon," from the French "melange," meaning "mixture;" perhaps from *melas*, a Greek word meaning black. Its origin, like that of the people it specifies, is lost now. Already, it is entirely meaningless to most people even within a few dozen miles of Newman's Ridge; and presently, like the people of the ridge, who are constantly drifting away, intermarrying outside, never going home, saying nothing of the little ridge history they may know, it may be entirely forgotten. Except for a few curious people who like mysteries without answers.

The mystery of the Malungeons is basically simple. When the first Yankee and Scotch-Irish mountain men drifted down the Clinch River from its sources in Virginia toward the place where it meets the Holston to make the Tennessee River, they found in the rich farmland of the Clinch valley a strange people already settled. They were dark, tall, not exactly like Indians, certainly not at all like the escaped Negroes lurking on the outskirts of white slave-holding settlements. Even then they kept to themselves, had little to do with Andy Jackson's men and the others, the trappers, adventurers and farmers who came down the line of the river.

When they were first seen is doubtful. One Tennessee history notes that the journal of an expedition down the Tennessee River in the 1600s recorded an Indian story of a white settlement eight days down the river. The Indians said the whites lived to themselves, had houses and owned a bell which they sounded often, especially before meals, when all of them bowed their heads toward it. The journal was not clear about whether the location was on what is now the Clinch River. It could have been. These people could have been the Malungeons. But there is no record that any white man saw them.

Certainly they must have been there fairly early in the eighteenth century. Hale and Merritt's History of Tennessee and Tennesseans says a census of the settlements in 1795 listed 975 "free persons" in the East

Tennessee mountain area, distinguishing between them and the white settlers. As there never was any considerable number of Negroes in the mountains, these must have been the strange people of the Clinch valley.

But the other settlers apparently were unwilling to admit that they dark people were Caucasians, and the dividing line between "whites" and "Malungeons" began to be drawn—by the whites. Forty years later the division became serious. In the Tennessee Constitutional Convention of 1834, East Tennesseans succeeded in having the Malungeons officially classified as "free persons of color." This classification was equivalent to declaring them of Negro blood and preventing them from suing or even testifying in court in any case involving a Caucasian. The purpose was fairly obvious and the effect immediate. Other settlers simply moved onto what good bottom land the Malungeons had, and the dark people had no recourse except to retire with what they could take with them to the higher ridge land which no other settlers wanted and where no court cases could arise. Some may have been on Newman's Ridge previously, but now the rest climbed the slopes to live, taking with them their families, a few household possessions, some stock and a burning resentment of this and other injustices, such as the fact that their children were not welcome in the settler's schools, only in Negro schools, which they declined to attend.

On the ridge they built their small houses—log shacks without floors and sometimes even without chimneys—planted corn, and distilled whiskey. Now and then moving in he night in Indian fashion they descended on the richer farms of the valley. Now and then when strangers approached the ridge too closely or ventured into Blackwater swamp, they used the long rifles which seemed almost like parts of their bodies, so naturally were they carried. Now and then, valley farms lost cattle or hogs or chickens and never found any trace of the missing stock. Now and then, strangers failed to come back from the ridge or the swamp.

When the Civil War split the border states county against county and family against family, few of the Malungeons went to either army. They stayed home, brooding on their mountainside.

In the valleys, farm women told their youngsters, "Act purty or the Malungeons'll get ye." There is no record that they ever "got" any children, but old men still live who remember when no wandering hog was safe and few chicken yards secure.

What happened after the war is not entirely clear; nor the reasons for it. Revision of the state constitution took care of the old segregated status of the Malungeons, but nobody now seems certain exactly what made them welcome in the towns again.

Hale and Merritt, in their history, have the most fantastic explanation. They say, without giving any authority, that the Malungeons struck gold. Just when and just where are difficult to decide. The history declares flatly that the strike was made somewhere on Straight Creek, where ovens were built for refining the metal and for manufacture of technically counterfeit twenty dollar double eagles. But the counterfeit coins, the history continues, actually had nearly thirty dollars worth of gold in them and were welcomed by most storekeepers in the area. The storekeepers gave face value, more or less, for them, then sold the coins as gold by weight. Naturally, Malungeon business was more than welcome.

The only catch to the story is that nobody except Hale and Merritt ever seems to have heard of it. No other history mentions it and no trace of the coins remains in East Tennessee—at least, not in any of the expected places. Nor does Straight Creek appear on available maps. Milum Bowen, storekeeper at Kyle's Ford, says he has known the Melungeons all his life and "they're real friends if they're your friends, but will do you some kind of dirt at night if they don't like you." He has traded constantly with them during most of his seventy-some years, but never saw or heard of any such coins.

Only one ghost of a clue is in the memory of anyone in the area. That is a rumor—no on of the dozen people who will tell it as a rumor seems to know where it comes from—that there is silver—not gold, but silver—somewhere in the lowering mountains which ring Hancock County, somewhere in the half-mapped, heavily wooded ridges. "People say," they tell a stranger, "that it'll be found again someday."

Whether there was gold or whether there was none, the Malungeons, after the Civil War, seemed to enter a new phase of their lonesome existence. Bushwhacking declined, some few Malungeons came off the ridge to go to school, many more turned to distilling for their principal source of livelihood. Of all the stories of moonshining in the Hancock County mountains, the best seems to be the often-retold tale of Big Haly Mullins, a very real woman who became a legend herself. Milum Bowen testifies to the fact that Big Haly really did exist, really did make whiskey and most certainly weighed 600 or 700 poounds.

The legend is that in the early years of this century, Federal revenue agents time and again followed the steep paths to Big Haly's cabin, time and again found aging whiskey and the still for making it, and found Haly, peaceful and alone, waiting for them in her cabin. Each time she admitted ownership of the still and whiskey, and each time they officially arrested her.

There they stopped. Big Haly was in her cabin and was too fat to be got out the door. Even if they had been able to get her through the door, they had no method for getting her down the ridge to any court for trial. She was much too heavy for any combination of men who could go together down the trail, she was much too heavy for any mule, and she would not or could not walk.

So the revenuers went away and Big Haly resumed making whiskey as soon as the still could be repaired—that is to say, her myriad of relatives, who had vanished into the hills as soon as the Federal men left the highway, returned and began making whiskey again under Haly's directions, shouted from inside the cabin.

At least one supporting fact is attested by Bowen. When Mrs. Mullins died, he says, Malungeon relatives knocked the fireplace out of the end of her cabin in order to get her body outside for burial. It just would not go through the door.

Toward the end of the 1800s one person made an extended study of the Malungeons. This was a Nashville poetess, Miss Will Allen Dromgoole, who spent some months living with the dark people in the mountains and reported her findings in two articles in the *Arena* magazine, published in Boston in 1891.

Miss Dromgoole noted several strange facets of the Malungeon life, some of which she thought indicated Latin origin. Especially, she noted that there was a special veneration for the Christian Cross shown along the whole ridge. She thought this strange, in view of the fact that the ridge people, if they were religious at all, leaned toward the shouting types of Protestantism which used the cross symbol little, if at all. Too, she said the Malungeons commonly made and drank brandy rather than whiskey. This seems open to some doubt, as no one in the area makes any brandy now, and no one remembers any of it ever coming off Newman's Ridge or out of Blackwater Swamp. Possibly Miss

Dromgoole was a teetotaler and no authority on the subject. She also noted a common habit of burying the Malungeon dead above the ground, with small, token houses over the graves, much as the Spanish and Indian Catholics bury the dead in the Southwestern United States and Alaskan Indians, converted to Greek Catholicism, do in Alaska and the Aleutian Islands. Again, Miss Dromgoole's word must be taken for it, because no such graves are in evidence now.

Several peculiarities mar the poetess' account of the dark people. One is that she changed her mind. In the *Arena* article of March, 1891, she rejected the theory that the Malungeons might be Negroid, basing her rejection on their appearance and on what she stated as a fact—that continuance of such blood would be impossible because octoroon women never have children, and Malungeon families were traceable for numerous generations. She said then that she did not know where the Malungeons had come from or of what blood they were, although she was inclined to believe they were basically Portuguese.

Three months later, however, Miss Dromgoole signed another article on the same subject in the same magazine. But this time she had decided, among other things, that octoroon women were not necessarily barren after all. She no longer found the Malungeons interesting, friendly or pathetic. In June they were dirty, thieving, untrustworthy, decadent and not mysterious at all. In June she knew their exact history. There had been, said Miss Dromgoole, two wily Cherokee Indians with a big idea. First, they borrowed names from white settlers in Virginia and called themselves Vardy Collins and Buck Gibson. Then, in the woods near a Virginia settlement, Vardy covered Buck with a dark stain, led him to a plantation and there sold him as a "likely nigger," receiving in payment $300, some goods and a wagon with a team of mules. With this loot he promptly vanished into the forest again.

Whereupon Gibson made his way to the nearest fresh water, washed off the dark stain, then calmly walked off the plantation a free man protesting that he knew nothing of the sale of any "likely nigger" and certainly was not one.

In the forest, Gibson met Collins at a rendezvous where they split the loot and went their separate ways. Miss Dromgoole's article gives no hint of her authority, but she states flatly that Collins came to Newman's Ridge, Tennessee, where he begat a large family by a wife whose ancestry was not specified. Subsequently, an English trader named

Mullins came to the ridge and married one of the Collins family. A free or escaped Negro, one Goins—this is still quoting Miss Dromgoole—married another daughter and settled in Blackwater Swamp; ansd a Portuguese, one Denham, arrived from no one knows where, married still another Collins to establish one more related family on the ridge.

Miss Dromgoole completed her estimate of the Malungeons by noting that the most common names among them were still those four, along with Gorvans, Gibbens, and Bragans, or Brogan, and that all the families used a strange system of identifying their members, a system in which the wife of Jack Collins would be known as Mary Jack, his daughter as Sally Jack and his son as Tom Jack. She did not say what she thought this system proved, if anything.

Miss Dromgoole is gone and there is no practical method of checking her theories or even her facts now. But her final estimate of the Malungeons did not please them, and they had a sort of revenge. Milum Bowen remembers that the ridge people created a jingle about the poetess and repeated it endlessly to each other. "I can't remember the rest of the words," he says, " but the last of it was 'Will Allen Damfool.'"

Actually, Miss Dromgoole's theory of origin for the dark people has as much to support it as any of the others, which is virtually nothing except that the dark people do exist. Many theories have been advanced. One, which the Malungeons themselves like especially, is that they are descendants of the lost Roanoke colony in Virginia—although the only plausible link with that colony is the English-sounding names the Malungeons now bear. They could be the Lost Colony, of course. But there is no real indication that they are.

Woodson Knight, a Louisville, Kentucky, writer, professed to find in 1940 an indication in these same names that the people might be Welsh, and was bemused by the possibility that those along the Clinch River might have descended from the retainers of a certain early Welsh chieftan, one Madoc, who with his ship "sailed from the ken of men into the Western Sea" in the days of the Roman Empire's decline. Which could be, of course, but lacks any supporting evidence whatsoever.

Unquestionably the oddest theory of all was advanced by J. Patton Gibson, a Tennessee writer, and given an odd twist by Judge Lewis Shepherd, of Chattanooga. Shepherd's connection with the Malungeons

came through his employment as attorney for a half-Malungeon girl in a
land case near Chattanooga. The land had been owned by a Caucasian
who married a Malungeon woman who somehow had wandered far from
her native Hancock County mountains. A daughter was born, and
subsequently both the mother and the father died, the latter in an asylum.
His relatives sent the child away and claimed the land, basing their
claims on the theory that the Malungeon woman had been of Negro
blood, that the marriage therefore had been illegal under Tennessee
statutes and that the child was illegitimate and without rights of
succession to the property.

Shepherd was employed as attorney for the girl, by this time nearly
grown, and brought back to Chattanooga by friends of the dead man.
Like so many of the people who have written and spoken of the subject
of the Malungeon mystery, Shepherd nowhere quoted his authorities, but
what he told the jury was that the girl in question had no Negroid
characteristics and that she, a Malungeon, was a descendent of a lost and
hounded people, originally Phoenecians, who migrated to Morocco at the
time the Romans were sacking Carthage. From Morocco, he said, they
eventually sailed to South Carolina, arriving there before other settlers.
But when lighter neighbors came, these people could not get along with
them because the light South Carolinians insisted the Malungeons were
Negroes, and even attempted to impose a head tax on them as such, as
well as barring their children from Caucasian schools. So they fled
toward the mountains and stopped only when they reached Hancock
County, Tennessee. There was nobody then, and there is nobody now, to
support in any way his theory or to argue with him on any basis except
improbability. But he did win the court case.

One more theory is worth repeating along with the more curious.
Among others, James Aswell, magazine writer and Tennessee history
expert, has repeated it as a possible explanation for the Malungeons. This
is: that about the time of the Portuguese revolt against Spain, numerous
Portuguese ships were playing the Caribbean as pirates or near-pirates. A
common method of disposing of unwanted crew members was to maroon
them, sometimes on the Florida keys or coast. Some crews also mutinied,
and one may well have burned its ship, attacked some small Indian
village ashore and taken the women, then fled west to the mountains to
escape Indian wrath.

That these Portuguese could have reached the Hancock ridges is obviously quite possible, especially if their marooning or mutiny should have taken place on the North Carolina coast. To say that they did reach the ridges is another matter. The only evidences of it are the dark and Latin features of the present-day Malungeons—the differences between Indian and Latin are often difficult to distinguish, the rumors of cross veneration and near-Catholic habits of burial, and the possibility mentioned by some writers that a name such as Bragans might as easily originally have been Braganza as Brogan.

Whatever they are—Welsh, English, Phoenician, Portuguese or just Indian—the Malungeons still are on Newman's Ridge, in Hancock, Rhea and Hawkins counties of Tennessee, and a few across the border in Virginia. Many are scattered by ones or twos, miles from the isolated ridge to the occupied for so long. There are known to be hundreds and maybe thousands with variously diluted blood. And where they came from nobody knows. The old people left no records, no implements, books or relics to help in solving the mystery. They were uneducated, often illiterate people, and even what little the grandfathers knew or had heard of their own origin died with them, except for scraps of oral stories.

The descendants are still farmers, for the most part, still have occasional trouble about their color. Within the last dozen years, disputes flared briefly in certain Hancock County districts about whether Malungeon children should go to white or Negro schools and during both wars of this century, Malungeons have had color trouble upon reporting to Southern cantonments. They still make a certain amount of tax-evading whiskey somewhere up the dim ravines, and now and then are hauled into court for it. Generally, they still avoid schools, except for the mission at Vardy, from which the Rev. Chester F. Leonard sends a few on to the University of Tennessee or to church colleges. One such college, Maryville, has records of half a dozen entered, none graduated. Mr. Leonard, incidentally, says "The group is so intermingled that one cannot be sure of a typical specimen."

In the small Tennessee hill towns, now and then, a dark man will talk to a stranger, tell a few incidents heard or seen on Newman's Ridge or advise him, "See if anybody knows, he will." Only ___ never does. A lovely woman may even, looking straight at the visitor with gray eyes, say, "My own grandfather had some Indian blood and perhaps some

Spanish. We don't know much about the family, but there is a story that some of De Soto's men…"

The lady may have small hands and feet, high cheekbones, straight hair and olive skin, and a regal carriage. She may talk for some time and tell much that is written in no books, some hearsay, some the most fanciful legend. But one word she will never say. She will never say,

"Malungeon."[1]

---

[1] W. L. Worden, "Sons of the Legend," *Saturday Evening Post*, 18 October 1947.

Sources

Interviews and Oral Presentations

Alther, Lisa. "The Melungeon Melting Pot," presentation at Third Union, Wise, Virginia, 20 May 2000.

Beale, Calvin, Wayne Winkler, in-person interview, June 2002, Kingsport, TN.

Collins, W. C. "Claude," Wayne Winkler, in-person interview, January 2002; Sneedville, Tennessee.

Collins, W. C. "Claude," "The Vardy School," presentation at Fourth Union, Kingsport, Tennessee, 21 June 2002.

DeMarce, Virginia Easley, Wayne Winkler, telephone interview, August 1997, in-person interview, September 1998, Williamsburg, Kentucky.

Demeril, Suleymann, Wayne Winkler in-person interview, June 1998; Ankara Turkey.

Fields, Bill, Wayne Winkler, in-person interview, July 1997, Wise, Virginia.

Gallegos, Eloy J., Wayne Winkler, in-person interview, September 1998, Knoxville; Tennessee.

Goodyear, Mary, Wayne Winkler, in-person interview, July 1997, Wise, Virginia.

Gowen, Arlee, Wayne Winkler, telephone interview, August 1997.

Henige, David, Wayne Winkler, telephone interview, September 1997.

Jones, Kevin, Wayne Winkler, in-person interview, February 2002.

Jones, Kevin. "DNA Test Results," presentation at Fourth Union, Kingsport, Tennessee, 20–21 June 2002.

Kennedy, N. Brent, Wayne Winkler, in-person interviews, July 197, Wise, Virginia; April, 1998, Johnson City, Tennessee.

Lyday-Lee, Kathy. "Will Allen Dromgoole," presentation at Third Union, Wise, Virginia, 20 May 2000.

Mullins, R. C. "The Vardy School," presentation at Fourth Union, Kingsport, Tennessee, 21 June 2002.

Overbay, DruAnna Williams. "The Vardy School," presentation at Fourth Union, Kingsport, Tennessee, 21 June 2002.

Sizemore, Charles. "The Vardy School," presentation at Fourth Union, Kingsport, Tennessee, 21 June 2002.

Talay, Istemehan, Wayne Winkler, in-person interview, June 1998, Ankara, Turkey.

Welton, John Lee, Wayne Winkler, in-person interview March 2002, Jefferson City, Tennessee.

Williams, Troy. "The Vardy School," presentation at Fourth Union, Kingsport, Tennessee, 21 June 2002.

Wilson, Darlene, Wayne Winkler, in-person interview, September 1997; Johnson City, Tennessee.

Books, Periodicals, And Websites

Acton, Thomas A. "Gypsies in the United Kingdom," *Patrin Romani Web Journal*, http://www.geocities.com/~patrin/patrin.htm.

Allen, Garland E. "Flaws in Eugenics Research,"*Image Archive on the American Eugenics Movement*, Dolan DNA Learning Center, Cold Spring Harbor Laboratory, http://vector.cshl.org/htmp/eugenics/essay5text.html.

American Anthropological Association. "Statement on Race," http://www.aaanet/stmts/racepp.htm.

"An Exciting Scene," *Nashville Sunday American*, 7 September 1890, 7.

Aswell, James. *God Bless The Devil*, Federal Writers' Project. Chapel Hill: University of North Carolina Press, 1940.

———. "Lost Tribes of Tennessee's Mountains," *Nashville Banner*, 22 August 1937.

Ball, Bonnie. *Melungeons: Their Origin and Kin*. Johnson City TN: Overmountain Press, 1969, revised 1992.

Barr, Phyllis Cox. "The Melungeons of Newman's Ridge," Graduate thesis, East Tennessee State University, 1965.

Beale, Calvin L. "American Triracial Isolates: Their Status and Pertinence to Genetic Research." *Eugenics Quarterly* 4/4 (December 1957): 187–96.

———. "An Overview of the Phenomenon of Mixed Racial Isolated in the United States." *American Anthropologist* 74 (1972): 704–710.

———. *A Taste of the Country: A Collection of Calvin Beale's Writings*, Peter Morrison, editor. University Park PA: The Pennsylvania State University Press, 1990, 42–52.

Berry, Brewton. *Almost White*. New York: Macmillan, 1963.

Bible, Jean Patterson. *Melungeons Yesterday and Today*. Rogersville TN: East Tennessee Printing Company, 1975.

Bleakley, Fred R. "Appalachian Clan Mines Web Sites for Ancestral Clues." *Wall Street Journal*, 14 April 1997, B-1, B-5.

Burnett, Swan. "A Note on the Melungeons." *American Anthropologist* 2 (October 1889): 347.

Callahan, Jim. *Lest We Forget: The Melungeon Colony of Newman's Ridge.* Johnson City TN: Overmountain Press, 2000.

Cavender, Anthony P. "The Melungeons of Upper East Tennessee: Persisting Social Identity." *Tennessee Anthropologist,* 6/1 (Spring 1981).

Cohen, David S. *The Ramapo Mountain People.* New Brunswick NJ: Rutgers University Press, 1974.

Converse, Paul. "The Melungeons," *Southern Collegian* (December 1912): 59–69.

"Crawford Story Brings Comment." *The Coalfield Progress.* 4 July 1940.

Dane, J. K., and Griessman, B. Eugene. "The Collective Identity of Marginal Peoples: The North Carolina Experience." *American Anthropologist* 74 (1972): 694.

Davis, Louise. "Why Are They Vanishing?" *Nashville Tennesseean Sunday Magazine,* 29 September 1963.

———. "The Mystery of the Melungeons," Nashville *Tennesseean Sunday Magazine,* 22 September 1963.

Deacon, Richard. *Madoc and the Discovery of America.* New York: George Braziller, 1966.

DeMarce, Virginia Easley. "Verry Slitly Mixt: Tri-Racial Isolate Families of the Upper South—A Genealogical Study." *National Genealogical Quarterly* (March 1992).

———. "Looking at Legends—Lumbee and Melungeon: Applied Genealogy and the Origins of Tri-racial Isolate Settlements." *National Genealogical Quarterly* (March 1993): 24–45.

———. "The Melungeons" *National Genealogical Quarterly* (June 1996): 134–49.

"Distinct Race of People Inhabits the Mountains of East Tennessee." *Kingsport Times,* 7 August 1923, 1.

Dixon, Thomas. *The Leopard's Spots.* New York: Doubleday, Page, & Co., 1902.

"Don't Fraternize," *Nashville Daily American,* 6 September 1890, 2.

Dromgoole, Will Allen. "Land of the Malungeons." *Nashville Sunday American,* 31 August 1890, 10.

———. "A Strange People." *Nashville Sunday American,* 15 September 1890, 10.

———. "The Malungeons." *The Arena* 3 (March 1891): 470–79.

———. "The Malungeon Tree and Its Four Branches." *The Arena* 3 (June 1891): 745–751.

Elder, Pat Spurlock. *Melungeons: Examining an Appalachian Legend.* Blountville TN: Continuity Press, 1999.

Emory University. "Race and Racism," http://www. emory. edu/COLLEGE/ANTHROPOLOGY/research/race. Html.

Estabrook, Arthur H., and Ivan E. McDougal. *Mongrel Virginians*. Baltimore: Williams & Wilkins, 1926.

"Eugenics/Sterilization," http://member.aol.MRandDD/eugenics/htm

Evans, E. Raymond. "The Graysville Melungeons: A Tri-Racial People In Lower East Tennessee." *Tennessee Anthropologist* (Spring 1979): 1–31.

Everett, C. S. "Melungeon History and Myth." *Appalachian Journal* (Summer 1999): 358–404.

Fetterman, John. "The Mystery of Newman's Ridge." *Life Magazine* (26 June 1970): 23. (Not in all editions.)

"First English Settlement," http://statelibrary. dcr. state. nc. us/nc/ncsites/english1. htm

Gallegos, Eloy J. *The Melungeons: The Pioneers of the Interior Southeastern United States*, 1526–1997. Knoxville: Villagra Press, 1997.

Garner, Hallie Price. 1890 Census of Union Veterans and their Widows, Hancock County, TN, htttp://www. rootsweb. com/~tnhawkin/1890vethan. html.

Gilbert, William Harlan, Jr. "Memorandum Concerning the Characteristics of the Larger Mixed-Blood Racial Islands in the Eastern United States." *Social Forces* 21/4 (May 1946): 438–77.

Glenn, Juanita. "Hancock Countians Prepare For Drama About Melungeons." *Knoxville Journal*, 1 May 1969, 5.

Glenn, Juanita. "Hancock Countians Aiding Dream With Drama." *Knoxville Journal*, 11 March 1971.

Goins, Jack H. *Melungeons: And Other Pioneer Families*. Rogersville TN: Jack Harold Goins, 2000.

Goodspeed's History of Tennessee. Nashville: Charles and Randy Elder Booksellers, 1887, reprinted 1972.

Grohse, William Paul, papers (Microfilm Roll # 7) East Tennessee State University.

———. "Hancock County—'The Land of Mystery,'" *Hancock County (TN) Post*, 4 July 1968, 10–12.

Guthrie, James L. "Melungeons: Comparison of Gene Frequency Distributions to those of Worldwide Populations." *Tennessee Anthropologist* XV/1 (Spring 1990).

Hale, Will T. and D. L. Merritt. *A History of Tennessee and Tennesseeans*. Chicago: Lewis Publishing Company, 1913.

Hancock, Ian, *Roma Slavery*, http://www. geocities. com/Paris/5121/slavery. Htm.

Hardin, Peter. "Eugenics in Virginia." *Richmond Times-Dispatch*, 26 November 2000, online edition.

Haun, Mildred. *The Hawk's Done Gone*. Herschel Gower, editor. Nashville: Vanderbilt University Press, 1968

Heinegg, Paul. *Free African Americans of Virginia, North Carolina, South Carolina, Maryland and Delaware*. http://www. freeafricanamericans. com/introduction. Htm.

Henige, David. "Origin Traditions of American Racial Isolates: A Case of Something Borrowed." *Appalachian Journal* (Spring 1984): 201–13.

———. "The Melungeons Become a Race," *Appalachian Journal* 25/3 (Spring 1998): 270–86.

———. "Henige Answers Wilson." *Appalachian Journal* 25/3 (Spring 1998): 297–98.

"His Just Deserts." *Nashville Daily American*, 5 September 1890, 1.

Ivey, Saundra Keyes. "Oral, Printed, and Popular Culture Traditions Related to the Melungeons of Hancock County, Tennessee." Ph. D. diss., Indiana University, 1976.

Johnson, Mattie Ruth. *My Melungeon Heritage: A Story of Life on Newman's Ridge*. Johnson City TN: Overmountain Press, 1997.

Kennedy, N. Brent with Robyn Vaughan Kennedy. *The Melungeons: The Resurrection of a Proud People; An Untold Story of Ethnic Cleansing in America*. Macon GA: Mercer University Press, 1994, revised 1997.

Kennedy, N. Brent. "An Update on Melungeon Research." 22 May 1997, online letter at www. melungeons. org (site now defunct)

———. letter to Elizabeth Mills, editor, *National Genealogical Quarterly*, response to DeMarce review, 15 August 1996.

Kessler, John S., and Donald B. Ball. *North From The Mountains: A Folk History of the Carmel Melungeon Settlement, Highland County, Ohio*. Macon GA: Mercer University Press, 2001.

Loewen, James *Lies My Teacher Told Me*. New York: The New Press, 1995.

Martin, Ken. "First European Contact." *History of the Cherokee*, http://cherokeehistory. com/firstcon. htm.

McCulloch, Richard. "The Races of Humanity." http://www.racialcompact.com/racesofhumanity.html.

———. "The Preservationist Imperative." http://www.racialcompact.com/preservationimperative.html.

"Melungeon Drama Goes On Despite Money Problems." Kingsport *Times*, 19 April 1972.

"Melungeon Line Almost Extinct." *Kingsport Times*, 26 November 1964, 9-C.

Messick, Mary Ann. *History of Baxter County, Centennial Edition, 1873–1973*. Mountain Home AK: Baxter County Historical and Genealogical Society, 1973, reprinted 1998.

Miklos, David. "Eugenics Research Methods." *Image Archive on the American Eugenics Movement*. Cold Spring Harbor, NY Dolan DNA Learning Center, Cold Spring Harbor Laboratory, http://vector.cshl.org/htmp/eugenics/essay3text.html.

Mira, Manuel. *The Portuguese Making of America*. Franklin NC: Portuguese-
   American Historical Research Foundation, Inc, 2001.
————. *The Forgotten Portuguese: The Melungeons and Other Groups*.
   Franklin NC: Portuguese-American Historical Research Foundation, Inc,
   1998.
Montell, Lynwood. "The Coe Ridge Colony: A Racial Island Disappears"
   American Anthropologist 74 (1972): 710–18.
Morello, Carol. "Beneath Myth, Melungeons Find Roots of Oppression."
   Washington Post, 29 May 2000, online edition.
Mullins, R. C. and Macie Mullins. "My Rock Candy Christmas." *The Vardy
   Voice* (December 2001).
"Mysterious Melungeons: No Origin, No Color." *Bristol, Herald Courier*26,
   October 1970, section 2–1.
Nassau (McGlothlen), Mike. *Melungeons and Other Mestee Groups*. 1994,
   online in several locations, including
   http://www.multiracial.com/readers/nassau.html. McGlothlen changed his
   name to Nassau in 1997.
Nelson, Bruce. "Lumbee Indians of N. C. Think They Have Answer." *Atlanta
   Journal and Constitution*, 15 May 1977, online edition.
Nordheimer, John. "Mysterious Hill Folk Vanishing." *New York Times*, 10
   August 1971, 33,38.
Oldpath, Obadiah. *Jewels of the Third Plantation*. Lynn MA: Thomas Herbert
   and James M. Munroe, 1862.
Overbay, DruAnna Williams. "Museum's Contents Reflect Vardy's Past, Part
   Two." *The Vardy Voice*, Vardy Community Historical Society, June 2002.
Pollitzer, William. "The Physical Anthropology and Genetics of Marginal
   People of the Southeastern United States." *American Anthropologist* 74/3
   (1972): 719–34.
Price, Edward. "The Melungeons: A Mixed-Blood Strain of the Southern
   Appalachians." *Geographical Review* 41/2 (1951): 256–71.
Price, Edward T. "A Geographic Analysis of White-Negro-Indian Racial
   Mixtures in the Eastern United States." Association of American
   Geographers, *Annals* 43 (June 1953): 138–55.
Price, Henry. "Melungeons: The Vanishing Colony of Newman's Ridge."
   lecture presented at the Spring Meeting of the American Studies
   Association of Kentucky and Tennessee, 25–26 March 1966, Tennessee
   Technical University, Cookeville, Tennesseee, transcript from Grohse
   Papers, Roll 7, East Tennessee State University, Johnson City, Tennessee.
Public Broadcasting System. "From Indentured Servitude to Racial Slavery."
   Africans in America, http://www.pbs.org/wgbh.aia.part1/1narr3.html.
"Race War Breaks Out." *Nashville Daily American*, 9 September 1890, 1.

Reed, John Shelton. "Mixing in the Mountains." *Southern Cultures* 3/4 (Winter 1997): 25–36.

Rountree, Helen C. *Pocohontas's People: The Powhatan Indians of Virginia Through Four Centuries.* Norman OK: University of Oklahoma Press, 1990.

Selden, Steve. "Eugenics Popularization." *Image Archive on the American Eugenics Movement.* Cold Spring Harbor, NY, Dolan DNA Learning Center, Cold Spring Harbor Laboratory, http://vector. cshl. org/htmp/eugenics/essay6text. html.

Shepherd, S. L. *Memoirs of Judge Lewis Shepherd.* Chattanooga TN, 1915.

Sims, Leah C. *Unraveling a Deceptive Oral History: The Indian Ancestry Claims of Philip. S. Proctor and his Descendants.* http://www/eskimo. com/~lcsims/tayacfraud. ht~.

"Stony Creek Baptist Church Minute Books, 1801–1814," http://searches. rootsweb. com/usgenweb/archives/va/scott/church/stonycrk. txt (32 pages). Copied from original document by Emory Hamilton of Wise, Virginia, 1966, contributed for online use by Jenny Stillwell.

Stuart, Jesse. *Daughter of the Legend.* New York: McGraw-Hill, 1965.

"Tennessee Ernie Ford Is Chairman Friend of the Melungeons [sic]." *Hancock News Journal,* 5 February 1971.

"Two Colored Lovers." *Nashville Daily American,* 6 September 1890, 2.

"The Melungeons: A Peculiar Race of People Living in Hancock County." *Knoxville Journal,* 28 September 1890, 1.

"The Melungeons." *Littel's Living Age* 254/31, March 1849.

"The Moors of Delaware: A Look at a Tri-Racial Group." http://www. mitsawockett. com/MoorsOfDelaware/trirace3. html

"The Nanticoke People," http://www.graydovetrading.com/Nanticoke.html#Fight.

Vande Brake, Katherine. *How They Shine: Melungeon Characters in the Fiction of Appalachia.* Macon GA: Mercer University Press, 2001.

Vardy Voice, The, newsletter of the Vardy Community Historical Society, January 2002.

Walk Toward the Sunset. Souvenir program, Hancock County Drama Association, 1971.

Weals, Vic. "Home Folks." *Knoxville Journal,* 24 July 1953.

"Who Were The Mysterious Yuchi of Tennessee and the Southeast?" http://www. geocities. com/Capitol Hill/Lobby/3486/tenn-asi. html.

Williams, Samuel Cole. *Early Travels in the Tennessee Country 1540–1800.* Johnson City TN: Watauga Press, 1928.

Wilson, Darlene. "Miscegenation, Melungeons, and Appalachia: A Virtual Case Study in Documentary Racism." project proposal, University of Kentucky, online at www. melungeons. org (now defunct), 1997.

————. "A Response to Henige," *Appalachian Journal* 25. 3 (Spring 1998): 286–296.

Overbay, DruAnna, editor. *Windows on the Past*. Sneedville TN: Vardy Community Historical Society, 2002.

Winkler, Wayne. *The Melungeons: Sons and Daughters of the Legend*. radio documentary, aired January 10, 1999 on WETS-FM, Johnson City TN.

Wood, Karenne, and Diane Shields. *The Monacan Indians: Our Story*. Madison Heights VA: Monacan Indian Nation, 2000.

Worden, W. L. "Sons of the Legend." *Saturday Evening Post*, 18 October 1947.

Yarbrough, Willard. "Melungeons Ways Are Passing." *Knoxville News-Sentinel*, 26 April 1972, 33.

————. "Maligned Mountain Folk May Be Topic of Drama." *Knoxville News-Sentinel*, 8 January 1968, 1.

————. "Melungeon Story Revived." *Knoxville News-Sentinel*, 21 June 1973, 25.

Zuber, Leo. "The Melungeons." WPA Federal Writers' Guide MSS, McClung Historical Collection, Lawson-McGhee Library, University of Tennessee, Knoxville, Tennessee.

INDEX